五千年专制到此可告一段落！

个人崇拜从今可以休矣！

DENISE CHONG

EGG ON MAO

—

THE STORY OF
AN ORDINARY MAN
WHO DEFACED AN ICON
AND UNMASKED
A DICTATORSHIP

COUNTERPOINT
BERKELEY

Published by arrangement with Random House Canada, an imprint of the
Knopf Random Canada Publishing Group, which is a division of Random House
of Canada Limited.

Library of Congress Cataloging-in-Publication Data

Chong, Denise.
Egg on Mao : the story of an ordinary man who defaced an icon
and unmasked a dictatorship / Denise Chong.
p. cm.
ISBN 978-1-58243-547-3
1. China—History—Tiananmen Square Incident, 1989. 2. Mao, Zedong, 1893-
1976—Portraits. 3. Lu, Decheng. 4. China—History—Tiananmen Square Incident,
1989—Biography. 5. Political activists—China—Beijing—Biography. 6. Mechanics
(Persons)—China—Biography. 7. Political refugees—Canada—Biography. I. Title.

DS779.32.C516 2009
951.05'8—dc22
2009032949

COUNTERPOINT
2117 Fourth Street
Suite D
Berkeley, CA 94710

www.counterpointpress.com

Distributed by Publishers Group West
Printed in the United States of America

10 9 8 7 6 5 4 3 2 1

For Wae Hing and Arlett, with love

PROLOGUE

IF THE OTHER BOYS relished the competition, his desire was only ever to best the river. The routine was always the same: select a pebble for the right weight and roundness, hurl it, and eyeball the distant *plop!* in the water. More scouring for pebbles, more talk of technique. That day, as every other day, it was Decheng's pebbles that faded farthest in the distance.

Discouraged, some would seek an advantage by wading into the shallows, invited by the softness of the yellow sand underfoot. The far shore beckoned, shimmering with specks of mandarin oranges ripening in the grove of the commune there. The sweet oranges hinted at another favourite pastime, a swim across (for those who could manage both the distance and the fast-flowing current), a savoured stolen fruit or two, and then a swim back.

When the challengers tired of the Liuyang River swallowing their pebbles, Decheng and his friends, Hongwu and Zefu, played on. Of all his friends, they were the two he admired most. In Hongwu, who came from one of the poorest families in town but was clever at school and wily on the streets, he sensed a destiny of greatness. In Zefu, whose gentle manner and slight physique others ridiculed, he saw kindness. As for himself, he excelled at play. Rather, whatever he enjoyed, he did well.

On the far bank, a lone figure trudged into view, following the river's grassy edge along a footpath that led to the village at the base of Heavenly Horse Mountain. Decheng, confident of having a better throw in him yet, plucked another pebble from the sand. He tested its weight, arched his back, and unleashed.

The boys looked for the splash.

Across the river, the tiny figure halted his progress, straightened his posture. He turned his head warily, to one side then the other. He peered into the orange grove, as if expecting someone to show his face from behind a tree and confess to the prank of tossing whatever had dropped into the tall grass nearby.

A throw right over the river. Surely the record would stand.

ONE

THE REACTION OF ONLOOKERS caromed wildly between praise and condemnation. Many remained incredulous, not knowing what to make of what they had just seen the two young men do.

The curious lobbed questions.

"Who are you?"

"Who do you represent?"

"Why would you do that? What do you want to achieve by doing this?"

"The suffering in China today can be traced to Mao Zedong and to the dictatorial rule of the Communist Party—" Decheng was surprised at the confidence in his voice.

A brawl of words broke out around him.

"He's right. Down with Mao!"

"How dare they! There's no need to abuse Mao like that."

"What they did is an insult to all of China!"

Decheng felt a rush of exhilaration. He and Dongyue had succeeded in throwing every single one of the more than thirty paint-filled eggs. Even now, there was not a single policeman coming through the crowd for them. Just ordinary people, startled, arguing, awoken.

He'd never felt so alive.

NO MATTER WHERE one stood on Beijing's Tiananmen Square, to look north toward the portrait of Mao Zedong that hung on the gate to the Forbidden City was to meet the Chairman's steady gaze. The composition of the painting made sure of that: the subject's head is dead centre, his shoulders are square to the front, his eyes stare directly outward. That the portrait should dominate Tiananmen Square befitted a man who'd had so many titles in life: the Great Teacher, the Great Leader, the Great Helmsman, the Great Supreme Commander, the Great Saviour, Beloved Leader, but most commonly, Chairman Mao.

For fifty years, an oil painting of Mao Zedong had been mounted on the gate there. Successive versions subtly aged the Chairman and each altered something—taking away the cap, changing the jacket, realigning the gaze. The first was painted in 1949. A new portrait was commissioned in 1950, in 1952, in 1963, and for the last time in 1967. Sunlight and harsh weather took their toll on these paintings and at least once every year, the management office of Tiananmen Square was obliged to take the current version down and replace it with a freshly painted copy. Often the replacement was an overpainting on an old canvas, each of which was reused as many as five or six times. By 1989, the painter of the Tiananmen portrait, the third person to hold that post since 1949, had been turning out a painting every year for the past thirteen years. Just after two in the afternoon of Tuesday, May 23, 1989, in the sixth week of the pro-democracy protests in the square, that portrait maker's schedule was disrupted.

It was the fourth day of martial law in the capital, ending another night during which citizens and students alike had rushed to erect barricades to keep the People's Liberation Army from entering the city centre and reaching the square. By now, the students' routine was to use the morning for sleep then return to the square at lunchtime. Those from Beijing rolled out of their bunks at university dormitories; others, sheltering in tents on the square, awoke, ready for another day's occupation. Throughout the city, families and their children, workers and managers and intellectuals, less afraid with each day that downtown streets remained free of a military presence, felt almost celebratory. "Have you been to the square yet?" became frequent words of greeting. By one o'clock, some

300,000 Beijingers—about equal to the number of troops sitting on the city's outskirts and the largest crowds yet since martial law—had converged on the square. The weather continued to buoy the festive mood, the cloudless days and 30-degree heat more like what Beijing could expect at the height of summer.

WANG QIUPING HAD LAST SEEN her husband, Lu Decheng, on the morning of Tuesday, May 16, a workday for them both at the Liuyang Long-Distance Bus Company. He'd left for the vehicle-repair garage, where he worked as a mechanic, and she had gone to the station's administrative offices to start her shift as an on-board ticket seller. That day, her rotation had her on an overnight trip.

On Wednesday evening, she returned home to find a note on the table, a green enamel cup holding it in place. A pen weighed heavily in Decheng's hand, so, not surprisingly, the note was brief. *Wangping, don't worry yourself. We'll come back soon. Lu Gao.* He used the names by which they called each other, a combination of their family names and given names or, in his case, a nickname "Gao" meaning "tall," a holdover from his boyhood.

She wasn't troubled if she was the one on the road because she knew him to be safe at home, but she couldn't handle the reverse. An anxious Qiuping immediately made the rounds of colleagues and neighbours to ask if they'd seen her husband. She learned that Decheng and two friends, the tall Yu Zhijian and the young, bespectacled Yu Dongyue (they shared a surname but were unrelated), had been seen that morning boarding the first bus to Changsha.

Qiuping could guess why Zhijian and Dongyue would want to go to the provincial capital. They were intellectuals. Zhijian was a teacher, and Dongyue was an arts editor at the *Liuyang Daily*. Liuyang was a small and backward town in Hunan province, with one high school that served the entire township. But Changsha had several modern colleges and universities, and was home to the famous Yuelu Academy, a gathering place for great scholars for the past one thousand years. Decheng's two friends could count on meeting like-minded people who would be now rallying there, and obtaining uncensored news of what was happening in the student pro-democracy movement in Beijing.

Ordinarily, Qiuping had no concern about Decheng going to Changsha. Town folk typically made it a day trip, although the 80-kilometre bus ride took from two to three hours, because of potholes in the road. However, these were not ordinary times. Last month, angry crowds had protested in Changsha's streets. People had shouted and waved *dazibao*, placards on which they'd written "anti-inflation" and "anti-corruption." That same night, a similar demonstration had taken place in Xian, the capital of Shaanxi province in the northwest. Such public anger was unheard of in China. The bigger news was the central government's reaction. In an editorial in the *People's Daily*, the government lumped these demonstrations together with the student pro-democracy protests on Tiananmen Square—then one week old—and denounced them as *luan*—turmoil. Equally ominous was an accusation that students were instigating this *luan* in order to overthrow the Communist leadership. For a regime that above all valued stability, there was no more politically charged term.

Qiuping didn't know what her husband thought of the student pro-democracy movement. They didn't talk politics because she had neither mind nor concern for the subject. In the days before Decheng left, she, like everyone throughout China, had been mesmerized by television images of three thousand hunger strikers in Tiananmen Square. She watched because, to her, it was a story of heartache, of the possibility that these young people might die.

Early Thursday morning, Qiuping hurried to the home of Li Hongwu, her husband's best friend. He was the person she and Decheng turned to any time there was a crisis in their lives, and he had never failed them. Qiuping planned to ask Hongwu to go to Changsha and bring her husband back.

Hongwu wasn't at home. Within her wide social circle, Qiuping found another friend who was willing to leave immediately for

Changsha. The friend was gone overnight. He returned Friday morning. He had no news of Decheng or his two friends. Qiuping was left to wonder: the country's main north–south rail line passed through Changsha; had they decided to go to Beijing to join the student protests there?

Few people in Liuyang contemplated seeing the nation's capital in their lifetime. The north was different in geography and climate, dialect, cuisine. The journey by train from Changsha covered more than 1,500 kilometres across several provinces. If indeed Decheng and his friends had boarded the train in Changsha, would they have even made it as far as the capital?

That evening's television news and late-night radio bulletins only heightened Qiuping's anxiety. For the second night running, the news reported rumours that the government was about to declare martial law in Beijing. Now it appeared it was really going to happen. At midnight, the mayor of Beijing announced that People's Liberation Army troops and vehicles had moved into position on the city's outskirts.

The next morning, Saturday, May 20, Beijing was officially under martial law.

Qiuping could not bring herself to ask anyone to risk travel to the capital to find her husband. Not knowing what else to do, she listened intently to the radio, and peered at television images from Beijing, searching faces in the fleeting crowd shots, waiting for close-ups of protestors. She saw nobody familiar.

Saturday night passed. Sunday night. Monday.

By Tuesday morning, tension eased as the army remained outside Beijing. By now, Qiuping had been apart from Decheng for seven nights. In their eight years together, they had been separated this long only once before. He'd been one of several bus station workers chosen for a ten-day trip to the provincial head office in the distant mountain village of Shaoshan in southwest Hunan. She hadn't wanted him to go. Decheng had no interest in going either, mainly because he didn't see any privilege in visiting the village famously known as the birthplace of Mao. But in the end, he went, knowing that if he didn't, he'd be criticized for slighting the Chairman's memory. While he was away, she had found their separation trying; she'd imagined the worst, in the way someone does when possessed by love.

MOST WITNESSES WOULD SAY they saw two young men throw the eggs at the portrait. By their drab, dated clothing, they appeared to be from the provinces. One was handsome with large eyes, the other wore heavy, black horn-rimmed glasses. Two teenage boys had joined in, briefly. They each picked up an egg, threw it, then disappeared.

Few realized that another young man had been involved. The tallest of them, he had been steering passersby away from the area below Mao's portrait so the other two would have space to throw the eggs.

In the aftermath, crowds had pushed the tall man to the margins. Some who'd seen him arrive on the scene with the other two approached him, seeking an explanation for their action. One stranger pulled him aside. He spoke in a low urgent voice: "We have the money and means to get you out of the country; we can put you on a plane to Hong Kong." Then, pressing his point, "You should come with me, *now.*"

The tall man, unfazed, did not respond. Before the stranger faded into the crowd, he levelled a warning. "What you have done is a serious thing," he said. "You'd better *run.*"

DECHENG MET VOICES of confusion and skepticism head-on: "The goals of the student democracy movement are too limited—"

"Don't blame them, they did it because of the students."

"—we did this to demonstrate to the Chinese people that we must confront this regime."

"Students wouldn't do that kind of thing! Who are they?"

Though Decheng had a sense that what he was saying was going over the heads of most of those around him, he wasn't disappointed.

After all, he and his two friends saw their action as aimed not at ordinary people, but at the leaders of the student movement. They had faith that the leaders would see that what the trio had done was a political act that carried symbolic meaning. They had targeted an icon to challenge the despotic rule of the regime. Now it was up to the student leaders to mobilize the people and make them see that, like the stained portrait of Mao, the dictatorship was flawed, even finished. The only goal was democracy, and nothing, not even martial law, could stand in its way.

As Decheng argued with the onlookers, the most extraordinary feeling washed over him; something that he'd never imagined he would experience, or that he had sought to experience. *I have done something great*, he told himself. *I have achieved something.*

A COUPLE OF STUDENTS who were members of the picket squad on the square noticed the suddenness with which a massive crowd had formed under the portrait of Mao. A gathering that large had to be more than the usual gawkers and sightseers. Sensing trouble, they rounded up a half-dozen other pickets and students, and ran over to investigate.

The student pickets came from Beijing's many universities and provided security and maintained order on Tiananmen Square. The word "picket," perhaps better than "marshal," which they were also called, reflected the historical context of picket outposts on China's frontiers, to report and warn of contact with the enemy. During the week-long hunger strike on Tiananmen Square, these picket squads were particularly helpful in forming cordons around hunger strikers to protect them from spectators and keeping "lifelines" open for ambulances. Once martial law had come into effect, their role changed. Their main task, student leaders stressed, was to make sure the protest was conducted peacefully so as to give the regime no excuse to argue that force was needed to restore order.

Even as they crossed Changan Avenue, Beijing's widest thoroughfare, the pickets could see the reason for the crowd: Mao's portrait had been defaced. Blobs and streaks of what appeared to be ink marred the painting, like dark birds in flight, smashed against the canvas. A conspicuous black stain perched lopsidedly on Mao's left eyebrow. Two long streaks blotted his neck. One large yellow gob hovered over his left shoulder. Yet another splat of red dirtied his jacket below his chin like a remnant of a sloppily eaten dinner.

Bystanders pointed out the culprits to the pickets, the two men deep in the centre of the crowd. The first student picket came at Decheng from behind, grabbing the neck of his woolen sweater. Decheng whirled around, swinging his arm violently to free himself from the offending grip. "If I had wanted to run away," he said menacingly to the picket, "don't you think I would have done so already?"

The pickets told Decheng and Dongyue that they were taking them to the student command centre. "You have to explain yourselves!"

"I am going willingly," Decheng declared. "I have no wish to conceal my views."

The picket who'd grabbed his sweater seemed to think it necessary to manhandle him. This time, Decheng fixed him with a stare: "Do you even *know* the meaning of our action?" Apparently not. The picket alternately pushed and dragged him. Decheng had a flicker of self-doubt; perhaps the faith the three of them had in the student leadership was misplaced.

Only when Zhijian saw the phalanx of student pickets on the other side of Changan Avenue did he realize they had his two friends in custody. He grabbed his jacket and the backpack that he'd left on the ground and hurried to try to catch up with them. He called out, "Hey! I'm with them! I'm one of them."

ON TUESDAY EVENING, Qiuping went to the workers' club at the station. Besides a television set and a shelf of books, there was a ping pong table and mah-jong. Several workers and their families were gathered there, like her, awaiting the evening news at seven o'clock.

The broadcast began with the day's top stories. In an update on Tiananmen Square, the announcer said that three men had vandalized Chairman Mao's Tiananmen portrait by throwing ink at it. The visuals showed two workmen, dwarfed by Mao's huge face, standing in an elevated cherry picker. They were at work anchoring a long dark green canvas tarpaulin over the portrait. Several large stains and blotches were plainly evident on the painting.

The announcer went on to say that the students themselves had apprehended the three vandals, all from Hunan province, and turned them over to the police. Qiuping, her heart pounding, saw images of several students, their trademark red cloths tied round their foreheads, tugging roughly at the arms of two men, to make them stand beside a third. She knew all three. She felt herself willing the one with the large eyes to turn his face to her so she could look into them. One of the men, said the announcer, portrayed their action as a protest against the cult of personality worship.

The stunned silence and stillness in the room was like the aftermath of an explosion.

The announcer identified the three men as their names appeared on the screen: Lu Decheng, Yu Dongyue, and Yu Zhijian. Everyone in the room turned to look at Qiuping. They all knew her husband, Decheng, as a talented mechanic. Everyone knew of his father, Lu Renqing, a driver who'd been with the bus company since it started up more than twenty years ago.

Decheng and the other two were shown again in the second half-hour of the news program, which featured interviews with people in the daily news. Decheng spoke animatedly about the technique he had used to throw the paint-filled eggs. Qiuping wailed so hard and long that her co-workers were convinced she was having a nervous breakdown.

LU RENQING AND HIS WIFE, Meilan, had only one luxury in their one-room flat at the staff dormitories of the bus station: a black-and-white television set. As they did every evening, once Renqing was off shift, the couple sat down to watch the news. When Renqing heard that the portrait of Mao Zedong overlooking Tiananmen Square had been vandalized with ink, he took it as an insult. From his chair in front of the television, he admired a pristine poster of the exact image of Chairman Mao on his own wall.

Feeling loathing for the three perpetrators who were being brought forward, Renqing was astonished to recognize the defiant look on the face of one of them, because it was his son's.

"Decheng's never been a good son," Meilan said, repeating her favourite reference to her stepson.

All Renqing could think was that now everyone in town would see him and wonder why Driver Lu couldn't control his own son.

He turned to his wife. "It's over."

When the characters for "Lu Decheng" appeared on the screen and the announcer spoke the name aloud for all the world to hear, Renqing fainted.

A DAY LATER, his rage ignited by his wife, the distraught bus driver marched down Station Road to People's Road and up Plum Tree Alley. He banged on the door of the home of Ironworker Li, Hongwu's father.

"I have only one son!" Driver Lu yelled at Ironworker Li, as if the man should feel guilty for having several. "It's your son that makes my son like this! It's your son's fault!" He stormed past Mr. Li into his house, and went on a rampage, toppling furniture and smashing dishes.

From there he headed to Number 35 Clear Water Alley, the home of Grandmother Lu, the woman who'd raised him and, one generation later, helped raise his own first-born, Decheng. The old lady had heard the news of what her grandson had done and had expected Renqing would come.

Renqing hurled blame her way. "You've been leading him astray since he was small and now look what he's done! You're the one who's filled his head!"

The old lady's penetrating stare expressed utter contempt for Renqing's predictable bullying. Had he raised his son in his own image, he would have yoked him to authority.

Renqing's rage crumbled into self-pity before her. He searched for some concession that for once in their lives the two of them belonged on the same side of an argument.

"These are different times," he said pleadingly. "Things are fine now in China. Life is okay. What does Decheng have to complain about?" When still she didn't reply, Renqing broke down. Between sobs out came what terrified him most, that his only son would be sentenced to death.

"What for?" shot back Grandmother Lu. "What did he do wrong?"

When Driver Lu left, the old lady, feeling the wear of her eighty-five years and the fatigue of her long widowhood, shuffled off to the homes of each of Decheng's two younger sisters. They had all been together a month earlier, when they had joined Decheng and Qiuping to celebrate the fourth birthday of their daughter, Little Xinfeng.

Grandmother Lu had one message for the two sisters. "You mustn't blame your brother," she said.

TWO

How many turns are there in the Liuyang River?
How many miles does it wend to Xiang River?
What county is there on the riverbank?
Who grew up there to lead us to the Liberation?

There are nine turns in the Liuyang River,
It takes fifty miles to reach Xiang River,
There is a Xiangtan county on the riverbank.
Chairman Mao grew up there and led us to the Liberation!

"Liuyang River" to the tune of a Hunan folk song
Revised lyrics by the Music and Dance Unit,
Hunan Province, Literary Work Troupe

THE SLEEPY TOWN OF LIUYANG sat unremarkably along the banks of the Liuyang River in a hilly area just shy of several mountain ranges in Hunan province. The river was famous in all of China. Everyone had heard of its legendary nine bends from the lilting folk song that became an anthem of the Revolution, when new lyrics turned it into a song about Chairman Mao, a native son of the province. The river and the people of the town that shared its name had much in common. Since Liberation, when the Communists took over in 1949, their lives had mimicked the winding river and its fickle ways. They were seldom sure that their lives were on the right course, much as oarsmen on the river experience the odd sensation of having gone round one of those nine bends only to have the scenery they thought they had passed come back into view. Or their good fortune could change without warning into adversity, the same way that oarsmen, enjoying a calm stretch of the river's shallow waters, could find themselves caught in a current moving deceptively fast.

People here, as in much of China, had become more and more accustomed to feelings of powerlessness. After Liberation, much came to depend on the dictates issued from faraway Beijing, where the powerful resided and whose job it was to protect the Revolution. Yet, perhaps the river could offer another metaphor for one's fate. Each drop from the spring melt that feeds the Liuyang from high in the mountains above the town will eventually reach the famous Xiang River, then, the great river of China, the Yangtze. People from this backwater would be mistaken to regard themselves as insignificant players in China's history. A single drop of water can lead the way to the future. Like the tributary of a tributary that becomes a mighty river, one person steps forward and becomes a force of many.

NORMALLY, FOR A WOMAN TO BE WIDOWED was to find herself in a dreadful and pitiable state, especially if left without a son to support her into old age and sweep her grave when she was gone. Zhou Zhaolin, the mother of a young girl—the only one of Zhaolin's five children to survive infancy—was in her late twenties when she learned abruptly of her husband's death. During one of the ruling Kuomintang's campaigns of "annihilation" against the Communists, which had them on the run to their guerrilla base in the mountains of neighbouring Jiangxi province, Kuomintang soldiers captured her husband, condemned him as a bandit, and executed him. Because he'd held a high position—he had been trusted enough by Mao Zedong himself to serve as head man of a west Hunan "soviet," the name given to Communist-controlled townships—the Kuomintang undoubtedly delivered death with great cruelty.

Fortunately, Zhaolin's spirited personality caught the attention of Lu Qiubao, and she remarried quickly, and well. Their names suited his affections for her. His was "Autumn Protector"; hers, "Lotus Inviting the Dawn." He liked the widow rather a lot and was unperturbed that she didn't entirely reciprocate his affections. But he had qualities she admired. Eleven years older than she, and born in the same year as Mao, 1893, Qiubao had left his family's home in the remote mountains as a youth and made for the Xiang River to earn his living. He started with a crooked-stern junk, good for negotiating the sudden twists and turns of the river, and made short trips transporting goods. He moved into collecting timber and steering his great log booms downriver to Changsha, and went on to own barges that carried cargo as far as the Yangtze River. He did well enough to take one of his two brothers into his business. Travelling the waterways, however, was not without risk. His brother once lost a load of salt, worth sixty times the price of rice, to thieving Communist soldiers.

For all the worldly wealth that came to Lu Qiubao and his wife, Zhaolin, children, especially the all-important son, seemed not to be in their destiny. But in 1939, when he was forty-six and she was thirty-five, fortune smiled. Two beggars, a twelve-year-old and his four-year-old brother, walked 60 *li* (one *li* is two-thirds of a kilometre) from the mountains to the Liuyang River, looking for their two uncles, whom the boys knew to be boatmen. Their father, the third of the Lu brothers, had been dead a year from typhoid fever. Qiubao took in the younger boy and his brother took in the older one.

Four-year-old Renqing, whose fortuitous name meant "Celebrate Humanity," stepped onto the older couple's barge and into a comfortable life. The boy had lived in such a remote village that modernity confused him. The first time he travelled down the Yangtze at night, he mistook kerosene lanterns and torch lights on the riverbank and other boats for the eyes of animals.

In 1944, tragedy struck his older brother and the uncle and aunt who took him in. In one of their last offensives of the Sino-Japanese War, the Japanese attacked along the Liuyang River in a drive toward Changsha. A Japanese plane bombed and sunk the uncle's barge, killing all on board.

When Liberation came in 1949, the Communists elevated Zhaolin's status, even though she was remarried to Boatman Lu, to that of a "martyr's widow." The Party wanted to remind society of sacrifice in the name of the Revolution and rewarded Zhaolin with a certificate verifying that her first husband was a Revolutionary Martyr. To have died for the cause was not enough; such heroes had to have died under extraordinary circumstances and in a noble and defiant way. A martyr's widow was supposed to not only command respect, but also to receive material benefits to compensate for her loss. Cadres, the name that applied to all government officials, were expected to watch out for her, even to help her meet health-care expenses or to help pay for her children's schooling.

Despite the recognition, Zhaolin and Boatman Lu would not hear of it when their son, fifteen at the time of Liberation, asked if he could join the Party. Like so many young people at the time, young Renqing was willing to put his trust in Chairman Mao. His parents invoked the popular saying of parents who wanted their sons and daughters to stay clear of the Party: "Good people don't join an organization." Hardly was the new China born when Boatman Lu was himself called upon to make a sacrifice in the name of the new China. One year after Liberation, in 1950, the government made a "compulsory purchase" of his fleet of barges for use in the Korean War.

Qiubao chose to settle in the quiet river town of Liuyang. In the early days of his bachelor life on the river, he had purchased a narrow row house in the town, intending it to be a foothold for his future. The town's modest boast was that it was the birthplace of fireworks and that it had been making them for thirteen centuries. That manufacturing fireworks was still the most important local industry showed the relative backwardness and poverty of the area; those were jobs of last resort as the factories were notoriously unsafe and accidental explosions often maimed or killed workers. Qiubao took the proceeds of the sale of his river business, purchased a building in town, and opened up the Good Fortune Shop, a general store. He invested in a modest twenty *mou* of land (one *mou* is about one-sixth of an acre of cultivated land), a holding typical of a poor to middle-class peasant, and rented it to a farmer. He installed his family across the river in a rural settlement called Tang Family Pier, below the village of Swallow's Nest on Heavenly Horse Mountain. They lived in a house that had once been the wealthy Tang family's ancestral clan temple.

As Lu Qiubao entered his sixth decade, his future seemed secure. His business was thriving. In the attic of his house he kept planks of the finest wood that would one day be made into coffins for him and his wife. But as sure as the Liuyang River cut a bending course, Qiubao's life turned unexpectedly again. In 1954, local Party cadres paid him a visit. Ominously, they said to the enterprising business-man that he could find himself on the wrong side of the Revolution. The Party had been waging a two-year-old political campaign against the capitalist class and thousands had been fined, sent to labour camps, or executed.

The cadres told Qiubao that to avoid persecuting him, they would classify him as a "small trader." He expressed his gratitude, but they were not done. Of course, they said, he would still want to set a good example by honouring his wife's status as a martyr's widow. He could, therefore, "happily donate" his house, the Good Fortune Shop, and his land to the people.

Lu Qiubao's former home became a storage depot, his general store a biscuit factory and warehouse, and his farmland part of an agricultural collective. A martyr's widow and her son could not be thrown out onto the street, so the Party allowed the family to keep the row house in town. The old man, his wife, and their son brought from their old house across the river only what the cadres permit-ted: pots and pans, bowls and utensils, clothing, and the wood intended for the couple's coffins.

Qiubao's downfall precluded his joining the revolutionary working class and getting a state-assigned job. Nothing, however, stood in the way of his nineteen-year-old son or his wife. Renqing and Zhaolin found employment at the Liuyang Bamboo Products

Factory. He made furniture. She joined other girls and women making blinds from scraps of bamboo. For the rest of her life, Zhaolin would be embittered at the reversal of fortune: "We could have had oceans of rice; instead, we have nothing!"

IN LIUYANG, only the beggars' lives didn't change. The town's most familiar vagrant was Small Head Not Proportional to His Body. Clever enough to stake out his begging territory and strong enough to muscle out interlopers, he was the sole helping hand to unload the cart of coal that arrived daily for his neighbourhood eatery. In return, he kept his stomach full with the noodles that departing patrons left swimming in the lick of soup in the bottom of their bowls. If Small Head was but treading water, at least he felt in control of his fate.

The Lu family's row house was in an older part of town between the South and East Gates. Liuyang was once a walled town. The gates were gone now, but their former locations still served to orient the people who lived there. Their neighbourhood was called Zhou Family Pier. Little remained of the original family settlement of the Zhous—tycoons who'd once controlled the upper river—except a sloping slab of concrete at the waterfront, which a descendent put in to ease the work of hauling water and washing laundry.

The Lus' house was located at Number 35 Clear Water Alley, situated among three blocks of identical two-storey row houses, home to about a hundred families. There were two ways to reach the alley. Approaching from the riverbank, one would turn sharply uphill at the gnarled camphor tree. The dirt path turned into a stretch of stone slabs that became Clear Water Alley. A much easier approach, and the only access by vehicle, was uphill from the house. Turning off People's Road onto River Road brought one to the back door and the second floor of the house; the road was carved into the hill.

The neighbourhood of Zhou Family Pier had the look of generations of neglect. The brick exteriors of the century-old houses had mostly fallen away to reveal rotted wood, clumsily repaired here and there with planking. Walls made of thin bamboo stakes separated one row house from another. In places, tacked-up bamboo matting covered holes that were large enough to step through.

Renqing decided he would try to escape this diminished life. He took it upon himself to enlist in the People's Liberation Army. The army was one of the few ways out of rural poverty; it offered the security of a wage and new recruits were sent to Beijing to learn a trade, so enlisting held the added appeal of seeing the capital. Qiubao and Zhaolin only found out what their son had done when the order came for him to report to Beijing. They were not happy. Parents had as much disdain for their children becoming soldiers as joining the Party. "You don't turn good iron into nails," went the saying.

As far as the army brass were concerned, Renqing was a good prospect. They regarded revolutionary offspring as "good roots and shoots." Qiubao and Zhaolin could not stop their son from going. Had they done so, the Party would have condemned their reactionary attitude. Of all people, a martyr's family was expected to know how to comport themselves.

Renqing was happy in Beijing. He looked the part of an army man, tall, with a strong physique. The army trained him to be a driver and assigned him to the personal staff of an officer. Renqing was as pleased with this start to his army career as he was to be in Beijing. To stand in Tiananmen Square with its portrait of Chairman Mao, to watch the October 1st National Day celebrations when Mao himself stood at the Tiananmen Rostrum and waved to the crowd, was exhilarating. The capital embodied the glory that was new China. In 1958, the last stone was placed on the massive Monument to the Revolutionary Martyrs. On the heels of that unveiling, in what seemed to capture the meaning and spirit of Mao's new Great Leap Forward to turn China into a modern industrial power, Beijing launched the construction project of Ten Great Buildings. Two of those were part of the redesign of Tiananmen Square: the Great Hall of the People, which would house the National People's Congress, and the Museum of Chinese History formed a pair to flank the west and east sides of the square. The others were away from the square, including the Beijing Railway Station.

In the end, Renqing's parents got their way. In 1959, three years into his fledgling army career, they sent him a letter summoning him home to Liuyang. "We're old," Qiubao wrote. "We need you to come home." In the army, there were few acceptable grounds to ask for a discharge; caring for one's parents in their old age was one. Though bitterly disappointed, Renqing did his filial duty.

Renqing came back to the dingy row house on Clear Water Alley and back to wearing out the footpath to the bamboo workshop. The business was now a co-operative. Collectivization had come to China. The township of Liuyang operated as a commune, every worker now a member of a brigade or a production team. Nobody worked for themselves; everyone served the state. The Party found ways to turn even the smallest concern into the people's business. A raft that once sat at the river's edge at Zhou Family Pier, there for the use of anyone who had to cross, had now become the People's River Transportation Company. Some found it laughable that once they could pole themselves across the river for free, but now they had to pay the ferryman who had the new state job.

Zhaolin moved swiftly to find her twenty-four-year-old son a wife. She needed a daughter-in-law to help her find food. The Great Leap Forward had brought on severe shortages. She selected from among the girls she worked with. Fifteen-year-old Zhang Xizhen was a sensitive, gentle, and inward-looking girl. Her name, "Delicate Treasure," suited her; she was slight and plain but for her strikingly large and expressive eyes.

From the start, Zhaolin was the overbearing mother-in-law. Delicate Xizhen was hapless and without fight, and also ill pre-pared for the domestic responsibilities of a daughter-in-law. The last of five children, she had lost her mother at an early age. Her widowed father and an older brother had lovingly raised her, doting upon her and indulging her. Now, the older woman was left to fume at how her daughter-in-law lay sleeping while she herself was awake and busying herself before dawn. The chores were endless. Besides foraging for food, keeping the house clean, and cooking, someone had to haul heavy buckets of water from the river and wash clothes at its edge.

Renqing added to his mother's litany of complaints about his new wife. As if to emphasize the lovelessness of the match, he also put her down at every turn. He belittled her standard of cleanliness. He never shut up about his aversion to her body odour. Between her mother-in-law's hectoring and her husband's insults, Delicate Xizhen was often reduced to tears. To cope, she made frequent trips across town to the North Gate, to her birth home. She would confide her woes to her father and her brother, Mingxian. In keeping with his name, "Bright, Worthy," her brother would brighten her mood and restore her sense of self-worth. She would dry her eyes, laugh, and for a little while feel happy.

IN 1963, DELICATE XIZHEN fulfilled her first duty as a wife and produced a son. Traditionally, the honour of naming a child went to the grandparents. On his own initiative, old Qiubao took his grandson to a fortune teller, who predicted that the boy would achieve "great things even before he leaves childhood." What he foretold of the boy's character pleased both grandparents even more: "He will be a man of his own sphere. He will follow his own way." Qiubao named his grandson Decheng. Its meaning, "Virtuous Success," embodied his hopes for the child.

The women from the Residents' Committee were among the first to visit upon news of a birth in the neighbourhood. The government set up these committees everywhere in the 1950s. Two or three "reliable and warm-hearted retirees," in other words, elderly women whom the Party trusted, were given the job of getting to know every family in their neighbourhood, while making sure neighbours behaved as good comrades ought to. In the towns, each committee was responsible for, on average, three-hundred households, and in the country, entire villages. By the 1960s, the committees had grown, typically, to four elderly women. Their tasks expanded; they took orders and instructions from the Party then reported back on residents' compliance with Party dictates and their sympathies for the Revolution. As a consequence, residents began to see these female cadres with the red arm bands as snoops who would get them into trouble.

Tensions eased at Number 35 Clear Water Alley when provincial cadres sent Renqing to work as a driver in the mountains near Shaoshan, because he was now absent from Liuyang for months at a time. The Hunan Provincial Transportation Company required a skilled man to drive 4-ton trucks loaded with minerals or timber. During the four years Renqing spent mostly away from home, he and Delicate Xizhen had a second child, a daughter. A third was on the way in 1968 when the province brought long-distance bus service to Liuyang. Needing drivers, the company transferred Renqing back to his hometown.

He had a new status in town; now he was Driver Lu. A popular phrase, "Four wheels and a knife," summed up the two occupations that the average person coveted—driver and butcher. A discreet slip of the blade could ensure that meat appeared on the family table. A driver, admired for his rare skill, had access to vehicles and could offer a lift for later favours in return. Being a long-distance driver also gave Renqing a way to top up his salary. On out-of-town trips, if he scrimped on what he ate, he could pocket what he didn't spend of his meal allowance.

With this new assignment, Driver Lu had the security of belonging to a "work unit," the all-important *danwei*. Assigned to one, a person could expect lifetime employment. A work unit wasn't just a means to regular wages; it was the organization by which the Party and the government controlled almost every aspect of a person's life. It provided dormitory housing, so that colleagues were also neighbours. Depending on how well off the work unit was, it reimbursed the full costs of health care for workers and usually, at least partial costs for their immediate family. It distributed the ration coupon books for grains and oil and cotton and any other goods that came under rationing if in short supply, such as bicycles. It issued permits for travel, gave permission to join the Party, enter university, marry—and later, when the one-child policy came into effect, become pregnant. The work unit held political study classes. Even recreation was often centred around the work unit. At the end of an individual's working life, the work unit paid the pension, sometimes even the funeral expenses.

The new Liuyang Long-Distance Bus Station opened up on the north edge of town. A new route, called Station Road, joined the terminal to the highway that locals called "Changnan Road," because it connected two provincial capitals, Changsha to the west and Nanchang, the capital of Jiangxi, to the east. The station's wooden dormitories were built to house employees and their families. They had electricity but no running water. Each block contained forty units, twenty on each of two floors, accessed by an exterior corridor with a staircase at each end. The front of each unit had one window and a door and each floor had a communal latrine. An outbuilding served as a communal bath for the entire compound.

Driver Lu and his family were given Unit 6 on the ground floor. The single room measured 5 metres by 5 metres, and at the back was a nook for the hearth. Faced with such cramped quarters, Driver Lu and his pregnant wife arranged for their first-born, Decheng, then five years old, to stay behind at Clear Water Alley to be raised by his grandparents. The couple moved to the dormitory with their three-year-old daughter. In short order, Delicate Xizhen gave birth to a second. The first daughter was Dongmei—"Winter Plum" for the season of her birth—and the newest baby was Xinhui—"New Rays."

YOUNG DECHENG DIVIDED HIS DAYS between his mother and Grandmother Lu. A day with the old lady always included a walk along the riverbank to visit Auntie, her only surviving child, who lived with her own family in a rundown house at the river's edge.

Delicate Xizhen would sometimes collect her son from Clear Water Alley on her way to the bamboo workshop, where children of the women workers played at their feet, or on her way home. Occasionally she'd keep him at the station dormitory overnight; if his father was away there would be extra sleeping room.

Every day at Clear Water Alley, Decheng wandered next door to Number 34, the home of old Carpenter Yi and his wife. The couple loved children and their own were long grown. Carpenter Yi's wife enjoyed playing chess with the neighbourhood children and he was a gifted storyteller. Other children, quickly bored, would wander off, but not Decheng. He sat at the carpenter's knee, listening raptly. His favourites were mysteries featuring Judge Di, a fictional character in Tang dynasty fables, which had been collected and popularized in China by Robert Van Gulik, a Dutch diplomat in the 1930s. In one of the stories that Decheng liked best, the judge, who regularly stumbled on wrongdoing and righted it with his cleverness, is convinced a man was murdered, yet the corpse reveals nothing. The widow, trying to be helpful, suggests he check the skull. Judge Di finds an embedded nail and, his suspicions roused, orders the exhumation of the widow's previous husband. Sure enough, he finds a similarly placed nail and he fingers the widow in both murders.

Come evening at Clear Water Alley, Grandmother Lu would allow her "Little Treasure," as she called Decheng, to fall asleep downstairs, and when she herself was ready to retire, she took him in her arms and carried him up the narrow stairs to his bed. The boy slept securely. His mother left him comforts—a mosquito net, an extravagance that no one else in the family enjoyed, and a quilt that she had sewn for him and patched whenever necessary.

Whenever Decheng stayed at the station and saw his parents together, he saw how cold they were to each other. It hurt to see his mother's tears, but they invariably meant a visit to her birth home, one of his favourite places. Uncle Mingxian was married now so it was his household. But as before, aunts and uncles and cousins were constantly coming and going.

The relatives always fawned over Decheng and his little sisters, who were the youngest of the cousins. Hands constantly ruffled his hair or stroked his cheek. "You are the most lovable little boy," the relatives would say. Decheng had many nicknames, and they addressed him by whichever one he had going, most of them his family name together with endearments of the relatives' own invention. Besides Lu Chengpi, which played on another meaning of *cheng*—wrinkled orange peel—they called him Lu Popo, meaning "pickled egg," which then became Lu Bobo, describing an egg about to become an embryo. Later, seeing how much Decheng loved to eat any kind of *doufu*, not only the watery variety but also a regional specialty and one-time staple of soldiers known as "stinky *doufu*"—bean curd fermented in a vegetable and fish brine and deep-fried to a crisp, with a smell so bad that people would cross the road to avoid it—they called him Lu Doufu. Finally, a growth spurt inspired Lu Gao, "tall."

The young Decheng got some of the same fussing-over at his mother's bamboo workshop, and he considered the trip there to be a reward in itself. After a long walk along the riverbank, Decheng and his mother turned to follow a fast-flowing stream that branched off the river. The bridge they had to cross to reach the workshop had no rails and was only two stone slabs wide, requiring them to walk single file, so that Decheng faced rushing water on either side and could see it between the slabs at his feet. Every time he crossed, his mother extravagantly praised his bravery.

The shared joys of these walks ended when Decheng was seven or eight. Delicate Xizhen had to stop work. What began with episodes of spitting up blood grew into several emergency trips to the hospital. Doctors diagnosed rheumatic heart disease. With rest and the aid of traditional herbs, Xizhen hoped to regain her strength and eventually return to work. Reduced to a one-income household, the Lu family was chased by hunger. Sometimes Decheng and his sisters gnawed on their mother's medicinal herbs and roots, despite their bitter taste.

By now, Decheng was old enough to haul water from the communal water pump and refill the supply of coal bricks for the dormitory unit's hearth. He could also accompany his mother on her daily walks to shop in the market just off People's Road. One of those trips gave him an early sense that his mother had qualities that were anything but ordinary. He was walking hand in hand with her in the crowded market, when his mother stooped to pick up a ten-*yuan* banknote that he had also noticed lying on the ground. A ten-*yuan* note was a rare sight; nothing larger than a five—for most, an entire week's wages—would ever pass through most people's hands. His mother caught up to a man walking just ahead. She tapped him on the shoulder and showed him the ten-*yuan* note, and asked if he had dropped it. Decheng had not seen the note fall to the ground and he was sure his mother hadn't either, so who knew who it belonged to? Seeing the relief that flooded the man's face, however, filled him with guilt that he should have doubted his mother.

On another trip to the market, the two were on an errand to buy his mother cotton slippers with a rope sole. A pair cost two *yuan.* When Delicate Xizhen found and paid for her purchase, the clerk gave her an extra ten *yuan* in change. His mother immediately realized the mistake and handed it back. Decheng's large eyes widened. *What a good person my mother is*, he thought. After all, this was a state shop, the clerk was a state worker. It wasn't her money. Not like the man in the market, who had dropped a ten-*yuan* note of his own. Later, back at the dormitory, Decheng was excited to share the story. He told a neighbour how his mother had returned the extra ten *yuan.* The neighbour was scornful. "What a stupid woman your mother is!" Confused, Decheng said no more.

DELICATE XIZHEN'S STAY AT HOME lasted a year. Her condition worsening, she was admitted for a convalescence at the Hospital of Chinese Medicine. Because the work unit's health insurance didn't cover all of her bill, the family opted for this hospital over the adjoining People's Hospital; traditional medicine was cheaper than Western drugs, which made up most of a patient's bill. Driver Lu's parents helped the beleaguered family by taking in all three of the children.

When summer holidays ended and time came again for school, Grandfather Lu gave his grandson three *yuan* to pay his fees. All that summer Decheng had lingered in front of a shop window on People's Road, admiring the toy tanks and fighter jets. An idea came to him; he could work the distractions of his grandparents and his parents to his advantage. He went to his father and collected money for the same school fees, took the extra back to the shop, and bought the toys. He hid his purchases at his grandparents' house, but it was only a matter of time before he was found out. Grandfather Lu was so upset that he jumped up and down, shouting, "You have cheated adults. Even worse, you have cheated your own parents!" Decheng had never heard his grandfather raise his voice before nor seen him so angry. It was then that he understood the high expectations the old man had of him. He took his punishment: his grandfather bound him to the staircase and paddled his backside. It was the first and last time his grandfather would physically discipline him.

Grandfather Lu let Decheng keep the toys. The boy asked, had he ever had to beat his father? "I never had to lay a hand on your father," the old man said. When his grandmother added, "Your father always listened to us," Decheng was sure he heard disappointment. Then, unable to hide her pride, she said, "You are such a naughty boy!" His own father behaved toward him as men thought a father should— distant, remote, and stern. Any interaction was intended strictly to demonstrate authority: "When you stand, stand up straight! When you sit, sit up straight! Your hands, out of your pockets!"

Comparing his father's bland admonishments with his grand-father's lessons on life, Decheng had a sense that there were strengths and weaknesses that set one individual apart from another. He realized that his grandparents had already been reduced to poverty and that taking in his sisters and him had to be a strain on the old couple. But he saw that poverty didn't have to mean a loss of spirit, which he'd seen little of in his father.

LIKE OTHER CHILDREN, Decheng passed his time at the river's edge watching some of the poorest fathers of Liuyang wade into the water with their homemade basket traps. Everyone in town used to rely on the river for food. That changed after the new steel bridge was raised and people were seduced by progress. The fishery co-operative gleefully used dynamite charges so that carp and grass fish floated belly up on the surface of the river, there for the taking. Within a few short years, the fish were so small that the co-operative abandoned the river to the poor. Every year, before the spring torrent carried the melt down from the mountains, two of those poor fathers drove bamboo poles into the river bottom and anchored a net, its holes stitched smaller than the year before. On the day the river was running the fastest, they pulled up the net. All eyes watched for even a single large fish. If one emerged, a runner was sent to sell the fish to any family in town having a wedding or a funeral. In summer, when the waters of the Liuyang receded, the children awaited the return of the poorest fathers, who planted vegetables in the rich silt left behind.

Grandfather Lu, too old to challenge the river or to stoop in the silt, strapped a basket to his back and plied the ditches in search of a different bounty. Decheng joined him, rising early in the morning. The old man taught him to follow the wind in chase of waste paper, which Decheng snared with a bamboo stick rigged with a nail protruding from its end. Grandfather Lu took a sharp knife and scraped off faded paper banners printed with propaganda slogans and outdated *dazibao* left on walls. Sometimes the posters were from the first years of the Cultural Revolution, typically denouncing teachers, who were gone from Liuyang because they'd been sent to the countryside to do physical labour. In some places, they were several layers thick. Grandfather Lu and Decheng also picked up pieces of broken bottles. Once the old man had collected enough glass and paper, he sold it to the waste reclamation depot.

Though against the rules of collective agriculture, Grandfather Lu kept ducks. His seven or eight spent their days on the river, but he'd trained them to return to the house at day's end. So that they might avoid attracting notice from neighbours inclined to report him, he dug the birds a hidden passageway under the threshold. His ducks delivered the eggs that made festival days special. Grandfather Lu made sure nobody took for granted the blessings one had. At every meal, if even a grain of rice fell from someone's chopsticks or slipped between the bowl and the lips, either onto the table or floor, Grandfather Lu expected it to be retrieved and eaten gratefully.

At mealtimes Decheng saw what a favoured position he occupied. Meat was a luxury and fish a rarity. Usually, the protein for the table was one or two blocks of "watery *doufu*," fresh-curdled soy milk, which people lined up for daily at the co-operative. It didn't matter if one had money to buy more; daily purchases were limited. Grandmother Lu served Decheng even before her husband. Decheng always got the largest portion. If there was a piece of juicy fat among the vegetables, it was his. Any time a special treat was to be had, say crystal pears in season, Grandmother Lu would hold it back from his sisters until he arrived home from school.

THE EDUCATIONAL REFORMS of the Cultural Revolution had shortened the number of years children spent in school. In Liuyang, primary schooling was cut from six years to five, and junior middle school from three years to two. Decheng did not enrol until he was seven. Three times a week, or sometimes more, half the school day was devoted to learning by physical labour. The youngest children gathered mulberry leaves to feed a silkworm operation. Older students did heavier work, most often making bricks to build dormitories for teachers. Decheng preferred the physical work to studying Chairman Mao's thoughts in the classroom. In fact, he enjoyed it immensely. He was strong for his age and growing quickly, and quite ably carried mud on a shoulder pole, fed the fiery kiln, and loaded finished bricks into baskets.

Outside of school, Decheng devoted himself to a purer sort of play. He and his friends transformed alleyways and the riverbanks into a playground. In summer, the river level dropped and revealed pebbles that begged to test the boys' throwing arms. In winter, they waited for days when fat snowflakes drifted down like goose feathers and a thin layer of ice formed at the river's edge, so they could break shards off to eat. Day and night, the young Decheng played and played, stopping only at the sound of his grandmother's voice. She'd come within shouting distance, call him and wait for him to appear, and then they would walk home together.

One early morning, in his second year of primary school, Decheng was, as usual, making his way to school along People's Road. When he reached Plum Tree Alley, he saw Li Hongwu, new to school that year. For the last several weeks, the boy hadn't been seen in class and Decheng had assumed that he'd dropped out. Now he saw why: one leg and one eye were heavily bandaged. The boy was holding a bench and struggling down the solid rock slope of the alley. He repeatedly lifted and planted the bench in front of him, leaned on it for support, and dragged himself forward. Decheng rushed to help.

When Decheng had first seen Hongwu in school, he had figured that the boy was one of many late beginners from the countryside. That would have explained his appearance: malnourished, short for his age, his clothing dirty and ragged. As it turned out, Li Hongwu, two years older than Decheng, had been born in the same neighbourhood of Liuyang. Both of his grandmothers were martyrs' widows. Hongwu had indeed lived in the countryside working alongside his father for the past year and a half, picking up stones in a gypsum mine. He had decided to take the job to pay for his school fees in town.

Hongwu had not quit school; he'd been injured playing hide and seek in the courtyard of a neighbour's home. On that day, heavy rainfall had made the stone slabs slippery. He'd tripped, dislodging a stone that concealed a deep hole and jammed his leg. Hongwu's playmate tumbled into him, forcing his leg deeper into the hole. Hongwu screamed in pain, sweat running off him like water. The neighbour sent for the injured boy's father, while he worked to free Hongwu's trapped leg.

Li Hongwu's family was much gossiped about in town: Ironworker Li had a fondness for drink; his wife had gone mad. In an oft-repeated story, Mrs. Li once took four of her ten children down to the river's edge and threw them in, but the water was so shallow they walked out. She wandered the town mumbling nonsense and—"If you need any more proof she's crazy," people said—scribbling slogans on the outside of houses like "Let's fight Mao!"

Ironworker Li arrived in the courtyard. Hongwu was howling. His father took one look at his mangled leg and lost his temper: "We're so poor! How can we pay for the doctor? How will we survive?" He drew a fist, wound up, punched his son in the eye, and went home.

The neighbour, a high official in the commune, had privileged access to health care. Senior cadres like him went to designated hospitals and saw the best doctors, and their medical costs were fully covered. The official took Hongwu to emergency at the People's Hospital and pulled rank to have him seen immediately. A doctor said the break in the boy's leg required the expertise of a big-city hospital. Fortunately, the neighbour also had access to a car and driver. Two hours later, after a tortuously bumpy ride, Hongwu was attended to by a top surgeon at a hospital in Changsha, where again, the official had been able to press his privileges. After three weeks at home, Hongwu had been so anxious to return to school that he'd resorted to using the bench.

Decheng hoisted the smaller boy onto his back and, at day's end, carried him home and deposited him at his doorstep. He enlisted Yu Zhijian, a childhood friend who lived nearby, to help until Hongwu's leg healed. Zhijian was one of the brightest students in the school and loved studying; he appreciated as few other boys would Hongwu's effort to get to school. This gesture of kindness on

Decheng's part worked a kind of alchemy that bound him and Hongwu in an uncommon friendship.

ONE SUMMER MORNING, nine-year-old Decheng was absorbed in a game that neighbourhood boys invented using marbles and chess pieces. The pieces were set up against a wall, and players collected points according to the worth of the piece their marbles hit. Everyone wanted the King and his Mandarin, but first you had to get the Soldiers, the Minister, the Elephant, the Cannon, the Horse, and the Chariot, or whatever figures the contributing chess sets yielded.

Decheng's game was interrupted.

"Lu Decheng! Lu Decheng!"

A neighbour was calling urgently. "Come with me. Your mother has died."

Not a week ago, Decheng had visited his mother in hospital. She had been there almost a year now, so he'd grown accustomed to her absence. On that day, her condition had seemed no different than the last time he'd visited.

"See you again, Mama," he said upon leaving. "I'll go now."

She held him back a moment. "I have a favour to ask of you." She gave him a twenty-*fen* coin. She wanted him to go to the market to buy her some preserved *mugua*. At the mention of the sour fruit, Decheng's cheeks puckered and his mouth watered. *Mugua* was a delicacy, more expensive than meat, and considered to have medicinal value as an aid to digestion. About the size of a small pear, it grew wild in the mountains outside of town. To prepare it for eating, it was steamed in syrup and dried in the sun, nine times over.

I haven't been to the market, Decheng thought as he followed the neighbour to the hospital. In fact, he'd forgotten his mother's request until now.

They passed the market on their way. Decheng thought of how his mother would have been confident that her son knew his way around the many stalls and vendors and could find her the *mugua* on his own.

In the peace room, a windowless room on the first floor of the hospital, Decheng saw his mother's body, surrounded by her family. Grandfather Zhang had collapsed in a faint. Uncle Mingxian's tears and those of his wife flowed freely.

Renqing's eyes were dry.

My father was never good to my mother, Decheng thought. He gazed at his mother's face. Her expression looked peaceful, more so than he'd ever seen. It struck him that she'd been released from a trying life. He looked back at his father and thought he looked as if he were feeling sorry for himself.

"Decheng, why aren't you crying," an adult chided. In keeping with the rituals of death of a family member, grief, if not heartfelt, was nonetheless to be feigned as a show of respect.

Delicate Xizhen's coffin was brought to Clear Water Alley. Tradition holds that a mother's or father's coffin be brought to the home of the eldest son, where it remains for three days for mourners to pay their respects.

Neighbours and colleagues from the bus station spoke in hushed tones. "Three young children with no mother!" "How old was she?" "Twenty-eight." "Apparently she was sickly even as a child."

Visiting mourners glanced over at the dead woman's boy and remonstrated him. "Why aren't you crying."

By custom, the husband and eldest son had to keep vigil until the funeral. Someone spread straw on the floor for them to lie on. Nearby, two candles burned beside a framed portrait of Delicate Xizhen. A metre-long stick of incense, long enough to last the night, burned slowly, its straightness intended to keep her spirit from wandering on its way to the afterlife.

Decheng lay beside the coffin unable to sleep. In his hand, he fingered the twenty-*fen* coin his mother had given him. On the third night, exhausted, he fell into a deep sleep.

Slap! SLAP! He woke to his father hitting him, hard, across the face.

"You're such a bad son!" Renqing yelled at Decheng. "You can sleep so soundly beside your dead mother!"

In the echoing silence, Decheng thought about how he both wanted his mother and yet was happy she was freed from this world.

THREE

THE THREE FRIENDS described the photograph as "a family portrait." In family was a sense of shared origins, shared destiny; in taking the picture, the intention of putting down a historical marker: three men, two slogans.

The trio assembled, looked solemnly into the lens. Tuesday, May 23, 1989, a little after two in the afternoon, in Zhongshan Park, the Forbidden City, Tiananmen Square, Beijing.

The self-timer triggered the camera and it recorded their image. At thirty *yuan* a roll, film was expensive, so they took only one frame.

With family, for every parting, there is a hope, if not a promise, of reunion.

THE STUDENT PICKETS marched Decheng and Dongyue away from Mao's spattered portrait, toward the Monument to the Revolutionary Martyrs. The 37-metre-high granite obelisk sat on a double terrace with marble balustrades, in the exact centre of the square. It was designed to face north toward the Tiananmen portrait of Mao. His painted visage, therefore, looked toward the adorned side of the obelisk, which carried a gilded inscription in his trademark calligraphy: "The Revolutionary Martyrs are immortal."

The students and their captives reached the cordon of pickets ringing the monument. Their job was to strictly control access to the terraces, where the tents of the student leaders were. More than once, other students had tried to climb over the balustrades to get to the two tents, where the student movement's broadcasting centres were set up.

Three days earlier, Dongyue had presented himself at this check-point. Decheng and Zhijian had been watching from a distance with Li Hongwu, who had travelled with them to Beijing. Dongyue had their proclamation in hand, signed by the four of them, with hopes of delivering it personally to a student leader. The four had decided he was their best chance of getting through security. His heavy, horn-rimmed glasses gave him the air of a scholar. To lend an element of professional credibility, he hung his expensive camera round his neck and had at the ready his reporter's card from the *Liuyang Daily*. The other three saw him immersed in discussion with the pickets on duty, but after several minutes, he handed over the proclamation and walked away.

Today, the pickets turned Decheng and Dongyue over at the checkpoint. Others escorted them beyond. They herded the two up the stone steps to the first terrace, with its hodgepodge of makeshift tents, mostly anchored nylon tarpaulins or plastic sheets. Additional security guarded entry to the upper terrace to which there was even more restricted access, granted only to special pass holders among the student leaders. The picket guards with the two men in tow proceeded, unimpeded, to the second terrace.

Decheng was eager to meet the student leadership. The indignities he'd suffered at the hands of the pickets accumulated, beginning with the grab at his sweater, the manhandling across the square, and now, their guarding him and Dongyue as if they were common criminals. Decheng hadn't seen what had happened to Zhijian, but he wasn't concerned. He was certain that the three would be together soon and would have the opportunity to meet one or more of the student leaders. Decheng believed that when the students recognized that they supported the ideals of the pro-democracy movement, they would receive the three with honour and respect, as a host would a guest.

The pickets led the two men into a small tent. In the cramped space, which served as the office for students in charge of security, Decheng and Donyue faced a row of filing cabinets separating two desks. Seated behind one was a man who appeared too old to be a student. Behind the other was a teenage girl. The picket guards strong-armed Decheng to stand in front of the man, Dongyue in front of the girl.

Decheng felt like they'd been hauled into a police station. *I am not going to wait to be asked*, he decided. He pulled his identity card from a pocket of his sweater, and thrust it, photo side up, at the man.

"I am LU DECHENG."

He thought his message was obvious. His words had been clear, his voice strong. *I am unafraid to speak the truth.*

The man seated behind the desk was unfazed. He took the card but said nothing. He turned it over and over, examining it. His manner was surgical and steely cold.

Decheng suddenly felt uneasy. He looked over at Dongyue, who had emptied his yellow backpack and arranged several items on the desk in front of the girl. He was explaining them to her. The camera was not his; it belonged to his work unit, the *Liuyang Daily*, it was very expensive, he wished that it be returned. The other items were his: a canister of exposed but undeveloped film, a stack of photographs and negatives, several personal notebooks, and a pad of writing paper. Then he asked her a favour: Could she find a student to package these other items and send them to a postal address that he would provide? But not just any student—rather, one whom she was confident was a responsible individual. The girl was obliging. Dongyue gave her his reporter's card so that she would know where to send the camera, and he wrote out the address of a former class-mate where the rest of his belongings were to be sent.

THE HEAD OF THE STUDENT PICKET squad was Zhang Jian, a muscular eighteen-year-old student at Beijing Sports College. He was alerted through his walkie-talkie that there had been a security problem: three men had thrown ink at Mao's portrait at Tiananmen Gate. However, the situation was under control. Student pickets had managed to surround them, capture them, and take them to the monument for questioning. They were now being detained in the bus, formerly the command centre for the hunger strike, parked near the Museum of Chinese History.

Security Chief Zhang, whose burly physique and square jaw suited his role as head picket, considered himself busy enough without distractions like this. Once the regime had issued the edict of martial law, the student leaders' primary concern became holding the army to the outskirts of the city. Zhang likened his work since martial law to that of a military strategist. He coordinated intelligence on the locations of troops and army vehicles, dispatched students to intersections and bridges, as needed. His work was hampered by the overlapping roles and territory of numerous picket squads. They had proliferated on the square with the influx of students from the provinces and with the presence of the Beijing workers' group, both of whom had established their security patrols.

Upon hearing that some unknown persons had vandalized Mao's portrait, Zhang was peeved: they'd managed to maintain a peaceful presence on the square, and now this. He went to see the portrait, saw the gawking crowd, then made his way toward the bus where the three perpetrators were being held. Worry overtook him. He wondered if these three could be agitators disguised as students and sent by the Party to damage the student movement.

An incident in the last week, during the hunger strike, and at the height of public support for the students, had put the student leaders on guard against *agents provocateurs*. On that particular afternoon, a million Beijingers had surged toward the square to show solidarity with the hunger strikers. Word reached the student broadcasters that Voice of America, the respected international radio network, was reporting that 100,000 Beijing steel workers had gone on strike to back the students' demands. The students considered this startling development and what their reaction should be. Their own actions played to a vast contingent of foreign reporters; 1,200 journalists had descended on Beijing to cover a historic state visit by President Mikhail Gorbachev, the leader of the

Soviet Union. But the story of the visit, which ended a thirty-year rift between the two Communist superpowers, was eclipsed by the drama in Tiananmen Square.

The students immediately determined that this was a false rumour; the student movement had never advocated strikes. It had gone only so far as to call for class boycotts and only during the early days of the protest. They thought that whoever was trying to bait them into becoming excited about a massive strike had an amateurish understanding of the student movement; strikes were about workers' rights, and the students, in order to keep their movement "pure," had struck no alliances with non-student groups, even avoiding intellectuals. The leaders saw a trap: the regime could be trying to trick them into broadcasting a lie so that the police could arrest them for rumour mongering and inciting subversion. The students manning the broadcast station acted quickly. They dispatched others to eavesdrop in the vicinity. They overheard two men repeating the strike story and apprehended them. The students suspected that by their appearance—clean-cut, with athletic builds—the two were undercover policemen. Moreover, both refused to give their names. A body search revealed that neither carried identification. Some student leaders wanted to rough up the two to teach them a lesson, but in the end, they gave them a tongue-lashing and let them go.

When Security Chief Zhang arrived at the bus, pickets told him they were holding only two detainees, that the third man was being held by the workers' group. They said that these two had handed over their identification and that the students and the workers' group had agreed to hold a press conference to make clear that the three men weren't students.

Zhang looked at the two men squatting in the aisle of the bus. Despite the heat, one had on a jacket and a woollen sweater, evidence that he'd travelled to Beijing and was wearing everything he'd left home with. The other man couldn't possibly be a government agent; no one would be so foolish as to don such conspicuous heavy, black horn-rimmed glasses or carry a bright yellow backpack.

Zhang challenged the two men: "A true man would have the courage to tell the whole world who was responsible—"

"I take full responsibility for what I did. I have nothing to hide," interrupted Decheng.

The other man, Yu Dongyue, was as insistent that what the three of them had done was entirely their own idea. They had written a proclamation for broadcast by the students, it had not been aired, they had wanted to express their anger at what Mao and the regime had done to the Chinese people.

Zhang was awed by both men. *Someone could be so honourable as to step forward so readily, could be so unambiguous, so clear-cut in his attitude? This was something extraordinary.* He thought the two men deserved the courtesy of an explanation. They should know why defacing the portrait had so upset the students. "We're under great pressure to maintain a peaceful and orderly protest in the square," he told them. "Tiananmen Square is the important flag of the national student movement and if we fail here then we will fail in the whole country." Before the security chief left, he offered them his opinion about their act of protest: "If it were up to me, I would choose a completely different way against the one you oppose. I would take along others with me and go to the mausoleum, disarm the guards, take out the corpse, and flog it."

UNABLE TO CATCH UP to the student pickets hustling his two friends away, Zhijian surrendered himself to pickets from the Beijing workers' group. The group's tent was at the northwest corner of the square, against the front wall of the Forbidden City. Nearby the workers' tent was that of a student leader. Zhou Yongjun was an adviser to the workers' group, helping to draft proclamations and speeches and to set up a loudspeaker system. Adviser Zhou, who was enrolled at Beijing's University of Politics and Law, had headed the initial group of protesting Beijing students and appeared in one of the early defining television images of the protest in the square. He was one of three students who kneeled on the steps of the Great Hall of the People, appealing to China's leaders to accept a petition of student demands. In the end, no leader emerged.

Even though the commotion at Mao's portrait had happened practically on the doorstep of his tent, Adviser Zhou heard nothing of it until the head of the workers' pickets showed up with the third culprit. The picket said he needed to use Zhou's tent as a place to hold the man, at least until the workers' group told him otherwise.

"Since he was here to cause trouble, we did a body search," the picket said, placing a wristwatch on Adviser Zhou's desk. "He caused damage, so his belongings should be confiscated."

Zhou looked over at the man, who had moved to the farthest corner of the tent and was squatting there. He looked utterly exhausted, and as though he hadn't washed in days. Zhou thought he looked like one of those who'd travelled great distances to be in the capital to support the student movement. They were typically poor and without friends in Beijing, so they slept out in the open in the square. Most, however, didn't stay more than a couple days.

Zhou felt overwhelming pity for the man. "Come over here," he said, his voice kindly.

Zhijian rose slowly and walked over to stand before him.

"Why did you do it?"

The man said nothing.

"You can speak freely about your thoughts."

Finally, Zhou bridged the silence by handing back the man his watch. Thinking he was probably hungry, he offered him something to eat. He had on hand only what had been donated by Beijing residents: bread, green-bean gruel, and soft drinks.

His voice weak and barely audible, Zhijian uttered, "Thank you." He took some gruel and drink.

Sometime later, the head of the workers' pickets returned to Adviser Zhou's tent. He gestured to the man squatting against the wall. "What should we do with him?"

"What is there to do?" said Zhou. "Let him go. Let it pass."

At that moment, they were interrupted by one of the leaders of the workers' group. The students had called for the third man.

Like Security Chief Zhang Jian, other leading activists and leaders among the students kept odd hours, coming and going from their tents on the monument, and from the square itself. However, one hub of activity was the tent of the Voice of the Movement, the students' main broadcast station. Ever since the students had begun their occupation on the square, the station was manned twenty-four hours a day. Students were constantly receiving documents, writing scripts for broadcast and editing them, deciding what to broadcast, and doing the broadcasting itself.

Feng Congde, a twenty-two-year-old graduate student in physics at Peking University, was in the broadcast tent when word came that the picket squad was holding three men who had defaced Mao's portrait. Like him, every student there was alarmed that, yet again, someone was trying to damage the movement. Many saw a historical parallel between the damage to the portrait of Chairman Mao and the burning of the German Parliament building, in the fire of 1933. Some were convinced that the Communist leadership had sent these three agitators to pose as students and defile Mao's portrait, the iconic national symbol of modern China. They feared that just as Hitler may have plotted the arson at the historic Reichstag in Berlin and then created panic by blaming German Communists and declaring a state of emergency, so too could the Communists in China use the damaged portrait to discredit the voice of students and bring the pro-democracy movement to a halt. "If those three men are really students," Feng fretted, "then all our work in trying to keep out the troops will be for nothing."

Zhijian joined Decheng and Dongyue on the bus. The pickets kept them separated along its length, each under guard.

Students came on board and asked the three for the same information as was on their identity cards: name, birth date, work unit, residence. They were then told to write it down and sign their names to it.

One of the students asked Decheng a single question: "Why did you do it?" Decheng was expansive in his reply. But the entire time, he couldn't tell if what he was saying was making any impression, one way or another.

The afternoon wore on. Decheng's guard was kind enough to offer him a bottle of water. Never having tasted bottled water before, he found it salty and undrinkable. Around four o'clock, gusting winds blew up. Intense windstorms, carrying clouds of swirling dust from the Gobi Desert, were typical of springtime weather in Beijing. A violent, twenty-minute downpour followed. When it was over, the temperature had plummeted. Decheng's guard, noticing him huddling to stay warm, rummaged through the piles of used clothing. He returned with an old black cotton jacket. It was a child's size, but Decheng gratefully draped it over his shoulders.

After the storm passed, pickets came to take the three off the bus.

Decheng hoped that finally a meeting between the three of them and the student leaders was going to happen. The pickets said nothing, however, about where they were leading them. The group walked east, toward the Museum of Chinese History. As they passed a portable public toilet, Decheng said he needed to use it. When one of the guards followed him inside, he sighed. *They know perfectly well that if we wanted to run away there has been opportunity enough!* The guard, a young, slight student whom he towered over, stayed awkwardly close. Decheng turned on him. He couldn't contain his sarcasm: "Do you think, you—on your own, one person—could really stop me if I wanted to escape?"

Decheng rejoined the waiting pickets and his two friends. The group approached the central facade of the Museum. Hundreds of reporters, Chinese and foreign, had amassed at the bottom of a set of twenty-one steps that ran 100 metres along the length of the central facade and served as the base of an enormous colonnade.

Decheng saw the waiting reporters and reeled. As the students led him and his two friends up the steps, he realized that the three of them weren't going to meet the student leadership. The students had already decided how to interpret their action, to not only the Chinese people but to the entire world.

A student spokesman stood at the top of the steps and read a statement to the press: earlier that afternoon, just after two o'clock, three vandals had thrown ink to deface Chairman Mao's portrait, the students themselves had apprehended the three men, and they would be handing them over to the Public Security Bureau—the police.

Betrayal.

Decheng's heart sank. Last evening, when they considered the worst that could befall them, they had spoken of the police felling them on the spot, shooting them or beating them. Now he saw their naivety. They thought they had read the situation in the square. They thought they were helping the students, who had the weight of history on their shoulders. They had convinced themselves of the symbolic nature of their action, and had thought that the student leaders would see it the same way. From the moment the pickets had waded through the crowds to grab him and Dongyue, Decheng had retained confidence in the leadership. Now he saw that Dongyue had understood right away that their action would have only negative consequences. In the pickets' tent, he'd been making sure that sensitive material in his backpack would find its way into safe hands.

The spokesman identified the three vandals: Lu Decheng, twenty-five years old, a bus mechanic with the Hunan Provincial Transportation Company, at the branch in Liuyang township; Yu Dongyue, twenty-one years old, an arts editor at the *Liuyang Daily*; and Yu Zhijian, twenty-five years old, a teacher at Tantou Elementary School.

The spokesman said one of the three would speak to the press. To Decheng's surprise, a picket led him forward to the microphone. The spokesman asked him to confirm that the three of them were not students. Decheng's face darkened. *No, they were not.* His large

eyes stared, unblinking. *No, they did not represent any school.* He struggled to keep a coherent mind. *No, they were not associated with any school
organization that had joined the student movement.*

Decheng looked out at the sea of reporters, television cameras,
long lenses, microphones, and tape recorders. On the one hand, he
was drowning in disappointment, and on the other, he was acutely
aware that this most certainly would be the only opportunity to
explain to the world press their political thinking, the reasons they
had undertaken their action.

*No, no one in the student movement had told the three of them to vandal-
ize Chairman Mao's portrait.*

If the three of them didn't get their views out now, they would
forever be misunderstood, their intentions misinterpreted. Yet, he
felt wholly inadequate to speak for his friends. Dongyue was the
one who helped turn Zhijian's ideas into speeches and into
the proclamation delivered to the monument. Zhijian was pas-
sionate about politics and a gifted orator, as much at ease with one
person as with hundreds. The two slogans that they had posted at
Mao's portrait had sprung from his fertile mind. As he faced
reporters, Decheng was possessed with one thought: the students
chose the least educated and the least articulate one among the
three of us to cast us in the worst light, in order to divorce themselves and their movement from us.

No, no one in the student movement was involved in their action.

Anger forced words of his own out of his throat.

He yelled into the microphone: "We have nothing to do with the
Communists either! No one gave us instructions to do this. No one
is behind us." He stabbed at the air for emphasis. "We did this of
our own initiative. We take full responsibility for our actions—"

The spokesman pushed Decheng aside. He ignored the raised
hands of reporters and ended the press conference.

THERE WERE NO WAITING POLICEMEN. Instead, the three were
taken by students to a nearby trailer belonging to Chinese Central

Television, which was broadcasting from the square. The trio sat, waiting. They were to be interviewed next. On the set, the host of the seven o'clock news, Chen Yi, as famous for his silver hair as for his mellifluous voice, was taping an interview with three students.

They told him that a new liaison group of student and non-student organizations had been established city-wide, and that a new single command structure would go into effect tomorrow on Tiananmen Square. They named two students who would lead them. Wang Dan—the twenty-year-old history student from Peking University was considered "the brains" of the student movement—would head the new city-wide group; Chai Ling—twenty-three-years-old, she was a graduate student in psychology at Peking University and the leader of the hunger strike—would command the square. When the interview finished taping, the atmosphere was convivial. The three students called the host "Uncle" and he addressed them with the familiar "Xiao," meaning "Little."

Next, the three from Hunan took their places on the set. The host turned first to Yu Zhijian. In his usual calm, thoughtful manner, Zhijian explained the symbolism of targeting an icon of the Communist regime. He carefully explained the slogans they had composed: "Five thousand years of dictatorship will cease at this point!" and "The cult of personality worship will vanish from this day onward!" Zhijian drew on Western philosophers to articulate a desire for freedom and democracy. He expressed the goal of the three, to motivate the student leadership to question the legitimacy of the Communist regime itself, and therefore its very authority to impose a state of martial law. Above all they hoped to inspire the students to return to the original ideals of their movement—democracy for the Chinese people.

The host turned to Lu Decheng. "What happened to your back?" he asked. He called the cameraman to come in for a close-up on the thick, droopy stains stuck to the wool of Decheng's sweater.

Decheng touched his back. Egg white mixed with paint was encrusted there.

To better explain the mess, he stood up to demonstrate what it had taken to compensate for the sharp angle of the throw. To reach the target, he'd had to lean way, way back. The force of the forward motion, he explained, created a corresponding backsplash, thereby spilling some of the paint mixture cradled in the eggs. When the cameras were turned off, Decheng felt content. They had explained themselves well.

THE DRIVER OF THE MINIVAN repeatedly checked his rear-view mirror, as if he were afraid they were being followed. He took a circuitous route from the trailer to the police detachment responsible for Tiananmen Square, turning what was normally a five-minute trip into a twenty-minute ride. Among the eight in the van, including the three captives and three student guards, were a man and a woman. Their identities were unclear; Zhijian suspected that they were security agents from the government.

Decheng and Dongyue rode in silence. Not Zhijian. His guard, Guo Haifang, a twenty-two-year-old graduate student at Peking University, was a student leader. Guo had come to prominence early as the first of the three students to fall to their knees on the steps of the Great Hall of the People. Guo whispered to Zhijian that the students had had a heated debate about what to do with the three of them. Some had argued that they had no right to arrest and interrogate them. Others didn't know whether to believe they really were who they said they were; their identification could be faked. Some thought they should let the trio go, others that they should be turned in to the police. Finally, the matter was put to a vote. "There were nine who voted. We lost by one vote," he said. The van pulled up to the police station and as each of the three men from Hunan disembarked, Guo asked for their autographs. Decheng thought the request odd, but he obliged.

Inside the police station, Guo Haifang became curt and officious. He brazenly identified himself to the police by name and position, secretary-general of the autonomous union of Beijing universities.

The word "autonomous" asserted that the group was independent of the government and the Party. By that very definition, it was illegal. Guo demanded that the police give him a signed document acknowledging that they had taken the three men into custody. The police acquiesced when he refused to leave without it. "In the future," he warned, showing his audacity again, "we may come back to find out what has happened to them."

Half an hour later, after having registered the criminal cases of the three men for investigation, the police transported them across town to a temporary holding centre. The driver's route took them along Changan Avenue past the front of the Forbidden City. A large tarpaulin completely covered Mao's portrait.

At the detention centre, the three new detainees were being processed, to be separately incarcerated. A teenage boy sauntered in. Judging by his familiarity with the place and his casual relationship with the staff, Decheng decided he must be a relative of a worker there.

"Hey!" the boy exclaimed to the three men. "You guys were just on television!"

He walked around Decheng to get a look at his back. "That's egg on your back." He was contemptuous. "You guys have a lot of *nerve.*"

FOUR

WHEN HIS MOTHER DIED, Decheng was one year short of his tenth birthday. The end of the first decade is considered the first coming of age and after that, a birthday is not marked until age sixty, the beginning of celebrated old age. Of much more significance in Decheng's formative years was his mother's death. Her passing came to delineate a time before, when he knew happiness and believed in goodness, and a time after, when he would see that this virtue had lost currency. As for becoming a man "of his own sphere," as predicted by the fortune teller, the boy first had to decide how he would abide his periods of unhappiness.

WITHIN MONTHS OF HIS WIFE'S DEATH, Driver Lu found a widow who was as pleased as he to be remarrying. Xun Meilan was twenty-eight years old, born in the countryside the same year as Delicate Xizhen. From the widow's perspective, two things worked in Lu Renqing's favour: the high social status of his job as a driver and his *hukou*—the household registration booklet that gave him legal residency in the town—and the food rations that came with being an urban resident. Instituted by the Communists in the late 1950s, the registration system (called *hukou*) classified residents, and their descendants, as rural or urban, and agricultural or non-agricultural, the latter intended to distinguish industrial workers as the only ones eligible for subsidized housing, education, and health care. The restrictions on relocation and moving about were so severe that peasants could be arrested just for entering an urban area. Marriage was not always accepted as grounds for a transfer of one's *hukou*, but on that score, the widow Meilan was lucky. For Driver Lu, what appealed was the prospect of a mother. And, because she was infertile, he would be giving her the gift of children, including the coveted son, who could care for them in old age and sweep their graves after they died.

Grandmother Lu learned that Renqing was to remarry only when he asked her to deliver his three children to the station dormitory the next day for a wedding ceremony. Decheng fumed that his father had not told his two sisters himself. Like Decheng, the girls were still grieving the loss of their mother, and he thought his father should not have waited until the wedding to introduce the woman moving in to their mother's house.

The thirty wedding guests were mostly workers from the bus station. The bride, Meilan, was tall and attractive like her name, "Beautiful Orchid." She impressed all the guests with her smooth manners. She was a tailor, which explained her fine wedding dress. Renqing congratulated himself on recognizing a sure investment, unlike his mother's poor choice of Delicate Xizhen.

At the end of the ceremony, Renqing asked his two oldest children to pay their respects: "Address your mama." Decheng couldn't get the word out. Like him, his sister stood silent.

Their new stepmother waited, expectantly.

Some guests scolded the children: "Don't be so stubborn. Address your mama." The situation grew tense. "Address her as auntie, then!" The children could only manage to mumble the everyday salutation, used for friends, relatives, and acquaintances alike.

After the wedding, there came an early occasion to smooth the waters between Decheng and his new stepmother. "Since it's your tenth birthday," Renqing told him, "come for a meal." Stepmother Meilan excelled at all domestic skills, including cooking. In other ways, Unit 6 in the dormitory was nothing like it had been when it was the domain of Renqing's first wife. Stepmother Meilan was fastidious to the extreme; she had a phobia of germs. She ate only her own cooking and only from her own dishes. The tables had turned on Renqing; now he was the one to be nagged about inadequate standards of cleanliness.

On Decheng's tenth birthday, July 1, 1973, he went to the bus station to share a meal with his family. Unexpectedly, his maternal grandfather showed up. Grandfather Zhang had gone first to Clear Water Alley but, finding no one home, had walked to the station. He came bearing traditional gifts: candy, a double stack of long noodles to represent a wish of longevity—one must be careful not to break any—and to signify life's changing cycles, hard-boiled chicken eggs dyed red. He had more, presenting his grandson with two one-*yuan* notes, two face towels, and a pair of socks—like the blessing of double happiness, good things come in pairs.

Stepmother Meilan intercepted the gifts. She hollered at Decheng: "This grandfather represents the *dead* side of your family. You don't take gifts from dead people!" She smashed the eggs to the floor and stomped on the noodles. Tears streaming down his cheeks, his heart breaking for his disappointed grandson, Grandfather Zhang beat his chest in frustration.

The two Lu girls fared no better in the new family order. Children often came home with head lice and Stepmother Meilan, appalled at the prospect, opted for the most drastic precaution and shaved her stepdaughters' heads. That the woman should care so much about her own appearance yet be so insensitive toward his sisters' upset Decheng.

Greater humiliation was to come.

He'd first noticed his littlest sister's puffy eyes, then discovered that her pillow was damp, and felt badly that she had been crying herself to sleep. Then bruises appeared up and down her arms and legs. A horrified Decheng came across his stepmother disciplining his little sister in the courtyard outside the dormitory block. "Kneel!" she ordered the little girl, then raised her 18-inch wooden tailor ruler and began to whip her.

"STOP!" Decheng yelled.

That evening, Renqing showed up at Clear Water Alley in a rage. He grabbed the laundry paddle and smacked Decheng viciously. "On all the earth, there is no parent who is wrong!" he bellowed.

One day, a neighbour of Driver Lu, Old Wang, cornered Grandmother Lu at the station. "I can't bear to see a small child kneeling in the dirt, being beaten by an adult!" he said. He'd intervened and got into a quarrel with Stepmother Meilan. A few hours later, Driver Lu banged on his door: "Old Wang, are you looking for trouble?" Grandmother Lu promptly rounded up her two granddaughters and took them across town to see Uncle Mingxian: "I want your male point of view on how the children of your younger sister are being treated by their stepmother!" Renqing came immediately, arriving in a company truck to pick up his daughters.

Some weeks later, Renqing ordered his two oldest children to gather discarded wood left over from a construction project on the station grounds, for use as fuel for the cooking hearth. They took their little sister with them. They returned to the unit, arms laden, to something they'd never seen before: their father weeping. He saw them and gathered the youngest into his arms. This too was something they were seeing for the first time—their father displaying physical affection.

"There are no more pictures of your mother," Renqing told his children, through his tears. "Your stepmother destroyed every one of them." So taken aback was Decheng at hearing a sentiment as raw and intimate as grief in his father's voice that the enormity of the loss didn't sink in until later. More concerned about his father, he went to the unit directly above his father and stepmother's, where he knew a girl his age whom he could rely on to tell him what she'd seen or heard from below. His father and stepmother had had a screaming match. Stepmother Meilan had run outside with the pictures and ripped them up then set fire to them. "Practically the whole station was watching!" said the girl.

Renqing, reduced to tears by his wife and with his authority in tatters, sent Decheng's two sisters back to living most of the time at Clear Water Alley, joining their brother there. Still, Stepmother Meilan remained single-minded about expunging the memory of Delicate Xizhen. One year later, Grandfather Zhang died. Renqing took all three children to pay their respects at the wake, held at Uncle Mingxian's. Stepmother Meilan found out where they'd gone and came rushing over: "You don't take children to a place of death! Their mother has been dead so long she's out of the family!" For months after that young Decheng couldn't understand why, whenever he had to go to the home of Stepmother Meilan and his father, his feet started to ache. But it was obvious that a heavy heart makes for a heavy step.

DECHENG LOST HIS PATERNAL GRANDFATHER at about the same time. Old Grandfather Lu died at eighty-one. With his passing went the moderating influence on Decheng's father's temper and iron rod of discipline. As the new patriarch of the family, Renqing had a freer hand of authority and he used it. When he showed up at Clear Water Alley, he acted as though every visit carried with it the obligation to scold and punish his son. Seemingly, Decheng could do nothing right. One day it could be, "Your hair, get it cut! What will people say when they see you like that!" The next, if Renqing saw Decheng combing his hair, "Why do you care so much about your appearance?" He berated and insulted him: "You useless boy!" Regularly, he would get so worked up that the veins on his head bulged: "Are you my son or are you not? Then act like it!" Always, there was an accompanying cuff or smack. Renqing would curse in the most coarse of terms, then hurl a last word: "Get out of my sight and don't come back!"

In contrast, Grandmother Lu's scoldings were affectionate and reserved only for her grandson's youthful misadventures. He once came home without his shirt. He explained to her that he'd pleaded with the ferryman to let him steer the raft and he ended up breaking the pole. The ferryman had demanded that the boy give him fifty *fen* to repair it, or else his shirt. "How many shirts do you own," chided Grandmother Lu, "that you can give one away?" She went back with him to the river and demanded the return of the shirt and refused to pay the fifty *fen*. She upbraided the ferryman:

"He's just a child; he didn't break the pole on purpose. It broke because of his inexperience!" In the end she handed over the money, but she and Decheng left feeling triumphant.

Grandmother Lu, widowed again at sixty-nine, had lost none of her fight. The more Renqing came after Decheng, the more she rose to his defence. She argued that the boy certainly did not deserve to be physically disciplined. Renqing argued back that the laundry paddle, his instrument of choice, was entirely appropriate to his purpose—an elder teaching a youth a lesson—because it had a big end and a small end. Yet, other times, his temper found its outlet in a piece of kindling or a broomstick handle, even a length of bamboo, which left behind painful, red welts.

The house on Clear Water Alley fit like a picture frame around the tensions that defined the Lu family. Grandmother Lu was fond of threatening Renqing with disinheritance, that she might leave the family home to Decheng instead of him. Perhaps owing to Stepmother Meilan's formidable ability to guard her own interests, the two families arranged that five days a week, from nine until five, she could use the second floor for her tailoring business. Most mornings, on her way over she would stop by the vendor selling fresh Western-style buns to buy one for Grandmother Lu and one for Decheng. The hot baked bread, with a heavenly aroma and a golden crust, was an extravagance; one baked bun cost as much as five *mantou*, the more typical breakfast fare, steamed buns with a texture like a dense sponge. Coming from Decheng's stepmother, however, the baked bun, which should have tasted sweet, went down sour.

GRANDMOTHER LU AND DECHENG got along like two steps on a flight of stairs. There came a day, after a routine trip to the ration store, when the old lady began to share confidences with Decheng and trust him to keep them.

Grain (where rice wasn't available, corn, sorghum, millet, soybeans, or tubers), pork, and cooking oil were rationed. In the 1970s, the monthly allowance of oil still amounted to only a single table-spoon per person. Consequently, those who could afford their monthly half pound of pork were anxious for the fat on it, so they could render it for cooking.

Normally, Grandmother Lu, who told time at night by the position of the moon, roused Decheng so he could go ahead to claim a spot in the queue at the ration store, and she toddled along later. On this morning, Decheng woke himself when it was still dark. Yesterday, he'd been too far back in the line and the meat had run out. Today, Decheng arrived to see not a soul. He placed a brick to mark his spot as first in line and ran home to wake his grandmother and tell her of their good fortune. Luckily, she sent him straight back. People who had since lined up had ignored his brick. Close to 6 a.m., the hour the shop opened, several Red Army veterans and retired cadres showed up and muscled their way to the front. A war of words erupted. Like Decheng and Grandmother Lu, many of the people in line had come the day before and left empty-handed. They were, understandably, furious.

The interlopers condescendingly waved off the crowd's protestations. "Who are you to say we can't buy meat? This world is ours! We fought for it!"

Grandmother Lu plunged into the fray: "I am a martyr's widow! I am lining up like everybody else."

"Shut up, you useless old woman. You should have been dead by now."

For the second straight day, Grandmother Lu and Decheng left empty-handed. On the walk home, once safely out of earshot of anyone, a subdued Grandmother Lu told her young grandson that what he'd seen in the queue was the contempt of the powerful for ordinary people. It was hurtful and wrong, she said. She wanted him to understand that her classification as a martyr's widow was not something to be wished upon anyone. "To be a wife and to receive news that your husband has been executed is a dreadful thing." It was not her choice that the Communists made her a martyr's widow, a status that would bind her forever to the Party's cause. This was something she had to accept. But, she emphasized, this did not mean that a person should lose the ability to think for themselves, to develop their own beliefs.

She continued these confidences whenever they walked along the riverbank to Auntie's home, when no one was nearby. "Of what I tell you, do not speak freely," Grandmother Lu cautioned. She shared secrets told her by her first husband. She never attacked Mao directly, nor did she malign the Party. Rather, she spoke of taking the measure of a man by his character, and of her sympathies lying with ordinary people.

Among her tales, Grandmother Lu exposed an ugly side of a Communist legend that earned Liuyang a place in the lore of Mao Zedong's rise to power. Everyone in Liuyang enjoyed the annual commemoration of the Autumn Harvest Uprising of 1927, when Mao launched peasant insurrections in south Hunan, turning the fledgling Communist movement into an armed struggle. Every September 20, a torch relay began in a mountain village and ended fifty *li* later in the Big Marching Ground in town. The last runner passed through the wrought-iron entrance to the large dirt field that functioned as the town square, and delivered the torch to a stage festooned with one of Mao's most famous quotations: "A single spark can start a prairie fire." Grandmother Lu retold her husband's stories from those early skirmishes. In one, Mao's men stole an ox from a peasant family, blindfolded it, and wrapped it in cloth, then set it ablaze and ran it against the wooden gate of a walled town to batter and burn their way in. "An ox is precious to a family," Grandmother Lu said to Decheng. "The loss must have been overwhelming." Thievery abounded in these accounts. Mao's men were not above using the peasants' stores of grain and rice as their own larder. And she told what her husband had confided in her, of Mao's betrayals and deceits that had delivered his own men to death by execution.

Decheng knew this kind of talk was dangerous.

At school, he was being taught that class struggle lay at the core of human nature. For inspiration, teachers took their primary students to the village where the annual torch relay began. Back at school, Decheng and his classmates made paper replicas of the long-haired red spears they'd seen at the memorial hall in the village, dedicated to the Autumn Harvest Uprising. The teachers chose the best spears for use by the school's Little Red Soldiers, students who were like young Communists in training. Every early morning and lunchtime, two Little Red Soldiers stood on ceremonial guard at the school's front archway, which framed a view of the plaster statue of Mao in the courtyard behind.

Teacher Tu was recruiting Little Red Soldiers when he called Decheng over to stand back-to-back with him. "You're taller than me now!" Teacher Tu had noticed Decheng not for his academic abilities—his marks were only ever mediocre—but for his athleticism. The boy had quite an arm; he broke the county record for juniors for the shot put and the hand-grenade toss.

"You're getting so tall," Teacher Tu said. "You'll be in junior middle school next year; it's your last chance to be a Little Red Soldier. Why don't you join today."

Little Red Soldiers went on to become Young Pioneers, the Party's formal organization for children and youth. They patrolled the grounds and the school and reported on anybody not showing proper dedication to class struggle. Decheng couldn't refuse Teacher Tu. He didn't say what he was thinking, that he didn't think joining the Little Red Soldiers was an honour.

Decheng felt awkward being the tallest Little Red Soldier in the school, and singing songs like "Youngsters Love Chairman Mao," "Little Patrol Soldiers on the Grasslands," and "The Little Red Soldiers Are Busy Sweeping the Grain." The next year, when he became a Young Pioneer, he dreaded National Day, Communist Party Founding Day, Army Day, and Youth Day when he had to don the trademark red neck scarf and take part in ceremonies at the Big Marching Ground. The county-level government, modelling its observance of those festival days on Beijing's mass events held in Tiananmen Square, filled the dirt expanse by making attendance mandatory for selected work units and schoolchildren. Town folk who showed up were, more often than not, members of the Party wanting to check out who was on the dais; this was the equivalent of seeing who appeared on the balcony of the Tiananmen Rostrum, sometimes the only way to know who was in or out of power. Always, Decheng couldn't wait for the ceremony to end, to pull the red scarf off his neck and stuff it in his pocket.

WHEN DECHENG ENCOUNTERED HIS FATHER in town, he'd see him chatting and cracking jokes with friends, but the moment his father spotted him, his expression turned severe. It was if he always saw in his son something else that irritated, yet another failing to correct. As much as Decheng dreaded running into his father in public, he hated the familiar squeal of Renqing's truck as it came to a stop outside the back door of Number 35 Clear Water Alley. It signalled a beating was coming his way.

Feeling that his father did not love him and searching for explanation, Decheng considered that he too might be adopted, as his father had been. Yet he surmised from a story that his grandmother had told him that she would have been prepared to love his father had he passed a test. She told Decheng that soon after Renqing stepped onto their barge, she teased the boy, telling him that when the boat was out on the waters, he should eat only one bowl of rice per day. "Any more and you'll have to pee or shit more. What if it's night and you have to go, you could fall in the water," she'd told him. She waited, hoped he would ask for more to eat. "Not once did your father ask!" Grandmother Lu recalled. "Finally, I had to say to your father: 'Eat!'"

Decheng himself began to test his father's limits. He saw Renqing as having only one approach to parenting: big beatings for small reasons. Certain he endured more beatings than other boys in the neighbourhood and more than he deserved, he felt an urge to live up to his father's disappointment in him. He joined with Hongwu in raids across the river, to help themselves to what belonged to the commune on the far side, a mandarin orange from the orchard or a sweet potato left behind in the turned-up soil. He knew this constituted theft, but he reasoned that he was on a mission in aid of his friend. Decheng took care of ferrying back the bounty Hongwu intended for his siblings by stuffing it down his trouser legs, then cinching them before making the dash to the river for the swim across. Being malnourished, Hongwu had a harder time outrunning farmers and he wasn't a strong swimmer. Despite a head start, Hongwu twice escaped a farmer's clutches only by wriggling out of his trousers. The third time, the farmer held on to him and tied him to a tree. Decheng returned with Ironworker Li, who shamed the farmer into contrition: "Why would you do such a thing to a poor student?!" By this time, Ironworker Li was regularly bringing the *People's Daily* home from the nitrate factory where he worked so his educated son could read it to him.

By the time he was twelve, when Decheng entered junior middle school, he was taller than his father and became braver about rebelling and provoking him. He joined older "bad boys" in their river escapades and was the only one who climbed to the middle of the wooden bridge, where the distance to the water below was greatest. More than once, when he popped to the surface, his nose was bleeding. In the most daredevil of the boys' antics, Decheng could disappear from sight under the front end of the log trains, the fan-shaped booms tied end to end, and several minutes later emerge at the back. The triumph was not only holding one's breath, but negotiating the dark gap, as little as a foot in places, between the boom and the river bottom, and to brave the potentially deadly risk of being hit by a log dropped from the boom.

Driver Lu heard the reproachful warnings from neighbours of what his son was getting up to and he despaired. None of it perturbed Grandmother Lu. "The young calf has no fear of the tiger," she said, invoking the proverb to explain what she saw as Decheng's privilege—to test the unknown.

Renqing's greatest fear was that his son would turn into a *liumang*, a "street rascal," "hooligan," or "hoodlum." Renqing came up with a way to keep his son busy in summers, so he could keep an eye on him. A popsicle factory in town sold wholesale and leased vendors' carrying cases, a wooden box tacked with a cotton liner that held four hundred popsicles. Renqing decided that whenever he had a bus route to remote villages, Decheng would accompany him and sell popsicles at stops along the way.

Decheng found the work demoralizing. The box was awkward and heavy and his personality didn't suit the hawker's role. He'd have to walk through a strange village and sing out: "Ice popsicles! White sugar! Mung bean! Ice popsicles!" Then there was the agony of deciding price. He'd try to ask at least four *fen* for one, which earned him half a *fen* each. On cool days, the popsicles didn't sell. On days when it was hot, unsold popsicles started melting, and Decheng would feel obliged to eat as many as he could manage since they were going to waste anyway.

Travelling on the bus and watching his father bully passengers gave Decheng more reason to wish he could give up selling popsicles. He cringed when his father scolded people for minor transgressions—they boarded or disembarked too slowly, too quickly, they didn't close an umbrella soon enough, opened one too soon. He was disappointed that passengers wouldn't stand up to his father. But what Decheng hated most about the popsicle business occurred at week's end, when he had to take his can of money to the bus station to his stepmother. She methodically counted the tinny coins and the wrinkled notes and calculated profit or loss. He'd have to explain either. The profit was never more than one or two *yuan*. She offered him not one *fen*; she said his earnings were for his school fees.

THE RIVER IN SUMMERTIME was a place to earn pocket money if one's father had connections. The river itself announced the arrival of opportunity: the banks lost their orange-red stain from iron-rich silt that washed down from the mountains with the spring torrent, and the slowing current settled sand in the river's bends. Three *li* from Liuyang, in one of the bends named Camphor Tree Pond, was a bank of sand that was extra fine, pebble free, and sun bleached, ideal for making bricks and concrete blocks. Locals would come with wheelbarrows to help themselves for their home-construction projects. Renqing and a couple of fellow drivers had contacts with construction foremen who needed sand by the truckload. When a job came up, the three men drove their sons and daughters to Camphor Tree Pond to load sand into baskets, then haul it on shoulder poles to the roadside, where they then shovelled it into 4-ton Liberation-brand trucks. The builders paid the fathers by the ton. In turn, the fathers paid their teenage children a *yuan* or two for their day's work. Decheng relished the occasional day's work on the sandbank. His father let him keep his earnings, which he took great pleasure in giving to his grandmother for household expenses. Best of all was the excuse to be at the river where he could dive in as he liked with the excuse of washing off the sweat and dirt, and enjoy the pleasures of a boy's summer.

One September afternoon in 1976, Decheng had one of those days when he could hardly pry himself away from the river. He had floated so long on an inner tube—from an old tire at the bus station—that his toes and fingers were wrinkled. He arrived home and could see through the bamboo slats of the wall that there was a crowd at the Zhous' next door, gathered around their radio. Owning a radio was a novelty and a rarity; the Zhous had come into money when their son was demobilized from the army and had received a payment to help him return to civilian life. Decheng went next door to investigate and caught the word "bulletin." He assumed it concerned—as was usually the case—a crime or an arrest, or both. When he was younger, he'd listen with nervous excitement when the ubiquitous public loudspeakers announced an "important and serious matter" of a criminal or crime. Almost always a public execution was not far behind. On the day the criminal was to be shot, he'd run to the Big Marching Ground, squeeze his way to the front of the crowd, trying to get a look at the condemned prisoner. But by now, at thirteen years old, he'd come to see the crime-and-punishment bulletins not as news, but as propaganda.

Wanting to return to the reveries of a perfect summer day, Decheng, his shorts still dripping river water, turned away from the radio. Suddenly he was aware of a deathly stillness in the room. He looked and saw the adults' stricken faces. Some fixed him with a glare. The radio announcer was reading a list of state organizations: " . . . the Central Committee of the Communist Party of China, the Military Commission of the Central Committee of the Communist Party of China, the National Committee of the Chinese People's Political Consultative Committee . . ." These were all organizations that Chairman Mao headed.

I'm in trouble, Decheng thought. He stood attentively, trying to make up for having appeared lighthearted, and listened to the rest of the official announcement of Mao Zedong's death. The Mandarin language gave him some difficulty, but there was no mistaking the reaction the Party expected: "The Chinese people and the revolutionary people the world over love him from the bottom of their hearts and have boundless admiration and respect for him. . . . His passing away is bound to evoke immense grief in the hearts of the people of our country. . . ."

Decheng had been in the market once when a crowd berated a man who'd accidentally knocked a porcelain Mao button off a vendor's table. They had made the man pick up every last shard. "It was nothing deliberate!" Decheng had wanted to say. One of his adult cousins got into similar trouble in the market when someone noticed that the old newspaper she'd used to wrap the vegetables she'd bought had Mao's photograph on it.

The announcement went on for another five minutes. Finally came the familiar ending to every bulletin: "Long live invincible Marxism–Leninism–Mao Zedong thought! Long live the great, glorious, and correct Communist Party of China!" Then, instead of concluding with "Long Live Chairman Mao!" the announcer said, "Eternal glory to our great leader and teacher, Chairman Mao Zedong!"

A day later, the Residents' Committee responsible for the neighbourhood ordered Grandmother Lu to bring her grandson before them. The severe and emotional scolding he got for disrespectful conduct and for not taking the death of Chairman Mao seriously terrified him. In a move that took the committee aback, Grandmother Lu rose to the child's defence. She repeated the explanation he'd given her, that he'd confused Mandarin with the Hunanese dialect, that he'd heard *bugao* for bulletin instead of *fugao*, for obituary. The head of the committee cut off Grandmother Lu: "You, from a martyr's family, of all people ought to know what reactionary behaviour is!"

The entire nation was in official mourning for the nine days between Mao's death and his memorial service. At the Liuyang Junior Middle School, every morning four senior students stood guard at the entranceway, to watch for any student who was not appropriately solemn—anyone seen laughing or being playful was asked for their name. Every morning that Decheng sailed by the guards, he thought, *Another day that they haven't caught me with the wrong kind of thinking.*

At the Big Marching Ground, the entranceway of the Great Hall had been draped in black cloth. Inside, in the foyer, town officials had propped up an immense portrait of Mao, black curtains on either side. There was an honour guard of armed militia, and urns of incense and herbs burned continuously. Party cadres assigned every work unit and school in the town a time to file by the portrait. Teachers at Decheng's school instructed the students beforehand: no talking, you have to cry—"It's just as if your parents were dead; you have to cry for Chairman Mao"—move slowly in a light-footed manner, once in front of the portrait, step forward two by two, bow to Chairman Mao, and then file out. A rehearsal was held in the school auditorium using an identical, but smaller, portrait of Mao.

Upon his school's return from their visit to the Great Hall, Decheng was called to the office. Teacher Lo had sent for him.

He chastised him: "You have no love for Chairman Mao! Why weren't you crying?"

Decheng's face was expressionless. "I didn't even cry when my mother died."

Teacher Lo exploded. "This is different! This is Chairman Mao!"

On September 18, the morning of the mass memorial service for Mao to be held in Beijing's Tiananmen Square, in Liuyang, the portrait of Mao had been moved from inside the Great Hall to a stage outside. By that afternoon, 45,000 people would fill the Big Marching Ground. Schoolchildren would come from around the county, dressed identically in a white shirt, a white paper flower of mourning in a button hole, a black arm band on the left arm, and blue trousers. Decheng marched with his school to the Great Hall, and by noon they had taken their places. For the next three hours, as instructed, they stood under the hot sun, eyes forward on Mao's immense portrait. Finally, the memorial began. As if on cue, Decheng's classmates began sniffling, then, particularly the girls, crying fervently.

Decheng remained stoic. Teacher Lo kept glaring at him the entire time, as if to say, "Cry!" Decheng found the teacher's behaviour entirely irritating.

Back at school, Teacher Lo was livid. "Lu Decheng! What's happening to you? You have to rectify your political attitude!"

As the last year of junior middle school drew to a close, students had to make a decision about whether or not to go on to high school, and to register and pay to take the entrance examination. Before the year was out, army officials visited the school, trying to interest junior middle school graduates to train as paratroopers. Unsure about going on in his schooling and lured by the physical challenge, Decheng decided to apply. He easily passed the required medical examination.

At the end of the academic year, the school told him that he would graduate but that he would not be allowed to attend graduation ceremonies, which effectively ended his last year of junior middle school on the same sour note with which it began. More disappointment was in store. That summer, to Decheng's surprise, the army turned down his application. He wondered if the rejection had anything to do with his year-end report card. Not for the first time did the comment appear: "Does not accept criticism in an open-minded manner."

DECHENG DREADED ANOTHER SUMMER of selling popsicles. But he balanced that loathsome activity by spending his free time running with an older, and mixed, crowd. He fit in by virtue of his height. One day, he and several boys, two of whom were with their girlfriends, were strolling in town when his eyes met his stepmother's peering down at him from a passing city bus. Late that evening, he was asleep when his father burst into the room. He began wildly slapping him, all the while yelling hysterically: "What do you think you're doing? At your age, carrying on with a girl in public! What's going on?"

Decheng knew that Stepmother Meilan had yet again added vinegar to goad his father. He felt only contempt: *He believes whatever he is told; he doesn't have an original thought in his head.*

The next time Renqing came at him, Decheng didn't take his blows dutifully, as he'd done every time before. Instead, he snatched the broomstick his father was brandishing and snapped it over his thigh.

Despite his son's show of strength, Renqing ridiculed him: "Are you trying to beat up your own father?"

The beatings stopped, but Renqing still expected his son to obey him. He decided that Decheng would continue to high school. Decheng did not score high enough in the entrance exam to enter straight from junior middle school, but he did qualify for a preparatory one-year tutorial program. That was enough to satisfy his father. Decheng, self-conscious about the year's setback, didn't see the point of continuing; he had no interest in going on to university. Only two of his childhood friends had scholarly ambitions: Hongwu and Zhijian. Hongwu wanted to study medicine. Zhijian loved reading so much he would often forget to eat or wash. Decheng had little interest in any subjects other than physical education and physics, the latter only because he liked figuring out how things worked.

The unexpected ruin that came that summer to a classmate's older brother left Decheng feeling glum. He'd always considered this boy similar in disposition to him—introverted, straightforward, and honest. The first sign of trouble came when the Residents' Committee called every household of Zhou Family Pier to a meeting. Everyone had to leave a handwriting sample, using both the left and right hand. Talk was that someone had written counter-revolutionary slogans on a wall in the neighbourhood. Decheng went to the wall in question, but found it freshly scraped and repainted. In short order, his classmate's older brother was arrested for his counter-revolutionary crime and sentenced to fifteen years in prison.

That summer a Chinese squadron commander, who diverted his MiG-19 fighter jet to Taiwan, made the news. Decheng looked up China and Taiwan on a map. He eyeballed the Taiwan Strait. Seeing that the gap even at its narrowest had to be 300 *li*, Decheng sighed, "You can see it, but you can't get there." Inadvertently, he found another form of escape, in a cheap transistor radio he'd bought. He had no interest in the revolutionary programming on Chinese radio, and buying batteries, which had a frustratingly short life, proved expensive. Instead, he wanted to see how the radio worked. One day he unscrewed the back to see what was inside and by accident, the touch of his screwdriver tuned in the Taiwanese station Voice of Free China. Instantly, he turned off the radio, knowing that to be caught listening to the enemy's broadcast would land him in serious trouble.

As September approached, Decheng felt anxious about returning to school. On yet another day when Renqing had scolded and insulted him, Carpenter Yi, the next-door neighbour, confided in Decheng that he'd spoken to Renqing. For years, the Zhous on one side, and the carpenter and his wife on the other, had put up with Renqing's vitriol. Only once before had Carpenter Yi made the goings-on next door his business, when he rushed across to break up a fight between Grandmother Lu and Stepmother Meilan. The two had been locked in a pitched battle of words and the younger woman had hurled her tailor's shears at the old lady.

Carpenter Yi shared with Decheng his exchange with Renqing: "I told your father, 'You shouldn't shout at your son; you ought to treat him better.' Your father said he had to make up for your grandmother spoiling you. Well, I let him know, 'This guy has a future, he's a good person.'"

Carpenter Yi's words gave him the confidence to go to his father. He told him, firmly, that high school was not for him. "I am not going," he said. That fall, on the day that school started for returning students, Renqing sent Stepmother Meilan to Clear Water Alley to fetch Decheng and accompany him to the school, to register him and to pay the eight *yuan* in dues. Decheng was embarrassed to be walked to school as if he were a first-time primary student. He ran away, having made up his mind that he was done with school. For a week, he stayed with his uncle Mingxian and his wife. When his father finally came for him, Decheng refused to go outside to talk to him.

Later, Renqing, resigned that his son was not going back to school, sniffed: "Your stepmother was nice and kind enough to take you to school and you didn't even appreciate it."

What a ridiculous man my father is, Decheng thought.

IN HIS NEW-FOUND IDLENESS, Decheng deepened his friendship with his neighbour. Carpenter Yi moved on from the fables of Judge Di to the story of a national hero from Liuyang, the young scholar and political reformer Tan Sitong, considered the first martyr to have shed his blood for the sake of the nation. Tan's ancestral home, with its twenty-four rooms built around an inner courtyard, was on People's Road. Tan's grandfather was at one time governor of Liuyang County, and his father was governor of Hubei province. In 1897, Tan Sitong, then thirty-two years old, after a decade spent travelling around China, meeting people and studying local adminstrations, returned to Hunan to help lead a democratic reform movement. In 1898, Emperor Guangxu, himself a young man of twenty-four, summoned Tan and two other prominent political thinkers to come to Beijing to begin work on the Hundred Days Reform. The emperor's ambitious plan was to turn China into a modern state, to be governed like a constitutional monarchy. Hardly had Tan arrived in Beijing when the Empress Dowager, Guangxu's aunt, seeking to bring the reform movement to a swift end, seized back power. Tan could have fled abroad like his cohorts, Kang Youwei and Liang Qichao, who eventually settled in Japan. Instead, he stayed to face the executioner.

Decheng saw that a sign on the Tans' ancestral home identified it as a work unit of the Party. Later, when Decheng took a day trip to the village of Zhaishui in search of Tan's tomb, he found the road in wretched condition and the tomb itself crumbling and overgrown with weeds. Carpenter Yi wasn't surprised to hear of the state of neglect. He had a succinct answer to Decheng's rueful complaint that the local government appeared not to care about honouring Tan's memory. "The Communists don't like reform," Carpenter Yi said.

Carpenter Yi wasn't the only adult who had grown fond of Driver Lu's rebellious son. Decheng spent most Saturdays and Sundays at Hongwu's and made a friend of his father. Ironworker Li lost his gruffness when he liked someone. He was always eager to chat with Decheng, more so when lubricated by *bai jiu* from the local rice liquor distillery. His past was a tale of misfortune. Both Hongwu's grandfathers had been veterans of the Autumn Harvest Uprising and both had died in the Long March when the Communists were in retreat to the mountains of Shaanxi province. Each had left behind a child. One fared badly and the other well. The young Mr. Li turned to begging to support his widowed mother; the future Mrs. Li, on the other hand, had a cultured and privileged upbringing as her mother had remarried well.

After Liberation, cadres from Beijing, on a campaign to "unite red siblings" in marriage in order to build the next generation into a military dynasty to fight for the new China, came to Liuyang county to marry the two teenagers to each other and take them back to Beijing. Only the newlyweds' mothers' pleas convinced the cadres to let the "red siblings" stay in Liuyang to first raise a family.

By the early 1960s, Mr. Li was a cook at a communal canteen and Mrs. Li had risen to head of finances for the commune. Everything changed for the couple when she reported a large theft of meat. Local cadres accused them of covering up their own crime. To force a confession, they left Mrs. Li tied to a tree for days. Dehydrated and near death, she identified one of her accusers as the real thief. For this, the cadres banished the couple to the mountains. By the time the army in Beijing got wind of their fate and ordered the cadres to allow the family to return to Liuyang, the impoverished couple had given away seven of their ten children. Of those, they would see only four ever again—including Hongwu—the same four whom Mrs. Li later tried to drown in the shallows of the Liuyang River.

Ironworker Li confided in Decheng that he had stopped believing in the Communists long before the family's mistreatment. In 1954, during the flood season on the Yangtze River, there was unusually high water in its tributaries, including the Liuyang. One day, an alarm was raised in the town: "Bodies coming down river!" A primitive earth dam upriver from Liuyang, at the village of Three Hills' Mouth, had been breached, sweeping away several buildings, including a primary school. Typically, such dams were so shoddily built that they were called "*doufu* dams." Mr. Li took his hoe and rushed to one of the sharpest bends, knowing the bodies would collect in the pond there. He joined a crowd already there, fishing bodies out of the water, many of them those of children. He lost count after he pulled out eighty. Several days later, the Communists released the official death toll of the burst dam: three. "They can't tell even one truth!" Ironworker Li told Decheng. "It's all a series of lies from their mouths. Trust them with the future of China and you won't have one grain of rice to eat!"

Decheng spent his idle time with other boys his age, like him out of school and without work. Typically, they played cards, pool, or mah-jong, usually betting a few *fen* to make it interesting. One day, he and two others were looking to make a foursome for mah-jong. As a fourth boy pulled up a chair, Decheng needled him about not having squared up on an old, but minor, debt with one of the other players. The boy became defensive: "Why do you have to keep bringing that up? Why can't you let go of things in the past?" To everyone's shock, including his own, Decheng grabbed the boy by the shirt collar: "You have to settle this before we let you play again!" It was Decheng, however, who chose never to play again. Even though he knew that his display of temper that day had been untoward, he felt a simmering anger that he couldn't explain.

At night, Decheng took solace in listening to his transistor radio. The reception was best in the dead of night, also the hour when the neighbours would be asleep and least likely to hear him listening to the Voice of Free China. Except that he wasn't interested in its anti-China propaganda; he wanted to hear the Taiwan station's haunting theme song. As a woman's voice crooned the opening lines—"I sing for you, I sing about the sorrow in your heart . . ."—a familiar sadness welled up in him. One night, feeling desperately sorry for himself, he allowed the thought of suicide to flit across his mind. Suicide needs a cause to die for, he decided. A pointless one wasn't worth thinking about.

DECHENG'S GENERATION HAD GOOD REASON to be anxious about the future. The "iron rice bowl" that guaranteed lifetime employment by the state was disappearing. At the end of 1978 Deng Xiaoping introduced two historic changes of direction for the country. He began an "open door" policy to the West that would permit foreign investment. And he announced the beginning of reforms to move away from a planned economy toward a market economy. The immediate changes were dramatic: communes were no more; private enterprise was now allowed. State enterprises would initially still operate in a planned economy while getting used to the lifting of price controls. All state-funded enterprises—factories, schools, hospitals, and even prisons—would eventually have to pay more of their own way. Deng Xiaoping declared that China had to turn from class struggle to modernization if it was to develop. He was, however, equivocal. He likened the regime's approach to the early days of economic reform to "feeling for stones" under one's feet "while crossing a river."

Uncertain what jobs could be produced by a private economy, many youths enlisted when the army came again on a vigorous recruitment drive, this time in aid of China's border war with Vietnam. Renqing wanted Decheng, then sixteen years old and still without work, to sign up. Although he calculated that the army wouldn't refuse him twice, Decheng worried about drawing attention to whatever had been held against him the first time. Grandmother Lu intervened. "How can you be so ignorant?" she berated Renqing. "You have only one son and you would send him to war?" Decheng saw his way out and sided with Grandmother Lu.

Renqing's worries about his son's idleness ended soon after. The bus station held an internal hiring drive for apprentices at the vehicle-repair shop. Mechanics were needed to service a growing fleet of coaches, trucks, and passenger cars. Renqing, in a test that confirmed to himself his sway with the company, landed Decheng a place in the three-year apprenticeship program. Decheng did as his father bid, but he was also content to be studying engines. He moved from his grandmother's, joining other trainees in a dormitory, where they slept four to a room and ate in the canteen.

Even on his first day on the job, Decheng was planning how he would spend his first month's pay. He asked Uncle Mingxian's wife if the family had any pictures of his mother. Six years had passed since her death, but his uncle's wife still harboured bitterness toward Renqing. "Your father didn't have a shred of feeling for your mother," she told Decheng. She collected some photographs from the family and Decheng selected one, took it to a famed artist named

Shao Changfeng, who worked at a collective in Liuyang that produced propaganda signs and posters, and had a likeness drawn.

As if spoiling for a confrontation, at New Year's, the one time each year when Decheng dined at his stepmother's table, he offered to make tea for her. He made a show of washing her cup repeatedly before pouring her tea and placing it in front of her. Still, it wasn't clean enough for her. She poured the tea out and rewashed the cup and then went to refill it. Decheng grabbed it from her and pitched it against the wall. His father was shocked: "You're acting like you want to beat someone up!"

At the bus station, Decheng's restless anger sought its own target. It settled on one of his roommates, Jinwei, also an apprentice mechanic and the son of a driver. Jinwei was clearly bright and capable. What irked Decheng was that he should feel the need to not only brag but to put others down as well. He seemed to want to intimidate with his strength—why else did he do his chest-expansion exercises in full view of his roommates, to a loud count? On that score, Decheng felt he could measure up; more than once at school he'd been named sports commissar and he held county-wide athletic records, although he'd have been hesitant to list his achievements even if asked.

Decheng arranged to transfer to another room, thinking avoiding Jinwei would end his irritation. It did not. Decheng could not stop thinking that someone ought to tame his former roommate's conceit, show him that not everyone was in awe of him or feared him. He wondered, maybe he could make use of his own strength, perhaps provoke him into a fist fight and trounce him. He rejected that idea; fighting would be punished and he had no desire to bring that kind of trouble to either of them. Finally, Decheng devised a practical joke that a clever mind such as Jinwei's would understand.

He obtained an everyday agricultural pesticide of the brand "666." Triple sixes made for an auspicious combination—six was a homonym for "flowing" or "smooth" and three sixes meant "Things are going smoothly." He slipped into his former room and beside Jinwei's bunk, found his thermos, emptied it of hot water, added a drop of the pesticide, and screwed the lid back on. He pictured Jinwei opening the thermos and being greeted by the familiar smell of a peasant's toil in the countryside.

Instead of opening his thermos in his room as Decheng had expected, Jinwei took it to the canteen to refill it, probably thinking it empty by its weight. As soon the lid was off, a foul smell came out. What was supposed to be a joke elicited panic among everyone in the canteen.

The bus station called in someone from the head office in Shaoshan to head a formal investigation. Not surprisingly, being from Mao's hometown, the official was a hardline Communist who declared that he would find the class enemy responsible. When Decheng's turn came to be questioned, he spoke up right away: "I did it." The official reported him to the police. Fortunately, the police chose to regard it as a minor wrongdoing, giving them the discretion to impose an "administrative detention." Decheng received a penalty of two months in the local detention centre. While Driver Lu was tremendously relieved that his son would not lose his job as an apprentice, he was also more furious with him than he had ever been. "This is a terrible loss of face for me!" he raged.

UPON DECHENG'S RELEASE, with the approval of one of the senior managers at the bus station, he did not go back to live with other workers. Instead, the station restored his *hukuo* to Number 35 Clear Water Alley and he returned to live with Grandmother Lu. Once he was back at work, Decheng lamented to Hongwu that perhaps his disposition didn't suit a collegial workplace. He thought private business might better suit because he'd be on his own. "You have an introverted personality. That won't be easy," said Hongwu. "You'd have to work at it." He told Decheng that a person in private business needed social skills and a network. But as a first step, he should acquire top technical skills. Decheng needed to be apprenticed to the bus station's best mechanic. On Hongwu's advice, Decheng went to Master Mechanic Zhang's home to ask if he would mentor him. He came bearing a carton of cigarettes and two bottles of the finest Liuyang liquor and, as coached, told the surly older man, "You and I have similar dispositions; I like to keep to myself." The station's master mechanic had a new protégé. Later, Hongwu's advice would work again when Decheng wanted to learn to drive, preparing for when he'd have to test drive vehicles in his own business. However, at the station, only master mechanics were allowed behind the wheel. Decheng had his mentor explain to him how to drive and he practised in secret on night shift. Though Decheng feared getting into an accident, Hongwu's answer to that was not to worry, and to rely on his mentor to take care of it: "He's an outstanding member of the Party." Hongwu had already asked around. "He's untouchable."

FIVE

THE STORM IN THE LATE AFTERNOON on May 23 in Beijing was a topic of conversation not so much for the brief, intense rain but for the wind that blew up with it. Gusts of gale-force strength swayed whole trees and snapped branches, removed roof tiles and sent chimney pots clattering to the streets below.

A guard on the evening shift at the Eastern District Detention Centre learned that the waning day had delivered another surprise: the three men from Hunan whom he had just seen on television. The three were isolated from each other. The middle-aged guard saw that the one who ended up in his wing was Lu Decheng. He wasted no time pronouncing his own verdict: "Even the heavens were angry at what you three did!" Other guards continued the teasing: "The students themselves turned you in, you must be *huai fenzi*!" "Bad elements" was a term coined in the 1950s, when households were classified as of good or bad class origins, but later became a catch-all for troublemakers and criminals. Bad elements were to be avoided. Nobody talked to them, and they didn't even talk to each other.

The guards locked Decheng in a tiny cell with three other prisoners. Immediately, his suspicions were raised. He wondered why they were in a cell that was clearly intended for solitary confinement— the 3-metre-by-3-metre space was windowless, and spongy mattresses lined the walls. He also thought it odd that petty criminals would be put in with him, a political prisoner. The worst of their crimes was selling counterfeit train tickets and their sentences ranged from one year to less than six months.

That evening, Decheng was taken from the cell to the interrogation room, where two male officers awaited him. Legal procedure required that a detainee's interrogation begin within twenty-four hours. Normally, this investigation lasted three days and, under certain circumstances, could be extended to ten. However, none of the deadlines or requirements applied when the crime involved two or more persons, or was considered to have been "particularly evil" or to have brought "serious harm upon the country." If the police believe their investigation establishes guilt and if the law dictates that the crime is punishable by imprisonment, the case proceeds to a formal arrest and charges.

The two investigating officers wore shirt sleeves typical of those with a desk job. They'd come from the National Security Bureau, the highest intelligence agency in the government. Decheng figured this to be an ominous sign that the regime had taken an exceedingly harsh view of what he, Zhijian, and Dongyue had done.

Decheng made his own calculation based on the two officers' grave manner and their age—both appeared to be in their fifties: *Maoists*, he surmised. *Party members, who've risen through the ranks.* Thinking his future bleak if left to these two, he needed to assert himself. Decheng decided to make the opening move, to ask a question before they did. *What is there to lose,* he thought.

Upon arrival at the detention centre, the guards had been kind enough to bring him a tray of the cold leftovers from that day's supper—rice and vegetables, with a couple of pieces of meat. Decheng didn't mind that the rice, hours old, was crusted over, but he was disappointed at the blandness of the meal, which he assumed had to do with it being northern fare. People of Hunan had a legendary fiery palate, rivalled only by those from Sichuan. However, the Hunanese prided themselves on theirs being the hottest: "The Sichuanese *bu pa la*"—are not afraid of hot—"but the Hunanese *pa bu la*"—are afraid it's not hot enough.

Decheng assessed which of the two officers to put his question to, the heavy-set one or the lean one. He decided against the fat one, lest he take mention of a penchant for food as a personal insult against his weight.

"You know Mao Zedong liked hot sauce, right? Because he's from Hunan? Well, so am I. I have the same tastes."

The officers appeared indifferent to his request. By their opening question "Why did you do it?" Decheng thought perhaps they actually understood the defacement of Mao's portrait to be a political act and that they were more opinionated than their impassive demeanour suggested. He seized the opportunity to expound on the symbolism of attacking the iconic portrait. But try as he might, Decheng could not draw them into conversation or elicit any opinion.

The next day, a can of chili sauce appeared with Decheng's food tray, which was passed through the 15-by-20-centimetre aperture in the cell door. He interpreted the favour as a way to loosen his tongue. The two interrogators now seemed to suspect a conspiracy beyond the three men: *Who helped you to carry this out? Who are you associated with? Who is behind you? Who is giving you instructions?* It was as if they thought that Decheng and his comrades were not capable of planning and executing the action on their own, and that a "black hand," someone cleverer than the three of them, had manipulated them to some other unknown and sinister ends. He wondered how his two friends were faring, and if they were facing the same line of questioning as he was.

IN LIUYANG, the local police, coordinating their investigation with authorities in Beijing, opened a file that focused on a meeting that had taken place on the night of May 16 at Yu Dongyue's flat, above the offices of the *Liuyang Daily*. The police identified nine males in that "May 16th Incident" and honed in on five of them. They were the five who had travelled by bus from Liuyang to Changsha, where they then boarded a train to Beijing. The police in the capital had three of those men in custody: Yu Zhijian, Yu Dongyue, and Lu Decheng. A fourth, Kong Zhongshen, had stayed in Beijing less than a day before returning home. The Liuyang police found him at his dormitory at the Liuyang High School, where he was a teacher, and brought him in for questioning. That left at large a fifth man, Li Hongwu. Upon visiting the cast-ironware plant where he worked, police learned that Hongwu had paid to hold his job for several months and had taken leave.

LEAVING ASIDE DECHENG'S interrogators and his daily sessions with them, he found staff and inmates at the detention centre were congenial and the atmosphere relaxed. Petty criminals all, the inmates were euphemistically called "labour guests"—each day guards escorted them outside the prison walls to work at various factories and workshops, where they made everything from batteries to plastic lunch boxes, before returning at night. The guards, some of whom were former prisoners hired on after completion of their sentences, were eager to meet their famous prisoner. One, a teenager, sought out Decheng: "What you guys did was great!" The middle-aged guard who'd teased him the first night returned to chat. His views turned sympathetic and he wondered aloud why the students had reacted the way they had. "What we three did was too advanced for the students," Decheng replied.

From the outset, Decheng's cellmates were friendly. They tutored him on prison life. The first and most important rule of survival: identify the cell boss, always the one in the bunk farthest from the door. They explained that in tougher prisons than this, the cell boss controlled other prisoners with muscle, threat, and intimidation. Decheng's fellow inmates also coached him on greasing the guards' palms to get contraband. Decheng had some *yuan* left, but as much as he craved cigarettes, he saved his money for chili sauce. Within days of his arrival, he needed it all the more. Martial law prevented fresh food from reaching Beijing and the prison diet turned even more bland, offering nothing but biscuits and preserved vegetables.

For all his cellmates' helpfulness, Decheng was wary. He knew they had a means to report on him, because they left the cell each day for forced labour. They were also chummy with the guards, who often unlocked the cell door to share a smoke or a drink with them.

The daily visit from Decheng's two interrogators did nothing to relieve his monotony. After the first week, he judged that they must finally have been satisfied that the three had acted alone, because the interrogation took another turn. The two officers wanted to know what other acts the three had carried out, what other actions they had planned.

One day, the prisoner who'd sold fake train tickets returned to the cell with a transistor radio. Several wires were broken inside, but he brought it to life by temporarily soldering them with a well-placed drop of candle wax, and he improved its reception by attaching a small wire. He used earbuds to listen and shared them only with his two friends. Decheng accepted that his cellmates weren't so foolish as to let him use the earbuds—after all, the news was dominated by the continuing state of martial law and the stand-off in Tiananmen Square, and the authorities probably still believed the three had planned more actions. Were he to be caught listening to outside news, most certainly all of them would find themselves in far more serious trouble.

Decheng's cellmates couldn't help themselves from passing on tidbits of information. On May 30, the students had erected a white plaster statue in the square, calling it the Goddess of Democracy. On June 2, some students had begun a second hunger strike. That day, guards let on that the detention centre had processed dozens of new detainees—peasants and workers who had posed as students in order to solicit donations, claiming the money would be used to help the newest hunger strikers.

On June 3, Decheng noticed his cellmates' grim faces as they listened to the radio through the night. They spoke only in the lowest whispers and only amongst themselves. The next morning, the prison imposed a lockdown; until further notice all prisoners were to be confined to their cells. A short while later, a guard entered the cell, picked up the cell boss's pillow, shook it, and out fell the radio. Without saying a word, the guard left with it. That day, Decheng's investigators stayed away.

WHATEVER HAD HAPPENED in the early hours of June 4 brought an abrupt and frightening change in the tactics of the two investigators. On their return, they became old-style cadres, wedded to Party doctrine, hardline and hectoring. When Decheng repeated what he'd been telling them all along, they now lectured him: "You should feel remorse, yet you seem proud you did it!" Their language turned menacing: "What you did was very, very serious. You know it was counter-revolutionary!"

June 6 brought a much-welcome break in a prolonged heat wave. For twelve straight days, the temperature had been in the mid-thirties. With the detention centre in a lockdown, the heat had added to the discomfort of the close quarters. On this day, Decheng's cellmates finally broke their silence about what they'd heard on the radio the morning of June 4: the People's Liberation Army had opened fire on students to clear Tiananmen Square.

Decheng felt sickened. He and his two friends had believed that the government had imposed martial law because it fully intended to use deadly force. Suddenly, he felt frightened, knowing that his fate rested in the hands of a regime with a callous indifference to brutality. Hoping to get some sense of the mood outside the prison, a nervous Decheng asked a hurried question of the middle-aged guard: Did he still have some sympathy for what the three had done? "It was too confrontational," was all the guard would say.

The guards and his cellmates, Decheng noticed, seemed to want to calm him. A guard who used to toss three cigarettes through the bars, now made it four. And with every evening meal pushed through the opening in the cell door came a paper bag, concealing four cans of beer. Decheng followed his cellmates' lead in flattening the emptied tins and working them into the cracks in the floor until they disappeared. Decheng thought the beer was an incentive for his cellmates to keep a closer eye on him. When he noticed a guard pass a tiny rolled-up piece of paper to one of the prisoners, he presumed it contained instructions on how to handle him.

Just when his investigators were ratcheting up their pressure, Decheng's cellmates began to talk about ways to outwit them. The train-ticket seller warned that investigators routinely tried to dupe detainees into admitting to crimes that carried a heavy sentence. He explained how he had avoided such a fate. He knew enough not to admit that he'd also *printed* the train tickets, which would have constituted an "economic crime that undermines the socialist economic order," and for which the death penalty could apply. Instead, he confessed only to selling the fake tickets, which was a lesser crime.

The cell boss told Decheng that the way to escape the death penalty was to downplay his crime. The other cellmates chimed in with advice. "Chat with the investigators," they said. "Tell them you're prepared to pay compensation for messing with public property. Tell the two of them that what you did had nothing to do with politics."

Knowing their conversation would find its way to the investigators, Decheng ventured little, other than "Even if it was Mao's portrait in Tiananmen Square that was damaged?"

"Ah! No big deal! You'll get six months or a year for hooliganism, two at the most."

"Maybe no time at all, or just a fine."

My category of crime is much more serious, Decheng thought. Hadn't the investigators said as much, calling what he did counterrevolutionary? At the same time, he was conflicted about heeding his cellmates' advice. Knowing that something terrible had happened on June 4, he had begun to grow fearful of death. Yet he was tortured at the thought of taking refuge from the death penalty by reducing his political act to an act of vandalism. And what if he took that course only to find that the death awaited anyway? Because of the time he'd spent in a Liuyang detention house as a teenager, authorities in Beijing might decide to label him as a dangerous repeat offender, a hooligan who could not be reformed, which would be cause to execute him. Not knowing the fate of Zhijian and

Dongyue weighed heavily on Decheng. Struggling with his predicament, he imagined they were thinking rationally through this, whereas he was letting emotions cloud his judgment. He saw his only choice, to stand in solidarity with his friends.

The next time Decheng faced his interrogators, he insisted that his act had been political.

"You're so self-righteous! If this was the Cultural Revolution, you would be put to death by the masses!"

"What we did might be unthinkable to some now," replied Decheng, "but twenty years or more from now people will see it in a very different light."

The two officers were incensed.

After June 10, they stopped coming. The prison remained in a lockdown. On June 15, after the evening meal, guards removed Decheng from his cell. Waiting officers violently slapped handcuffs on him. They shoved and dragged him out of the detention centre and into the night. Several army trucks, with canvas-covered tops, were idling inside the prison walls. Soldiers, helmeted and carrying rifles fixed with bayonets, stood nearby.

Decheng's captors ordered him to kneel on all fours on the ground behind a truck. One after another, soldiers used him as a stepstool to climb aboard. Then, the last of them hauled him into the truck, throwing him face down between the benches on each side. With the soldiers now using him as a footrest and their boots pressing him into the gritty floor, Decheng was convinced the army was secretly taking him to be shot. He knew how the condemned went to their death: kneel on the ground, head bowed, then a bullet from an assault rifle to the back of the head. Except that in his case, no one but the army would know that he had been killed, only that he had disappeared. Strangely, he felt devoid of emotion, holding on only to the certainty of death.

TWENTY MINUTES LATER, the army truck jolted to a stop. The engine shuddered into silence. Decheng was hauled off, and soldiers trod on the prisoner as they climbed down from the truck. Suddenly, a bright light pierced the darkness. Decheng saw other army trucks disgorging soldiers, and among them two other handcuffed prisoners, Zhijian and Dongyue. They were lit, like him, by a camera crew filming their arrival.

Soldiers marched the trio toward a small building. Inside were even more armed soldiers. Now Decheng considered death imminent. Soldiers called their names one by one and led each of the three forward to sign documents. Decheng assumed these were their death warrants. When his turn came, he saw that the document before him was instead to acknowledge his formal arrest and the charges against him. He felt his first glimmer of hope since the students had handed them over to police; a formal arrest meant a court proceeding, a court proceeding meant a public record of the sentence. If death came, his wife and family would learn of it, and would not be left to wonder about his fate.

The next evening, on June 16, the seven o'clock news reported that the three men from Hunan who had defaced Chairman Mao's portrait had been formally arrested.

In the days since June 4, the news had been full of images of police rounding up hundreds of "thugs" who'd taken part in the protest on that day. This week, the regime had begun naming names. It issued an arrest warrant for an astrophysicist named Fang Lizhi, calling him "the arch enemy of the nation and the Chinese people," and blasting the U.S. for sheltering "the criminal who created this violence" in its embassy. A day later, the regime issued several most-wanted lists, including a list of twenty-one student leaders.

The announcer said that Yu Zhijian, Yu Dongyue, and Lu Decheng were charged with counter-revolutionary propaganda and incitement, counter-revolutionary sabotage, writing reactionary slogans, and destruction of state property. Television footage showed three handcuffed men surrounded by armed soldiers.

On that same day, in Liuyang, the police delivered a fax to Driver Lu, sent from Beijing regarding his son.

Beijing City Public Security Bureau
Notification to the Family of Arrested Person

Capital PSB 186

June 15, 1989

Because Lu Decheng has committed the criminal act of counter-revolutionary destruction, the People's Intermediate Court of Beijing City has on June 15, 1989, approved his being held in legal custody. He is now detained at the Beijing City Public Security Bureau Detention Lock-Up at Banbuqiao 44, Xuanwu District.

Special Notification
Family of Lu Decheng
Address: Hunan Province, Liuyang, 35 Clear Water Alley

When Qiuping saw her husband on the news again, she was relieved to have confirmation, the first since May 23, that he was still alive. When she read the notification of arrest and learned of her husband's incarceration in a Beijing jail, she was consumed with finding a way to offer him moral support.

Decheng and his two friends were incarcerated—again, apart from each other—at Banbuqiao Prison, or, as it was also called, K-block, because of the shape of the building. It was Beijing's largest prison, with an inmate population of more than two thousand. Locally, it was known as the Half-Step Bridge Detention Centre. Built a century ago, it was a short walk across a bridge from the prison to the execution ground, so prisoners were said to be a half-step from death. It was in Banbuqiao in 1898 that the reformer Tan Sitong was held, and at this execution ground where the executioner's sword took off his head, which was then left in a cage on the ground to rot.

K-block held prisoners awaiting sentencing, but it also had a reputation for housing those most likely to be sentenced to death. If a prisoner's crime had involved violence, not only were his hands bound, but his feet as well. Decheng's jailer locked heavy handcuffs on him, then turned a screw to tighten them. Prohibitions against smoking and drinking were strictly enforced. Life at this maximum-security prison was starkly different from the Eastern District Detention Centre. Prisoners awaiting trial were shackled twenty-four hours a day. Rations were paltry. Breakfast was a bowl of congee made from ground corn, and a bowl of potato scraps and a few tough leaves of preserved cabbage, with a scattering of chili seeds. Lunch and supper were two *wotou*, steamed cornmeal buns called "barbarian heads" because of their pointed shape. *Wotou* were the poor man's food in the north; one alone made for a bloated stomach, yet the more one ate, the hungrier one felt. Decheng negotiated a trade with a prisoner, giving up one *wotou* at lunch and one at supper in exchange for ten chili seeds that the other prisoner retrieved from his breakfast.

On his fifth day, Decheng and a cellmate, Lu Guo, noticed their breakfast was enlivened with sugar. Lu Guo's crime had been to try to stop the advance of a tank in the early hours of June 4 by setting it on fire. After breakfast, the guards hollered out Lu Guo's name and took him away to court for sentencing. Later that day, a guard came to the cell and a respectful silence fell over the place as he cleared out Lu Guo's belongings. It was then that Decheng learned the sweetness of the congee served as bitter notice that this would be someone's last breakfast.

Dignity, the only sustenance that mattered, was a struggle to maintain. When he was processed as an arriving prisoner, authorities confiscated anything metal, so he lost his belt and his leather shoes—they had steel toes and heels—and the metal clips were cut from his jacket. The ever-present handcuffs cut deeply into Decheng's wrists and stiffened his hands and arms. Eating when wearing handcuffs was easiest if the bowl was placed on the floor. Going to the washroom was especially awkward for shackled prisoners. Twice a day, a guard would announce a ten-minute toilet break with a count, "One, two, three!" and thirty to forty prisoners of his cellblock made a dash for it. To help accommodate everyone in the short time, the cell boss would instruct inmates, in anticipation of the count, when to massage their stomachs to bring themselves to the verge of defecation. Once at the toilets, the handcuffed inmates needed help with their trousers, before and after. Regularly, while waiting for a space, one or more would panic and soil the floor. Hurling abuse at the unfortunate prisoners, the notoriously abusive guards of K-block would make them use their own clothes to mop up the mess.

UPON DECHENG'S FORMAL ARREST, responsibility for investigation of his crime shifted from the police to the public prosecutors' office. Daily, two prosecutors visited Decheng to verify if the facts were clear and the evidence was sufficient for the trial, and to decide on the correctness of the charges. A clerk attended these sessions as well, methodically recording Decheng's responses.

The prosecutors were intent on detailing Decheng's every movement from the moment he and his friends left Liuyang until they'd thrown the last paint-filled egg at Chairman Mao's portrait. Repeatedly, Decheng insisted that he was hiding nothing. It was they who revealed evidence that came as a shock. They pulled from the prosecutors' file the photographs that Decheng knew had been in Dongyue's backpack, before he'd turned it over to the students. He saw that everything had ended up in the hands of police. Wearily, Decheng confirmed that it was him in the photographs, at the Changsha railway station, on Tiananmen Square, on Changan Avenue. One photograph brought a tinge of heartbreak. It had been on a roll of undeveloped film, so he was seeing it for the first time— the "family portrait" of the three. He recalled their mood, one of great solemnity and hope, moments before they packed up their slogans and the eggs, and headed for Mao's portrait.

The prosecutors told Decheng they had evidence he had tried to corrupt and incite a young trainee at the bus station into going to Beijing. Decheng could only think they had to be referring to a chance encounter and idle chat after supper, which had happened before he'd even known there was to be a meeting at Dongyue's flat. Similarly, the prosecutors had evidence that the three of them had forced the clerks at the post office in Changsha to help them in their counter-revolutionary activities. Decheng could recall one particularly helpful female clerk, who'd been impressed with Dongyue's calligraphy. He wondered if she was now in trouble.

"You have no love for Chairman Mao!" the prosecutors said. "You did not cry for Chairman Mao at his memorial." One of the prosecutors was derisive: "You have been a reactionary right from the beginning!"

I'm doomed, Decheng thought.

At the end of June, after a second week of interrogation, the prosecutors put on the table a five-page charge-and-prosecution document. "Read every word," they instructed. He was told to ink his thumbprint at the bottom of each page as he went. Upon reading the opening line—"Lu Decheng is guilty as charged"—Decheng felt it was pointless to read further. But when the clerk rushed him to ink the pages, he was so irritated that he searched for a couple of incorrectly written characters and refused to sign his name on the last page, above "Confirmed as Fact," until she made the corrections.

Decheng assumed that the trial date was approaching when a judge from the Beijing Intermediate Court paid him a visit. Judge Ding Fengchun told him that the three of them would be tried together. The judge was perfunctory. He asked if Decheng thought anyone should be recused from the case or if he had any request of the panel. The judge was taken by surprise when Decheng replied yes. He said that he did not want a court-appointed lawyer, that he wanted someone from Liuyang named Mr. Zhu—Decheng had heard Qiuping mention him as a respected family friend. Judge Ding was stunned. "Are you joking?" His tone was reprimanding and dismissive. The justice ministry saw anyone wanting his own lawyer as trying to hide his guilt by seeking an attorney willing to manipulate the facts, unlike a court-appointed official who put the interests of the proletariat first.

A day or so later, three court-appointed lawyers, all young women, visited Decheng in the interrogation room. Lawyer Cui Yunhui, the one assigned to him, sat at the table while the other two remained standing by the door. "Since you are guilty," Lawyer Cui began, "my role is to ask for a lighter sentence." Decheng argued that what they had done did not constitute a serious crime. She did not respond, nor would she speculate on what sentence the three might get.

ON JULY 9, Qiuping boarded a train to go farther afield than she'd ever gone and to the north where she'd never been. Her destination was Beijing, a city still under martial law. Travel into and out of and within the city remained difficult, not least because of a heavy police presence and numerous checkpoints. The regime continued to heavily publicize its lists, complete with photos and physical descriptions of persons wanted for "counter-revolutionary rebellion."

On July 10, Qiuping arrived in the capital. Armed with only the information on the notice of arrest faxed to Driver Lu, she found the office of the public prosecutor. She asked for the date of her husband's trial and was rebuffed, and told she could not attend anyway. Qiuping spent the next several hours trying to hire a lawyer to represent her husband. There was not a lawyer's office that hadn't heard of the case of the three men from Hunan, but Qiuping found no one willing to take the case. She returned to the prosecutor's office, upset enough to shout and scream, demanding to be told the trial date. She made such a fuss that finally, the office appeased her by giving her the name of the presiding judge.

The next morning, Qiuping went to Judge Ding's office. Much to her relief, he agreed to see her. Qiuping insisted that she had to know the date of her husband's trial so that she could be in the gallery to support him.

Judge Ding was polite. He refused to disclose the date and explained that her attendance was not allowed. The trial for the three men would be a closed proceeding because the charges involved state matters.

Qiuping became hysterical. "What's so important about that picture?" She blurted out what to her was inconceivable: "Are you people going to sentence these three to death for a mere picture?"

"It's no good all this shouting and yelling," Judge Ding said, trying to calm Qiuping. Then, gently, "Doing that will only make matters worse."

At this, Qiuping began to cry uncontrollably. "If my husband is to die, I want to go to the execution ground with him."

"Go home to Liuyang and wait for news," Judge Ding said.

Qiuping tried unsuccessfully to visit her husband at the prison. She left that evening, boarding a train south on July 11.

THE NEXT DAY, guards removed Decheng from his cell and led him out to a waiting van. He was joined by Zhijian and Dongyue. The day of their trial had come.

At the courthouse, outside the door of the courtroom, they and their lawyers stood together as they awaited the signal to enter. Decheng seized this brief moment to tell his two friends that they should inform the court that they wished to be represented by a lawyer of their own choosing.

The armed guards led the three into the courtroom. Judge Ding and two assessors sat as a panel at the front of the courtroom, facing the prisoners' box. To the judge's left sat the two public prosecutors and a court cameraman recording the entire session. To his right was the court clerk and sitting beside him, the court-appointed lawyers. The three men from Hunan entered the prisoners' box and remained standing. Behind them sat armed guards, and behind the guards was a gallery of about a hundred people, all strangers to the defendants.

The prosecuters read the charge-and-prosecution documents explaining the case against each of them. In a lengthy presentation, they emphasized that everything in the documents had been verified by the three defendants: "Everything is factual," the prosecutors said. They presented the crime as well-organized and planned, offering evidence of photographs of the three friends in Changsha, at the railway station making speeches and soliciting donations, and in Beijing, on Changan Avenue, in the square, and finally, in Zhongshan Park. Equally incriminating were Dongyue's notes and speeches in his handwriting. Only once during the trial did Decheng listen with curiosity to the evidence—when the prosecution cited the dimensions of Mao's portrait—6 metres by 4.6 metres—and showed numerous photographs taken by the management office of Tiananmen Square, documenting where paint and egg had found their mark.

When Judge Ding signalled to the defense lawyers that the panel's interrogation would begin, the three defendants interjected in a chorus to request their own lawyer. The other two immediately gave way to Zhijian. He respectfully acknowledged the presence of the court-appointed lawyers, but submitted that the three hoped that they could be represented by a lawyer from Liuyang whom they knew personally. The two public prosecutors didn't know what to make of this. Judge Ding, seeing this intervention as Decheng's doing, shouted loudly: "Lu Decheng! How dare you! You better behave in this court!" Then he said sternly: "You have to be sincere and honest with the court; you have committed a very serious crime. You are in a very, very grave situation!"

The panel's few questions were mostly directed at Zhijian, as though they assumed he were the ringleader. After only two hours, the trial was wrapping up with an address to the panel from each of the defendants' lawyers. When Lawyer Cui spoke, she repeated much of what was said by her two colleagues: she cited their youth and immaturity, and argued that their political thinking was "not yet developed." Her suggestion was, therefore, that a prison term could remould Lu Decheng and reform his thinking. She could not ask for leniency, however, since she could not say Decheng was sorry for the crimes he had committed.

Judge Ding turned to the three accused: "What do you have to say about all this?"

Zhijian made an eloquent statement. He explained their political views, their motives, and what they'd wanted to achieve. He elaborated on why they attacked Mao's iconic portrait and interpreted the parallel slogans they'd posted underneath it.

Repeatedly, the prosecution interrupted Zhijian. "Stay with the facts! Stop speaking as if you are trying to defend your action!"

Judge Ding, growing impatient, asked several times, "Are you finished?"

Zhijian persisted and after twenty minutes concluded his discourse.

It was Dongyue's turn. If seized with inspiration, he could be given to speaking quickly and without pause. If not, he either spoke in monosyllables or remained silent. In this instance, he was succinct, saying only that he accepted responsibility for his actions.

Decheng reiterated what Dongyue had said, adding that he hoped the court would be fair in its judgment and sentencing.

The judge called a recess and the panel went into a closed session. Minutes later, the court reconvened and the panel gave its decision: guilty on all charges. The verdict was no surprise; defendants who got to the point of arrest and a trial were presumed to be guilty of all charges. The judge announced that sentencing would be held over to the following month.

The trial was over.

THE WAIT BEGAN TO EAT AWAY at Decheng. He was diminished physically. He felt his mental strength eroding. When he was a free man, he had been prepared to accept death, but he'd imagined it would come suddenly. Now, in prison, he found himself agonizing, not so much over whether his sentence would be death, but if so, how near or far the end was, if the execution would be immediate. He craved a cigarette to ease his nerves, but in K-block, it was reckless to bribe a guard for even something so small.

Some ten days after the trial, one of the guards took Decheng to the guards' room and in behaviour that was completely out of the ordinary, spoke with him in a genuine and civil manner. He informed Decheng that his wife, Wang Qiuping, had shown up at the prison. However, prisoners were not permitted visitors when awaiting trial, and sometimes not even until after sentencing.

"Most people wouldn't dare come all the way from Hunan," the guard allowed. "It's still very difficult to travel. Trains are hardly running. . . ." He said that the guards had, however, accepted a care package from Qiuping.

He showed Decheng items that Qiuping had brought for him: toothbrush and toothpaste, toilet paper, and some washing powder for laundry. After almost two months in prison, such ordinary things seemed foreign to Decheng. The guard said that Qiuping had also wanted to leave behind banknotes for him, but that was not allowed.

The guard had something else for him—a letter. "It shouldn't be handed over to you—"

The usual gruffness so typical of the guards was by now completely gone.

"—but, considering that you three have had your trial and who knows what the consequences might be or when. . . ." He stopped trying to explain himself. "We read her letter." Even though reading prisoners' mail was part of the guard's job, his voice was confessional and apologetic. "We passed it around. . . ."

His voice broke. "This girl loves you so much."

"Love" was not a word spoken often; Decheng had only used it himself for the first time with Qiuping and only in the few lines he'd written her on the chance they could be his last, sent just before he'd thrown the eggs.

The guard handed Decheng the one-page letter, written on both sides. He searched Decheng's face as his eyes flitted down the page, and then the overleaf. The expression on the prisoner's face didn't change, even when he came to the letter's last line. "If you are to die, I have asked to accompany you to the execution ground," Qiuping had written.

"You have no response?" the guard asked.

Decheng dropped his cuffed hands. He stared, emotionless.

"No response at all? None?"

The guards had talked. They'd told each other of the tall, slim, long-haired beauty, with fine bones and a pale complexion, who was the wife of Lu Decheng. They had been awed by her courage and overwhelmed by what she had written. This, they told one another, was a great love of passion and deep feeling, which many longed for and few would ever have.

Decheng's continuing silence exasperated the guard. "This girl loves you so much and you are not touched one little bit? You can't even bring yourself to show the tiniest bit of emotion?"

In the days since the trial, to cope with the crushing uncertainty of whether he was going to live or die, Decheng had fortified himself by holding to thoughts of Tan Sitong's last days and nights in this same prison. On the eve of his execution, Tan had written a poem that ended: *I cannot escape my fate / For the sake of ideals I have been striving for / I shall die joyfully.* But Decheng could find no joy in waiting. He was tortured on the inside and numb on the outside.

Decheng's hands were too stiff to refold Qiuping's letter. The disappointed guard did not help him.

I'm not a brave person, Decheng told himself, losing the struggle to contain his fear of death.

"LU DECHENG."

The way the guard called his name, everyone in the cellblock knew this was his day of sentencing. Prisoners fell quiet. Oddly, Decheng felt no tension. Why he should feel so relaxed he didn't know. A fellow prisoner helped him fasten the two top buttons on his jacket, which by now hung grotesquely from his skinny frame.

"Hey! Who's in charge of opening this door?!" Decheng called out. He couldn't recall, had the congee been sweeter that morning? When the guard came to unlock the cell door, Decheng's joking became macabre. "Do you want to pack up my things?"

Thirty days had passed since the trial. The same entourage reassembled in the same courtroom with Judge Ding again presiding. Decheng stood with his two friends in the prisoners' box to hear the judge announce the sentences: Yu Zhijian, life imprisonment. *He's going to live.* Yu Dongyue, twenty years. *He will too.* Finally, Lu Decheng, sixteen years. *All three of us.*

The judge offered no explanation for the difference in the length of prison terms. The brief court appearance concluded with the routine announcement that those convicted had ten days to make an appeal to the High Court. Rarely were appeals filed, partly because an unsuccessful attempt meant there could be no later reduction of a sentence. Further, lower-court judges faced sanctions if their decisions were overturned, which led many to secretly clear their verdicts beforehand with the High Court.

When Decheng returned to K-block, his cellmates greeted him with eyebrows raised in surprise, and whoops of delight. Some of the prisoners reacted as though they'd won the lottery. Indeed, as Decheng later learned, several had placed bets on the morning's outcome. The overwhelming consensus among the "legal experts"— long-timers who'd read many a charge-and-prosecution document— was that the language in Decheng's clearly indicated that the prosecution was going for the death penalty.

Some days later, his cellmates had to shake and finally kick him to rouse Decheng from sleep. No prisoner had ever snored so loudly, they said.

PRISON OFFICIALS WAITED ANOTHER MONTH, until mid-October, before ordering the guards to remove Decheng's handcuffs. Authorities had to be satisfied that a detainee was not going to react to their sentence with anger or violence or by attempting suicide. The screw and lock on Decheng's handcuffs were so rusted after four months' wear that the guards had to use a hammer to break them open.

To help regain use of his hands and fingers, Decheng offered to wash his cellmates' dishes every day. As soon as he had enough feeling to hold a pen, he wrote a letter to Qiuping. He told her that because of his feelings for her, he wanted to free her from waiting for him. He had received a long sentence, too long for her to be expected to live as if in widowhood. Knowing prisoners' letters were read, he didn't communicate his greatest worry, that the wait could well be a lifetime, that the authorities could decide at any time and for any reason to extend his sentence. Instead, he wrote that he felt it would be morally wrong for him to ask her to wait for him: "Out of concern for your welfare, I am writing to ask you to divorce me."

When Qiuping's reply came, the guards again fetched Decheng from his cell. They handed him her folded letter, inside of which was a 3-by-5-inch black-and-white photograph.

Already some of the guards were tearing up as they stood awaiting his reaction.

In the photograph, taken at a studio, Qiuping's long hair caressed her shoulders. She was wearing a jacket that he recognized. Both her cheeks were clearly tear-stained and the photograph itself was marked where tears had splashed and been left to pool. Decheng turned the picture over. On the back, Qiuping had written an inscription. "October 2, 1989." That was her birthday; like him, she was now twenty-six years old. "Lu Gao, We will never accept a divorce, neither in life nor in death. Wangping."

"Your wife is absolutely amazing," said one of the guards.

Decheng wept as never before. His tears gushed, coursing down his face and drenching his clothing. Later a guard told him that his crying recalled a line from one of Mao Zedong's famous romantic poems. In "The Immortals," Mao addresses a female friend who had lost a spouse decades before to an executioner of the Kuomintang, just as he had. The two couples had been friends in Hunan in the days when the Communists were on the run from Chiang Kai-shek and the Kuomintang. Mao refers to heavenly word received on earth of Chiang's defeat and in the last line writes of boundless joy, such that "Tears fly down from a great upturned bowl."

SIX

ONE SPRING DAY, seventeen-year-old Decheng took his badminton racquet and headed for the Big Marching Ground. For weeks, he'd been feeling low, and exercise was always a welcome distraction. He knew he ought to be feeling relieved, grateful he'd been given a second chance. His time in detention had not affected his job or his standing at the bus station. Under the tutelage of his mentor and with hard work, his future as a mechanic was secure. And he was pleased that Jinwei, the boy who was the victim of his foolish prank, had settled down and proven himself to be a valuable worker.

Yet, if Decheng's anger had dissipated, he still felt burdened by a responsibility that he could not define. For two months in detention he'd kept company only with Dmitri Nekhylyudov, a Russian count, the protagonist of *Resurrection*, by Leo Tolstoy. It was the first novel of any length he'd ever read. He had decided to use his time in detention to improve himself, to do something he'd never done before. He'd borrowed two books to take with him from the workers' club at the bus station, choosing them mainly for their length; each was several hundred pages long. The other book was *The Book and the Sword*, by the hugely popular Louis Cha, founder of *Ming Pao*, the Hong Kong daily newspaper, who wrote under the pen name Jin Yong. Bored by Jin's sentimental tale of ancient heroes of martial arts, Decheng set it aside in favour of Tolstoy's novel. He found the count's tale of redemption utterly absorbing. He was enthralled at how the aristocrat and a prostitute on trial for murder—a former servant girl he'd once seduced—had rescued each other, one by extending help, the other by allowing herself to be helped.

And when the count, becoming introspective, goes on to give away his money to the poor, Decheng was impressed. *This is real socialism.*

On the second reading, Decheng considered whether anything like that could happen in China. Society was so repressed that he couldn't see how anyone like the count could ever emerge. The braggarts and the bullies would get their way and no one would stand up to them. *I might cause trouble, I might not,* Decheng thought, reflecting on his own run-ins with authority. Still, he felt disappointed in himself; he was no better than anyone around him.

The Big Marching Ground was ten minutes' walk from Clear Water Alley. Year-round, town folk used the field for sports and recreation. There were regular school track meets, soccer games, and basketball on an outdoor court. Decheng always came out to watch the Liuyang men's basketball team in action. Its star player was nicknamed "Big Peasant," a freakishly tall man whom organizers found in a nearby village.

Inside the running track, at the field's southeast end, badminton players gathered. Decheng spotted some twenty teenagers, boys and girls, keeping several shuttlecocks in the air at once. They played without a net; no one owned one. He joined one side of play. This being a weekday, the teenagers had the field to themselves. On the opposite side, a girl noticed Decheng's arrival. This was not the first time that Wang Qiuping had seen the handsome, athletic youth with the large, soulful eyes. She had remarked to her friends on his good looks and asked them about him. She was impressed to learn that Lu Decheng was in a three-year mechanic apprenticeship at the bus station. Like him, she had only a junior middle school education, but she had yet to find a full-time job. Her father, the deputy director of an opera troupe in Liuyang, had used his connections with the cultural ministry to get her part-time work at the local New China Bookstore.

Qiuping observed Decheng's enthusiastic play, delighting in the dance of his eyes as they followed the action. How purely boyish was his enjoyment. Suddenly, as his racquet made contact with a shuttlecock, his trousers slipped to his knees. A button must have popped off. He pulled them up and hurried off to one side. Qiuping considered her good fortune that his mishap finally gave her the opportunity to approach him. She followed. She took her handkerchief, twisted it into a spiral, and told him to try threading it through two adjoining belt loops. It worked. As they both rejoined play, Decheng's mind was only on playing badminton. She, however, had hardly a thought for the game.

One month passed. Qiuping showed up at the vehicle-repair shop looking for him. She introduced herself. As soon as Decheng heard her smoky, gravelly voice, he recalled that day on the Big Marching Ground, playing badminton. He had been acutely embarrassed at what had happened to his trousers and hadn't remembered much more than that a girl, with a memorable voice, had come to his rescue.

Wang Qiuping presented a black-and-white photograph of herself and asked for one in return. On the back, she'd written a tender dedication. Decheng saw the meaning of the character for her name, *Qiu* meant autumn, and *Ping* referred to the lotus leaves that float on a pond.

Decheng was surprised at her forwardness; an exchange of photographs amounted to declaring themselves boyfriend and girl-friend. At that stage, usually both sets of parents wanted to be involved. Decheng had met other girls through older friends and family. Stepmother Meilan had once taken him to a nearby village, hoping to interest him in her niece. Another girl's parents had contacted Meilan to signal their approval for their daughter, who'd been sending Decheng long love letters, to spend time with her stepson. But never before had Decheng experienced his heart racing like this, as he stood chatting with this lively girl. He accepted the photograph from Wang Qiuping. To give her one in return, he went to a studio to have one taken of himself.

Upon meeting Qiuping, the blackness lifted from Decheng. Buoyed by her vivaciousness, he felt exhilarated, purposeful, and focused on having a worthwhile and loving life. Together, the couple brought out the romantic in one another. Many boys, and parents with sons, had their eye on Qiuping. She told Decheng that she believed in finding the one person from whom she would be inseparable for life. Decheng, already smitten, knew that he had found the only girl he would ever marry.

A bicycle that Renqing had splurged on for Decheng to get to and from work bought the young couple privacy that was otherwise hard to find. Society did not tolerate public displays of affection between lovers. Even holding hands constituted "unruliness and exhibitionism," cause for a complaint to the local Residents' Committee.

With Qiuping riding sidesaddle, the couple peddled out of town on day trips. He took her to places he'd first explored with Hongwu, when the two used to rent bicycles for less than a *yuan* a day and cycle up into the hills to the township of the Seven Treasure Mountains. The peasant family who'd kept the boys' bicycles safe did the same for Decheng and Qiuping. They'd climb Dao Wu Mountain, following "Leading The Way" path, which was marked by a line of ancient pines to a deep lake, overlooked by "Ring-the-bell Pavilion." Legend held that centuries ago, before it was lost to the bottom of the lake, the bell could be heard for miles around. The two teenagers would enjoy a picnic of sweet potatoes and rice balls. On shorter outings, they would swim in the river. Decheng insisted that Qiuping use an inner tube as she was not a strong swimmer and the current could be tricky. They cycled across the bridge in town to Heavenly Horse Mountain and hiked up to a valley that Decheng and Hongwu had named Shangri-La for its bounty of wild fruits, where they could see timid muntjac deer.

Qiuping trusted her heart and saw both a strength and vulnerability in Decheng that were deeply affecting. He considered her a superior being, especially compared to him. Where he heaved and sighed over most decisions, she was clear-headed, decisive, and quick to act. Where he kept his distance from people until he sized them up, she was open-hearted, warm, and generous. As she'd shown that afternoon in the Big Marching Ground, in matters requiring a practical mind, she took charge. But Decheng believed her greatest gift was a spirited embrace of life, which inspired the same in friends and strangers alike.

In Qiuping's family, only Elder Brother, the oldest and only male among six siblings, knew that Lu Decheng was more than a friend. As teenagers, however, his sister and her boyfriend were years from legal marriage. One year earlier, in 1980, the government had enacted a late-marriage law in support of the one-child policy, brought in a year before that. The law set the legal marrying age for a woman to twenty, for a man, twenty-two.

Elder Brother and Qiuping conspired against their mother, whom they knew would be displeased at anyone, her daughter included, trespassing on her authority to decide Qiuping's future. Mrs. Wang, an outspoken and capable housewife, anticipated a bidding war between matchmakers over her exceptional daughter. Her husband, Deputy Director Wang, was concerned only with keeping up appearances befitting a man of his position, a senior cadre reporting to the provincial cultural ministry. As for Decheng, he let his father, who had seen him and Qiuping together in public, think what he liked. Decheng told Grandmother Lu, however, that he had found the girl he was going to marry. The old lady was very happy for the couple. "I have never been in love myself," she said.

That summer, on his eighteenth birthday, Decheng took Qiuping to his mother's grave in the municipal cemetery halfway up Green Sun Hill. She was buried in the family plot, where Grandfather Lu was interred and where a place was being kept for Grandmother Lu. Decheng brought along a bottle of Liuyang liquor and two enamel cups. He spoke softly at his mother's graveside, his voice tinged with melancholy and pride: "Mama, this is Qiuping, your future daughter-in-law." He added words of regret and praise, "You would have made a wonderful mother-in-law." By the time they'd emptied the bottle together, Decheng was tipsy while Qiuping was as sober as ever. "You are an amazing girl," he told her.

DECHENG WAS THE FIRST among his childhood friends to have a girlfriend. His contemporaries worried more about jobs, Hongwu and Zhijian excepted. They remained devoted to study. In the end, only Zhijian would write the nationwide university-entrance examination. Only one in four would score high enough to gain entrance. After high school, Hongwu ended up working in a cast-ironware plant. University had been his greatest dream; he'd worked as a child labourer in a mine to make his first school fees and begged on Sundays for money to buy supplies. He'd scrimped on pen and paper, writing his characters so small as to frustrate his teachers— "I need glasses to read your writing!" Hongwu's dream ended in high school, when his father took up with a young widow with three children. Hongwu felt he had no choice but to stay in Liuyang, to find work and care for his younger siblings and bedridden mother.

Zhijian scored high enough to be assigned a place at a college. The Hunan Normal Teacher's College (the designation as a normal teacher's college was given to all higher institutions short of big-city universities) was in the city of Xiangtan, in Mao's home county of the same name, south of Changsha. Zhijian's only disappointment was the college's decision that he would study chemistry, when his passion was literature.

Decheng's former school chums still got together on occasion, when days off coincided. Like Hongwu, a few others had factory jobs. Some had to go farther afield to find work, which was still better than working at the local fireworks factories. Decheng's friend Qin Zefu, with whom he'd whiled away childhood days throwing stones from the riverbank, worked at a distant cement plant. He could come home to Liuyang only a couple of times a month.

One summer's day, at Renqing's request, Decheng assembled a half-dozen friends to replenish the stores of coal bricks of two households, the Lus' unit at the bus station and Number 35 Clear

Water Alley. With Driver Lu helping, they broke coal pieces into dust, added clay and water, and compressed the mixture into circular moulds, then laid them out in the sun to dry. Once the contents hardened, they punched out the finished bricks, stacked them, and delivered them. After a day of satisfying work, the happy crew retired to Driver Lu's, where his wife had agreed to reward them with a meal. Qiuping was meeting Stepmother Meilan for the first time. While Decheng was never at ease in the woman's presence, Qiuping's liveliness, together with the good food and flowing liquor, kept everyone's spirits high.

Perhaps no one was enjoying the revelry more than Driver Lu. At forty-seven, he was beginning to take stock of his accomplishments. In the bus company, he had been promoted as high as a driver could go. A man entering the last decade before old age ought to be well satisfied, were it not for the waning of his physical energies. But there was no need to dwell on this; he could be grateful for a robust son such as Decheng, with his youthful energy and strength. In that respect, Renqing savoured the knowledge that he had achieved as much as any man.

Suddenly, a woman's shrewish yelling interrupted the gaiety. Qiuping and Decheng froze. Mother and daughter had the same energetic voice.

"Driver Lu! Come out and face me!" Housewife Wang strung together several profanities. "Where's my daughter?"

Doors banged opened upstairs and down in the dormitory. Footsteps pounded above as curious neighbours rushed to look over the railing.

Housewife Wang had trekked thirty minutes across town from her home to Number 35 Clear Water Alley, thinking her daughter was there with Lu Decheng. Not finding her, she'd marched back uphill to the northwest end of town to confront Decheng's father at the bus station. By then, she had worked herself into a spitting rage.

She barged into Unit 6. When she saw her precious daughter sitting at the dinner table beside the bus driver's delinquent son and his vulgar friends, she turned her foul mouth on both Renqing and Decheng.

"Your no-good son has turned my daughter into a bad girl! Do you know what he's been up to?"

Driver Lu shrank from the woman.

"It's all your fault!" Housewife Wang roared at Decheng. She hauled her embarrassed daughter away, issuing threats as she left. "Lu Decheng, you stay away from her! I'm warning you, stay away!"

Silence fell heavily. Decheng saw no good in lingering. He rose from the table, and his friends followed him out.

After Housewife Wang's appearance at the bus station, Renqing's opposition to the young couple's relationship sprouted like a weed after a rain. Suddenly, he insisted that Decheng was too young to be getting into any relationship, let alone a serious one. For his part, Decheng saw the lecture as more proof of his father's submissiveness. *More mindless bowing to someone else's stronger will.*

RUNNING AWAY TOGETHER was Qiuping's idea. "Love is all that matters," she told Decheng. "What's the use of explaining that to my mother and father?"

Housewife Wang had been locked in battle with her headstrong daughter. "Name one good point Lu Decheng has. He's not worthy of you." She saw a different future for her daughter. "So many boys are chasing after you, why are you chasing after him? You are an exquisite creature, do you understand that? You're so smart, you're so pretty. You should be able to marry somebody rich and powerful."

Deputy Director Wang had his own solution for keeping his daughter occupied and under his family's watchful eye. He wanted Qiuping to follow Elder Brother into the work unit of the operatic troupe. When she was a young child, he'd cast her in bit parts and, when touring the ensemble across Hunan province, he had sometimes brought her along. Full-time troupe members had to be eighteen, and upon her birthday, on October 2, she would be eligible to join.

Despite her interest in the stage, Qiuping decided against applying. She told Decheng she didn't want to risk the medical examination. The two of them were intimate; what if she were found to be pregnant? Qiuping saw that she was cornered. Her impulse was to flee. But running away together would be fraught with difficulty, and living together outside of marriage was "illegal cohabitation."

When Qiuping made up her mind, she acted quickly. She spent her first night on the run at Number 35 Clear Water Alley. Grandmother Lu happily gave up her bed to her grandson and his girlfriend. The next morning, Decheng went to Hongwu, seeking his help finding a temporary hideout before Qiuping's parents and the authorities could catch up with them. Hongwu, foreseeing a long and trying road, asked the couple, "Do you really love each other? No matter what happens, are you really going to stay together?" Convinced of their resolve, Hongwu put a plan into action.

To put off her parents, Qiuping moved immediately to Ironworker Li's house. A friend was dispatched to tell the New China Bookstore that Qiuping would not be returning to work. Decheng himself went to work that day as if nothing were out of the ordinary. A day later, Ironworker Li and Hongwu arranged a ride for the couple to the home of a distant relative in the countryside. Father and son came along to make the introductions. When Ironworker Li said goodbye, he presented Decheng with a mortar and pestle for grinding chili seeds. "For your life together," he said.

Qiuping's mother reported to the Residents' Committee of Zhou Family Pier that Lu Decheng had run off with her daughter. The women on the committee did not harass old Grandmother Lu about the whereabouts of her grandson; it would be unbecoming to threaten a martyr's widow. But they took to pressuring Driver Lu: "If you don't find them, a lot of bad things will happen to you!" Being on foot, and old, the women had no means to chase Decheng when he hopped onto his bicycle at the end of each shift. The station managers did not concern themselves with the matter because his *hukou* listed Number 35 Clear Water Alley as his address, not the bus station. That made him the Residents' Committee's responsibility.

The teenage couple's new life was a peripatetic existence in the hilly reaches north and west of town. They had to stay close enough to town that Decheng could cycle to and from work every day. They developed a routine in looking for a place to stay. First, they scouted for someplace off a main road with no more than a handful of houses in the vicinity. They stayed away from any place advertised for rent. Instead, they asked if anyone knew of a spare room or vacant house that someone might be interested in renting. Decheng honed his instincts about whom to ask and whom to accept as a landlord. He looked for sincerity and something intangible that told him a person could keep an open mind—someone, therefore, less likely to go to the police about two teenagers living together. He avoided anyone who was overly welcoming or appeared well known locally, or who seemed puffed up with their social standing—they were the ones most likely to be Party activists.

When the time came to explain themselves, Qiuping did the talking. She introduced the two of them, never using their real names. She described their plight, and evoked love: "We are two people in love and our parents are against our relationship." She explained that they wanted to get away from their parents for a while. "What is most important to us is that we love each other. But, when the time is right, we'll go back and talk to them."

Peasants saw in the two teenagers a wide-eyed young couple from town—the youth had a bicycle and wore a watch—with some cookware, dishes and utensils, clothing and bedroll in a wooden crate, lashed onto a bicycle. The two seemed sincere. For some, they stirred memories of a first forbidden romance, and for others the elusiveness of love.

Sometimes, the couple stayed only overnight in any one place, sometimes a week and never more than two. Never did they move in somewhere without having scouted somewhere to go next. To their pleasant surprise, they found many sympathetic people. Some refused rent. Others advised them on whom to avoid. Some told them when suspicions had been aroused, and warned them it was time to move on. The arrival of winter made their life more arduous. Rural buildings, with their clay floors and mud walls, were uncomfortably damp. Rarely was there furniture. They cooked on a charcoal brazier that accommodated a single pot, around which they huddled for heat. "The most important thing," they said, "is that we have each other."

IN THE SUMMER OF 1982, word got back to the Residents' Committees that Wang Qiuping was pregnant. Those on the committee responsible for enforcing the one-child policy, the family-planning women, confronted Decheng. They ordered him to produce a certificate showing that Qiuping had had an abortion.

Her pregnancy was against the law in several ways: only married couples could apply for a childbirth permit; couples had to apply for the permit, good for one year, *before* becoming pregnant; and married couples were not eligible for permits until the wife was twenty-two *and* the couple's combined age was fifty. Decheng had just turned nineteen. Qiuping's nineteenth birthday was in the fall.

The teenage couple wondered who had betrayed them; people everywhere reviled informants. It was unlikely to have been anyone in the countryside. In rural areas, authorities had to step up prop-aganda in support of the one-child policy, where it was more unpopular than in towns and cities. Daily, Decheng cycled by bluntly worded roadside banners: "Raise fewer babies but more piggies" and "One more baby means one more tomb." Beijing's great policy reversal on rural health care gave peasants another reason to be uncooperative. The advance of Mao-era barefoot doctors was lost in the shift to fee-for-service health care begin-ning in 1979, when the dismantling of rural communes spelled the demise of the co-operative medical system.

Perhaps Housewife Wang or Stepmother Meilan, maybe both, got word of the pregnancy—the couple were keeping in touch with family on both sides—and reported it. Informants wouldn't have to appear in person at a Residents' Committee office. Signs that offered substantial reward money for reporting illegal pregnancies or births provided a telephone snitch line.

Whoever reported the pregnancy, the result was the same. Whereas illegal cohabitation provoked little more than moral censure, illegal pregnancies and births were treated as very serious violations. In the countryside, signs warned peasants: "Houses toppled, cows confiscated, if abortion demand rejected." The array of punishments for town and city folk was as ruinous: crippling fines, withholding of salary, or loss of employment.

Meeting the conditions of marriage and age was not sufficient to qualify for legal pregnancy. Every year, the National Population and Family Planning Committee decided the total number of births it would authorize that year for the country as a whole. That quota was distributed by province, then allocated by county and town, right down to individual work units and neighbourhoods. Local family planning people decided who received childbirth permits and who would be asked to wait. They kept track of menstrual cycles, pregnancies, and births, and could impose punitive and "remedial measures," even forced abortion—known to be performed right up to full term—and forced sterilization. Beijing rewarded local family planning people with bonuses if their neighbourhoods had a good record of compliance, and punished them with demotions if they did not.

Decheng and Qiuping were determined to have their baby. Decheng sought out Hongwu. Qiuping was in tears; she did not want an abortion. "She says she'll throw herself into the river if she has to," Decheng said.

Hongwu pledged to find a way for them go through with the pregnancy. As always, he had a connection, an obstetrician who worked at the People's Hospital. He paid a friendly visit to the doctor's home, eventually turning the conversation to the one-child policy. When speaking in confidence, people equated children with happiness and saw the three-year-old policy as cruel. Hongwu brought up the reason for his visit: he had two underage friends who wished to go through with their pregnancy. Hongwu had thought of a solution, although he confessed that he'd never actually heard of its being done: the couple could hand in an abortion certificate as though they had gone through with the termination.

"If I help you, I'll lose my job, my qualifications will be taken away," the doctor told him.

Hongwu persisted. "This couple is very determined. They'll jump into the river together if they have to have an abortion."

The doctor was not unmoved, but he felt powerless to help. "I cannot help you. You'll have to find a way yourself."

With another idea in mind, Hongwu, who lived only a few blocks from the People's Hospital, took to strolling back and forth in front of the building, keeping an eye out for a couple of the right age. As luck would have it, he spied a young man and woman exiting the hospital. Quickly, he went into the building and found out from a nurse that the couple had come seeking an abortion, but had not been able to get an appointment until the next morning. They were married, but below legal child-bearing age. Hongwu rushed outside and caught up with the couple. He told them about his determined friends and suggested a way the two could help: "When you go to the hospital tomorrow, you could register the patient's name as Wang Qiuping."

The couple hesitated.

"How much will the abortion cost?" asked Hongwu.

"One hundred *yuan*."

As part of the program of reform, Beijing moved from dictating hospital fees that bore no relation to cost to encouraging public hospitals to charge commercial rates for drugs and most procedures. As a consequence, abortions became a way to make money.

Hongwu offered the couple two hundred. As a show of good faith, he gave them his name and address. Two hundred *yuan* was an average year's salary for a local factory worker, but he had that much in savings. At the ironware plant where he worked, a long-standing problem of air bubbles in the cast iron had resulted in a rejection rate of 98 per cent. The plant had always lost money. Hongwu took it upon himself to study the factory's manufacturing processes. His suggested changes corrected the problem overnight, so that the rejection rate was reduced to 2 per cent. The plant managers rewarded Hongwu with a sizable bonus.

The couple remained uncertain about Hongwu's offer. Without a certificate of their own, they would be in a predicament. But 200 *yuan* would give them the means to smooth their way with a bribe.

"What time are you coming to the hospital tomorrow?" Hongwu asked.

"Eight-thirty in the morning."

The next morning, Hongwu stood waiting outside the hospital for several minutes before the couple appeared. As promised, he had the money ready. The couple accepted it and told him to come back at noon. Mid-morning, Hongwu slipped into the hospital and found the girl sleeping on a cot in the hall. He checked her identification tag. The name was "Wang Qiuping."

QIUPING PUT THE WORD OUT to her friends that she and Decheng needed a safe house in which to ride out her pregnancy. An acquaintance, Second Brother of the four Xiao brothers, came through for the pair. The brothers had a half-finished house in the countryside, intending it as an investment until such time as they married. The building was framed into four rooms off one central room, but since the ceiling wasn't in, the brothers had yet to look for tenants. They offered the house to Qiuping rent-free. The mud house was crude, but its location was ideal. Four kilometres from town, sitting halfway up a steep hillside and back 400 metres from a main road, the house afforded a clear view of anyone approaching. Best of all, there was a clinic 2 kilometres away in the hamlet of Ji Li Bridge. A friendly doctor there calculated that the baby would be born in late January.

Already struggling to support Qiuping and himself, Decheng needed money to pay for her health care, the delivery, and the mother and baby's stay at the clinic. Hongwu, who did not disclose to Decheng that he had paid double for the abortion certificate, advised his friend how to ask his superiors at the bus station for a loan: "Tell them you need money to pay for medicinal herbs to nurse Qiuping back to health after her abortion." Not only did his advice work, but their response was so generous that it gave Decheng an idea. He approached a senior administrator named Yu Zijun, whom he respected, and spoke of how he and Qiuping lived as husband and wife but wanted to formalize their relationship. He spoke vaguely about how they had *de facto* fulfilled the conditions of marriage: they lived together and they had had a pregnancy. He said nothing about being underage. He succeeded at getting the necessary letter of reference, which the marriage law dictated had to be obtained from either one's work unit or Residents' Committee. Qiuping showed Decheng's letter to a friend at her Residents' Committee and she too obtained a letter of reference that made no mention of her age.

Decheng and Qiuping timed their arrival at the marriage bureau for the dying minutes before lunch. A lone female staff member was in the courtyard hanging her washcloth on a line. She was annoyed that the couple was infringing on her lunch hour. (Meal breaks were so sacred to every worker that pilots of China Airlines were known to make unscheduled landings to eat.) The clerk took a cursory look at the letters, approved the application for marriage, and issued the couple their marriage documents. With that, Lu Decheng and Wang Qiuping were officially husband and wife.

From dawn to dusk, at the Xiao brothers' house in the country, Qiuping, her belly swelling, joyously tended a hillside of vegetables that she had planted. When Decheng and Qiuping had been living itinerantly, they'd kept only what could be transported in the wooden crate on their bicycle. Now they accumulated the belongings that made the house feel more like a home. For the next months, the couple lived blissfully.

With the approach of winter, Hongwu arrived with extra covers and blankets. Decheng stoked a brazier with diesel fuel, which he got free from the bus station, to generate heat. The acrid smoke was hardly worth what little warmth came of the fire. At night, the moss and lichen growing on the inner walls froze. By day, they seeped water. The air seemed colder inside than outside.

Late in January, on a particularly cold night, Qiuping's contractions started. Hongwu and Second Brother arrived to help Decheng take her to the clinic. They lifted her into a wooden cart of the kind that every rural household owns, and Hongwu pushed while the other two pulled, all the way to the Ji Li Bridge clinic. Dr. Bei, who'd accurately calculated Qiuping's due date, delivered a healthy baby boy. He announced the weight proudly: "Seven *catties*, two *taels*!"

Hongwu went to tell both sets of grandparents the good news. To smooth the way, he brought offerings of hard-boiled eggs dyed red to signify new life. He included firecrackers, choosing the smallest he could find to acknowledge the necessary secrecy that had surrounded the birth.

He visited Stepmother Meilan first.

She rejected his offering. "First of all, I don't believe you. And second, even if there is a grandson, I won't go visit."

Housewife Wang was shocked. "But she had an abortion! How can she be giving birth?" She said she wasn't interested in seeing any baby that Lu Decheng fathered, but she would go anyway because she wanted to see her daughter. She asked her husband to come with her.

"How can I go? I'm the deputy head of a state opera company! People will say, 'You cheated. You have an illegal grandson.'" Deputy Director Wang sat, shaking his head. "This will be very bad for all concerned."

ON THE THIRD DAY AFTER THE BIRTH, Hongwu and Decheng placed mother and baby in the wooden cart, and took them back to the house on the hill. Decheng gave careful consideration to a name, which Qiuping left to him. His inspiration came from the names old Carpenter Yi and his wife had given their children. Their first, a girl, "Spreading Out From The Centre," was adopted; the second, another girl, "Sacred Thoughts," was born to his wife at the late child-bearing age of thirty-four; the third, a boy, "The Dead Tree Suddenly Blossoms Again," was an unexpected pregnancy four years later. Similarly, Decheng appreciated Ironworker Li's prophetic choice of Hongwu, the name chosen by the founding emperor of the Ming dynasty, who rose from the poorest of peasant stock to the height of power and became known for his creativity, determination, strategic brilliance, and visionary mind.

Decheng chose *Jin* (will) to show strength of character, and *long* (dragon), the creature at once the symbol of exaltation and of the physical world, its undulating body representing hills, valleys, and rivers. Baby Jinlong's soft cheeks were rosy and plump. He nursed contentedly, oblivious to having arrived in the coldest month.

When the baby was eight days old, something seemed to be amiss. He was lethargic. Then he no longer wanted to suckle. Qiuping worried that maybe he'd stopped taking in milk altogether. She and Decheng were frightened. They were inexperienced with babies and lived far from advice or help. Both parents wanted to hurry to a hospital in town, but they were in a quandary: the People's Hospital would likely offer the most modern treatment available for the baby, but the Hospital of Chinese Medicine, in an adjoining building, was likely to be less stringent at admissions. If the People's Hospital found out that Baby Jinlong's was an illegal birth, they might refuse to treat him. The anxious parents decided on the Hospital of Chinese Medicine.

At emergency, to their relief, admissions staff did not ask to see their childbirth permit. Decheng paid the cashier the hospital registration fee—the price for just coming through the door—and the consultation fee. After a long wait, a doctor examined the baby. A newborn's skin should be soft and flexible, he said. Jinlong's was taut. He speculated cold to be the cause and he thought an incubator might help. The People's Hospital next door had one, he said.

The couple was relieved again when the admissions staff there did not ask to see the childbirth permit either. Decheng paid the necessary fees, and again a long wait followed. Finally, they received a second doctor's opinion. He said that their baby had impetigo, a bacterial skin infection. He wrote out a prescription for an antibiotic. Decheng asked about the incubator. The doctor agreed the baby would probably benefit from being placed in one. Decheng paid the cashier for the prescription and asked what the fee was to use the incubator. He reeled at the amount: a minimum of one thousand *yuan*.

Decheng took his receipt to the pharmacy and brought the antibiotic back to a nurse. The baby was placed in the Observation Room, where he would stay until the cashier had received payment or a deposit so that he could be formally admitted to hospital for treatment. Baby Jinlong was hooked up to a saline drip. The couple hovered over him, hoping that the rosy colour would come back to his cheeks, that his illness—whether born of the cold or impetigo— would pass and he would be fine. The baby lay quietly. Qiuping and Decheng stared silently at the drip of the intravenous. Every time the saline ran low, one of them would go find a nurse.

A full night passed like this. By dawn, the couple was exhausted. They were unsure if Baby Jinlong's condition had improved or worsened, or even if there was anything to worry about. Decheng wondered aloud why no nurse or doctor had come to check on the baby. He thought about how the nurses seemed annoyed at being pestered when it came time to replenish his son's saline bag. Suddenly the staff's indifference frightened the couple; perhaps the doctors and nurses had decided Baby Jinlong's case was hopeless.

That day, a frantic Decheng tried to raise money from relatives and friends to pay for the use of an incubator. There was no point in appealing to either of their parents for help. Decheng went to Hongwu's, but he was at work; his older brother gave what he could spare, which was a pittance. He went to Auntie's and found her eldest son there. He'd come to Ji Li Bridge clinic with fruit and candies to mark the birth, and he offered to see what he could raise, later returning to the hospital with forty *yuan*. Decheng continued to the homes of a few other friends before abandoning his appeal. He felt numb. All he had to show for his effort was a clutch of five-*yuan* bills and one ten-*yuan* note.

After his shift ended at midnight, Hongwu returned home covered in a day's sweat and grease to find Decheng waiting. He looked spent, his eyes red-rimmed, his face tear-stained.

"What are you doing, looking like this? What's going on?"

Decheng's voice was barely audible. "My son's dying. He might not survive. Qiuping says if he's not cured, she doesn't want to live."

Back at the People's Hospital, Hongwu tried to calm Qiuping. "Don't worry yourself too much or you'll be the one to be sick. We'll find a solution together."

Hongwu woke up a couple of neighbours, a nurse and a doctor who worked at the hospital. Early the next morning, he joined them at a meeting with the head of the department of pediatrics and a hospital administrator to discuss Baby Jinlong's condition. Afterwards, the chief pediatrician met with the parents. He offered another diagnosis, speculating that the baby had frostbite, then broke the bad news: "There's no way to save your son. You could scour the whole province and not find a cure. But, this baby could use some warmth." In his final hours, Baby Jinlong was admitted for treatment and placed in the hospital's one incubator. By early evening, he was dead.

Qiuping went berserk with grief. She made a dash for the stairs, to fling herself from the hospital's rooftop. Hongwu yanked her back and pushed her onto a cot in the hallway, telling her sternly, "If you jump, you will be betraying your friendship with me!" A doctor prescribed a sedative and, as recommended, Decheng admitted his wife to hospital for bedrest.

A wintry storm had blown in and knocked down power lines, throwing the town into darkness. By the light of a flashlight,

Decheng sat with his infant son's body in the peace room. Later that evening, he went upstairs to visit Qiuping. She wasn't there. Her hospital bed was empty. Staff told Decheng that her mother had taken her home.

SEVEN

O NE EVENING IN LATE NOVEMBER, a guard came to Decheng's cell in K-block at Banbuqiao Prison when all prisoners were preparing to sleep. Told to pack up his belongings, Decheng was taken to the main office, where he joined Yu Dongyue and Yu Zhijian. In the six months since their confinement, each time the penal authorities brought the three together, their fate had taken a turn. The hour was late, going on midnight. *What was in store for them now?* Decheng wondered. The three were handcuffed together, Zhijian in the middle. Three guards, the ranking one among them armed with a handgun, the others with rifles, rode with them in a prison van across town. The ride ended at the Beijing railway station.

"Are we going home?"

"You're going to Hunan."

By late fall in 1989, Beijing's jails were filled to overflowing with detainees who had taken part in the pro-democracy movement and protests. Authorities in Beijing decided to repatriate the "1989 inmates" to their home provinces to serve out their sentences. At the same time, they moved into the larger provincial prisons other 1989 inmates from the many smaller detention centres in towns and cities around the country. Most of them were workers arrested for organizing their work units to join in local protests.

In the crowded waiting room of the Beijing railway station, Zhijian and Decheng, seeing a casual indifference in their guards, asked a favour—to buy them a pack of cigarettes. The guards exchanged a look as if to say better to oblige than risk a scene in public. The two friends shared a cigarette, which after months of enforced abstinence in K-block, left them feeling drunk.

On board the train south, the guards paid little attention to their handcuffed prisoners. The three friends had a lot of catching up to do. They had no idea how long this reunion would last; they didn't know whether they would be taken off the train at different times, whether they were destined for the same prison, or, even if so, whether they would be separated, as they had been in Beijing. They did know they would be together at least until the train reached Hunan.

The train entered the tunnel of night, emerged into the dawn and another day, rolling across the grey November landscape. In those hours, the conversation of the three roamed from homesickness to their misfortune during the past six months. They longed to see their families. They yearned for rice and peppery food. They lamented the students' betrayal. Zhijian and Dongyue revealed that their interrogations had been harsh, that both had suffered solitary confinement. As the sun set on another day, the three prepared for their separation. Assuming smoking was prohibited in their next prisons, they emptied the tobacco from the remaining cigarettes, rolled it into balls, and awkwardly, given their handcuffs, worked it into the linings of Zhijian's and Decheng's jackets. The train reached Changsha, pulled out, and continued south. About five hours later, at three o'clock in the morning, when the train stopped in Hengyang, a bleak industrial city on the Xiang River in south Hunan, the policemen and their three prisoners disembarked. The night air carried a heavy metallic smell, sharp enough to make Decheng's eyes water.

THOSE WHO DID BUSINESS FROM AFAR with the facility at 48 Tongxin Road, on the outskirts of Hengyang, knew it as the Hunan Heavy Duty Automotive Manufacturing Plant. It was also a prison. Those who came to this address would see 6-metre-high brick walls topped with high-voltage wires, and sentries looking down from watchtowers. The walls disappeared into a steep mountainside, against which the complex of two-storey buildings was constructed. The prisoners knew the institution as Hunan Provincial No. 2 Prison or Yanbei Prison. They wore identification badges, pinned conspicuously on the upper left breast of one's outermost garment above the pocket, with the characters *laogai*, meaning "reform-through-labour." As many as three thousand were incarcerated at Yanbei in the early winter of 1989, when the facility received some fifty 1989 inmates.

Among them, Yu Zhijian, Yu Dongyue, and Lu Decheng considered their good fortune; they were assigned to the same cellblock. Each 25-square-metre block housed thirty inmates, and sometimes as many as forty. Several cellblocks shared toilets, classrooms, a television room, and a canteen adjoined to a small exercise yard.

Decheng was ordered to arrange for a prisoner labouring in the "daily living and sanitation" section to sew a yellow stripe down the length of his every item of clothing, including underwear and individual socks. He had three days to do so. The same would apply to any clothing given to him while he was here. Any prisoner found wearing or in possession of garments without the stripe could be deemed to be plotting escape, for which the penalty was death. Prisoners' families were expected to supply all basic necessities. To offset the cost, the prisoners themselves were paid a monthly allowance in certificates valued at three *yuan*—holding cash was forbidden. The certificates could only be used at the prison co-op, which sold basics like laundry soap and toiletries, as well as stationery, and foodstuffs such as canned fish, powdered milk, and biscuits. Decheng saw one improvement over life at K-block—the co-op sold cigarettes, which meant smoking must be permitted. But three *yuan* didn't go far; prices were two to three times what they were on the outside.

Prisoners who couldn't depend on their families scrounged from what other departing prisoners left behind. Clothing was most coveted, because the prison was unheated, and from November to February overnight temperatures dipped below zero. Tuberculosis was rampant in the prison, and those who could not get warm feared they would be next to start coughing and spitting up blood. Decheng had only his cotton jacket and his sweater. When he'd left home in May, he'd thought he'd be gone a matter of days, maybe a week.

Immediately, Decheng wrote to Qiuping to share the good news that he, Zhijian, and Dongyue had been transferred to a prison fewer than 300 kilometres from Liuyang. He gave his letter to the authorities, and waited, anticipating that Qiuping would make an early visit. Decheng even dared to hope he would see his young daughter again, now that he was so close. Of some small comfort these past few months was the time he'd spent with Little Xinfeng before going to Beijing. Some sixth sense had made him take four days off work so that they could be together.

THE THREE FROM LIUYANG, like all the 1989 inmates at the Hengyang prison, were enrolled in "study groups," to participate in what penal reform authorities called an "orientation" program. Run by an older inmate, study groups were made up of a half-dozen or more new detainees. A prisoner remained in a study group anywhere from two weeks to three months—depending on how long he took to confess his crime and demonstrate an acceptable level of repentance. They would then begin the next stage: reform-through-labour.

The study groups kept the same hours as the regular prison population, who laboured in workshops making car chassis, wheel rims, and other parts. Since lights stayed on twenty-four hours a day, the arrival of dawn went unnoticed and a loud bell ended prisoners' nights at 5:30 a.m. Guards burst into the cellblocks, yelling "Out of bed!" at laggards. Six mornings a week, after overseeing a hurried, twenty-minute breakfast in the canteen, they escorted the regular inmates to their workshops and the new detainees to their study groups in nearby classrooms, where they stayed until five-thirty or six. Most days, prisoners spent the hour before supper pacing the cracked concrete in the exercise yard. There was a basketball hoop there, but it was for the guards' use only. The prison allowed small doses of television: a half-hour before supper three days a week and two hours on Sundays. After supper, four evenings a week, from seven to nine, the new detainees returned to their study groups and the others went to political-study sessions. At nine-thirty, the bell sent prisoners to their bedsides for roll call, then to wash up. At ten, the bell rang again, and prisoners laid down immediately with their heads uncovered.

The first job of the study group's team leader was to distribute and lead discussion about the prison handbook, *Regulations Concerning the Behaviour of Criminals Undergoing Reform.* Produced by the central government, it covered the minutiae of daily life, compulsory labour in workshops, and compulsory political study. The "ten forbiddens" were foremost among the rules, beginning with, "It is forbidden to oppose the four cardinal principles." In 1979, Deng Xiaoping articulated these principles—keeping to the socialist road, upholding the dictatorship of the proletariat, the leadership of the Communist Party, and Marxism–Leninism–Mao Zedong Thought—to appease the hardliners who were nervous that his reforms would undercut class struggle. When the team leader opened with this rule, he'd confirmed for Decheng that hardline idealogues ran the prison. The forbiddens, apart from banning the obvious—no fighting, martial arts, concealing money, explosives, poisons, clubs or knives, and so on—extended to political activity. There were rules aimed specifically at political prisoners, like the three from Liuyang: "no creating or spreading political rumours," "no talking in a chummy fashion or advocating local ideas as a way of cementing friendship." The prison expected that new detainees should be able to recite passages of the handbook on demand before their first month was over. Team leaders rewarded those who could recite it cover to cover by the end of the second month. *I won't lay my eyes on that book,* Decheng told himself.

The study groups were organized around daily struggle sessions, targeting each prisoner in turn. The leader would grill the day's prisoner on his thoughts about his crime, verdict, and sentence. Others in the group were expected to ruthlessly admonish and criticize him. In turn, the prisoner was expected to display contrition. The "great, glorious, and correct Communist Party" could not make false accusations. Prisoners followed up these sessions by writing self-criticisms that revealed their "state of thinking," which would show their gratitude to the Party for its magnanimity. Decheng's instinct was always to say and write neither too much nor too little. It seemed to work, at least judging by how he escaped the fearsome wrath of his team leader.

GUARDS ESCORTED THE WIFE and daughter of the prisoner, Lu Decheng, into the visitation area, a wide corridor more than 100 metres long lined with opposing rows of wooden desks. They sat down and waited. Guards patrolled up and down. Qiuping had been told the rules: her visit could last only twenty minutes, prisoner and visitor had to speak loud enough for guards to hear, and no physical contact was permitted.

Guards led Decheng into the corridor. Both mother and child broke down when they saw him. Especially in the eyes of a four-year-old, he was a ghostly and frightening sight. His head was shaved, his frame was bony, and his clothing was marked by a garish yellow stripe. Decheng, determined that his wife and daughter see him strong and resolute, kept his tears from spilling over.

Qiuping had brought clothing, a carton of cigarettes, toiletries, ballpoint pens, and paper. She'd cooked a specialty Liuyang dish—uncooked food was not allowed—and she had purchased him an ankle-length winter coat, made of leather. He was enormously touched: she would have had to sacrifice a lot to buy such an expensive coat.

Twenty minutes, in a place without privacy, wasn't much time.

Sadness seeping from her, Qiuping told him how difficult it had been to read his letter asking her to divorce him: "My heart hurt so much to read those words."

To see the anguish he had caused pained Decheng. However, he still wanted to be sure she recognized the uncertainty of their future together. If he could have spoken freely, he would have reminded her of the vagaries of the justice system and that the authorities were treating their three cases as one. But now, he had to try to get that across without so many words. He did his best: "You could be making a gamble of a lifetime. It doesn't matter what the sentence is. I don't know when we will be released—maybe in a short time, maybe in a long time."

For Qiuping, the matter was uncomplicated. "My love for you is a deep, deep love." She wept for them both. "My love can reduce your suffering in this place."

An expression held that "you love with your heart, not words from your mouth." Even characters in an opera wouldn't say to each other, "I love you." Instead they showed their sentiment through their actions. But to hear Qiuping's voice now wrapping the word, and to hear it in so barren a place, penetrated Decheng's gloom like a ray of light from the heavens.

She has shown again that she is a superior being to me.

They had been through so much together, had faced so many obstacles. Even at his lowest, when Baby Jinlong died, it was she who had remained determined, despite opposition from the Residents' Committee and their parents, that they would have another child. Now his wife and their daughter faced only the certainty of his absence. Still, Qiuping was offering to share his fate. Decheng was convinced now that *yuanfen*, something greater than fate and more powerful than destiny, had brought them together.

PRISONERS WHO'D COMMITTED counter-revolutionary crimes were permitted visits only from family. Sadly, Zhijian's and Dongyue's were unable to visit. Zhijian's widowed mother was still ailing in hospital and his sisters had to stay near to nurse her. Dongyue's parents and brother lived 60 kilometres beyond Liuyang, in the countryside. Apart from the distance, they faced the expense of travel. Bus to Changsha and then rail was quicker, whereas going by road all the way took more than a day in each direction. Fortunately, Qiuping could travel on the bus and stay overnight at any local station for free. Decheng would always share what she brought in her care packages; he'd divide the cigarettes between him and Zhijian and give most of the writing paper to Dongyue. From the start, other prisoners noticed Dongyue's talent for drawing and calligraphy and lined up to have him sketch their likeness, which they could send to their families. Dongyue charged only a few *fen*, a fraction of a guard's price for taking a photograph.

Qiuping's cooking was a relief from the prison fare. At Decheng's first meal here, when he saw that one of the wooden vats contained rice, he could hardly wait to fill his bowl. He hadn't tasted rice for more than six months. He went back again and again. And when rice appeared at the next meal, he thought that he might never have to eat another spongy *wotou* again. It took several meals at his new prison before Decheng noticed the mould and the worms mingled in with the coarse, stale grains. The vegetables served with the rice were tough enough to scrape the inside of his stomach. He could look forward to every fifth day, when some lonely pieces of pork appeared in the vegetables, but only if he was also lucky enough to get to the front of the line before all the meat was picked out.

Cheered to be in one another's company again, the three friends developed their own rituals within prison life. Dongyue liked to start and end each day by standing several minutes under the icy shower. Only cold water came from the prison taps. Dongyue had always believed bathing in cold water was a good way to strengthen the body. In Liuyang, he'd go for an early-morning swim, even on wintry mornings when ice had formed at the river's edge. Now, daily, he dragged his two friends into the prison's shower and splashed cold water on them until they adopted the practice as their own.

Dongyue insisted they adopt another of his rituals at mealtimes. To prepare the vegetables, the prison cooks tossed them into a huge tub of stale, dirty water, scooped them out into an immense wok over a fire, raked them with a farmer's hoe, then emptied them into the wooden vats. The vegetables, entangled with weeds and pebbles, were so raw that they were still crawling with insects. Some new detainees shrugged. "The big bacteria in the food will eat the small bacteria," they said. Following Dongyue's lead, his two friends rinsed the vegetables before eating them. Prisoners dipped their cups into a trough to get their drinking water. Decheng drank a cup a day, believing that the body would become acclimatized to the water. Dongyue, though he would use it to clean his vegetables, avoided drinking this water; instead, he paid the cell boss for hot boiled water from his thermos.

The only opportunity the three had to speak with any privacy was the hour before supper allotted to the exercise yard. Rules dictated a maximum of three could walk abreast. They were careful to change their conversation to small talk when a guard or other prisoners came near. Whenever the three discussed their case, emotions flowed strongest at their betrayal by the students. Only once did they disagree. Uncharacteristically sharp in his criticism, Dongyue thought that they could have avoided being nabbed by the student pickets. He argued that they should have made speeches first in order to attract a protective wall of supporters, and then thrown the paint-filled eggs. "We did it the wrong way around," he insisted. Decheng didn't agree, believing that with that many people in their way, they might not have had the space they needed to throw the eggs. "What matters is that we did it," Zhijian said, "not that we should have gone about it differently."

Most of the talk among the three was of the world beyond the high prison walls. News from outside found its way in. The gates regularly opened for trucks and outsiders making deliveries and pickups. Prisoners watched television. Personnel and prisoners being transferred in and out fed the prison grapevine. Developments in the Communist world made for the hottest topic of conversation among the three friends. In K-block, they had heard nothing of the breach in the Berlin Wall on November 9. At month's end, when the three arrived in Hengyang, they were stunned to learn of the collapse of regimes in quick succession in East Germany, Czechoslovakia, and Hungary. In late December, they watched television reports of the capture and summary execution of Nicolae Ceauşescu, the Romanian president, and his wife, Elena. Such a rising tide of democracy gave the three friends from Liuyang hope. China was the odd nation out, using violence and imprisonment to preserve its regime. If Western governments pressed Beijing to account for the 1989 inmates, they'd likely focus on the high-profile cases, such as theirs, perhaps leading to their early release.

In February of 1990, Qiuping travelled from Liuyang to break the news in person to Decheng that his beloved Grandmother Lu had died. He wept openly and was so distraught that a kindly guard let his wife stay an extra ten minutes. To the end, Decheng's grandmother had been stubborn and strong-willed. Though ailing, she had refused Auntie's entreaties to move in with her and her family. She left Number 35 Clear Water Alley and rented a room across the river near where she and Grandfather Lu had once lived happily. She died there days later.

Decheng made a request of prison authorities. "I want to pay respects at my grandmother's grave," he said. They knew full well that she'd raised him, that his legal residence, as registered on his *hukou*, was hers.

"It's within my rights as a prisoner to return to Liuyang to honour her."

The authorities ignored Decheng's request. He thought of their hypocrisy, of how the death of a widow of a martyr was supposed to be mourned, her memory revered. *I will find ways to oppose them,* he resolved.

DECHENG'S TWO FRIENDS received no compassion themselves. To the contrary, prison authorities singled out Yu Zhijian and Yu Dongyue for a harsh denunciation. More than two thousand inmates assembled in the great hall and the two men, handcuffed and bound one to each other with thick rope, were led onstage. For the next three hours, prisoners stepped forward to upbraid the two for their counter-revolutionary crimes and their incorrect thinking. The escalating rhetoric evoked the fanaticism of the Cultural Revolution that Decheng had read about in old *Red Banner* magazines, of which he had a collection at home. Like the struggle sessions from that time, the truth of any accusation hurled at Zhijian and Dongyue was irrelevant. What matters is that the accuser, in his inventiveness, demonstrates his own allegiance to the Party.

Still, Decheng sat in silent fear that at any moment the guards would haul him up to the stage or that the vitriol might spill over to him. Two denouncers rose from their seats. To his horror, they were both 1989 inmates from their cell whom he had believed to be squarely on their side. First on his feet was Song, who told the room he'd overheard subversive conversations between the two. Then, Liu stepped forward, reinforcing the other's tales. Decheng wondered whether the two, like the petty criminals who had shared his padded cell in Beijing, had been put in there to monitor the three of them. He could live with that more easily than the thought that they were pro-democracy advocates who had sold out. In the end, he escaped mention.

In attacking Yu Zhijian and Yu Dongyue, the prison authorities seemed to be following the proverb, "Kill the chicken to scare the monkey." But the denunciation session did not intimidate either of the two. Nor did it succeed in making pariahs of them. In fact, as the study groups stretched into their third month, the charismatic Zhijian began to draw more and more admirers among the 1989 inmates. Some hung on his every word and respected him as a political visionary. Still others, mimicking the lackeys who formed a protective perimeter around a cell boss, made it known that they were ready to do the same for him and Dongyue.

Inevitably, there was trouble. Cell bosses were not going to stand back and let an interloper usurp their authority. The prison system entrenched the existing prisoner hierarchy. Every cell boss was a "corrected activist." Identified by red badges, they were prisoners whom authorities deemed to have "corrected their wrong thinking" and to be "making good progress on reform." The red badges gave them privileges, like a single bunk instead of 18 inches of space in a communal bed, in which prisoners slept ten across. They also had, reliably, meat on meat days and received whole meal portions on a tray. Other prisoners slopped theirs out of wooden vats, pulled into the canteen on carts. Corrected activists were assigned lighter work and lower daily production quotas in the workshops, or held the plum jobs in daily living and sanitation, education, the clinic, or administration.

Penal authorities considered corrected activists to have the capacity, and therefore the responsibility, to help ordinary prisoners to reform. Officials designated them as "trustees," and expected them to help the guards keep the prison running smoothly. In reality, trustees harassed and preyed on ordinary prisoners, though they were not above backing off for a bribe of food or cigarettes, or favours like washing their dishes or clothes.

Impossible to avoid were the attentions of the "Rigid Control Teams." Selected from the burliest of corrected activists, they roamed freely throughout the prison, easily identified by their red arm bands with the characters for Rigid Control Team written in yellow. Behind the closed doors of their office, they sometimes did the guards' dirty work, beating and torturing fellow prisoners, which the guards might not always get away with.

One day, some corrected activists cornered one of the new detainees. They accused him of stealing another prisoner's belongings, grabbed him by the earlobes, and marched him to the office of the Rigid Control Team. Immediately, Zhijian rallied his supporters. The prisoner they had taken was a stocky and sturdy fellow, but also quite simple. Their ploy was obvious: find any new detainee with no education or ability to express himself, and haul him off on a trumped-up accusation. Then return the victim to his cell bruised and bloodied to send a message to all the 1989 inmates: submit or suffer the same fate. Zhijian and Dongyue proposed to the new detainees that they band together, go to the Rigid Control Team office, and demand their fellow prisoner's release.

Zhijian and Dongyue intercepted Decheng: "Stay back. Let the two of us face up to whatever happens. One of the three of us has to be able to communicate with the outside world. Just in case."

Decheng's two friends were again a step ahead of him in thinking through the consequences. They could exploit the regime's apparent strategy to treat the two of them harshly, and him leniently. The prison-wide denunciation of only the two of them seemed to confirm that the regime feared the two intellectuals of the trio and regarded the third, the uneducated Lu Decheng, as the lesser threat. Better to keep Decheng in that protected position, so that he could be a voice should theirs fall silent.

More than thirty of the new detainees marched on the office of the Rigid Control Team. The eight or nine trustees there weren't interested in talking. A melee broke out. Noses were bloodied, eyeglasses smashed, teeth knocked out. Blood poured from cuts and gashes. Guards came running to rescue the trustees. They jabbed the 1989 inmates with their electric prods, beat them with their wooden batons, and kicked and trampled them.

The guards led away the beaten-up new detainees into their office. They were determined to teach them a lesson. It was one thing for ordinary prisoners to come to fisticuffs amongst themselves, but unheard of that prisoners should try to take on trustees. The guards contrived a punishment that was the ultimate degradation for a political prisoner, to kneel in submission.

Back in the cellblock, Zhijian was determined that this humiliation should not go unanswered. He urged the new detainees to respond with one voice, proposing that they demand an apology from the guards and, borrowing a tactic of the students in Tiananmen Square, stage a hunger strike until it was forthcoming. Again, he and Dongyue told Decheng to stay on the sidelines.

A dozen of the 1989 inmates participated in the fast. To keep his mind from hunger, Zhijian recited Tang dynasty poems. Dongyue composed poems to commemorate the strike. Decheng asked him for one and, as was typical of Dongyue, he pondered, then took up his brush and wrote with a flourish. *Hunger can nourish the flower of democracy.* He added a closing punctuation mark of his own invention, a question mark and an exclamation mark that shared the same anchoring dot.

Prison officials were loath to concede any wrongdoing, but feared that word of the protest would get to the outside world. The last thing Beijing would want is attention drawn to the plight of the 1989 inmates. The hunger strike went into its fifth day. Officials from the provincial ministry responsible for prisons arrived in Hengyang to negotiate an end to the dispute. They proposed that two apologies be made: the guards would apologize to the strikers and the strikers would apologize to the Rigid Control Team. Neither side would hear of it. Finally, the provincial negotiators decided that the corrected activists who'd seized the prisoner in the first place would write self-criticisms for having wrongly accused him of theft. The negotiators called a meeting of all new detainees to announce the decision, and they forbade them to speak of it.

Word flew through the prison anyway. Ordinary prisoners sought out all three from Liuyang, clapping them on the back.

"Wow! What a victory!"

"This has never happened before!"

"You three guys are record-breaking!"

No need to make me into a hero, thought Decheng. *I didn't sacrifice myself.*

DAYS LATER, a couple of common criminals from Liuyang, who laboured as cooks and cleaners, slipped word to the three that their transfers were imminent; penal authorities had decided to separate them. The three friends were not disheartened. In the USSR,

Lithuania had declared its independence and other states in the union could not be far behind. Germany was preparing for reunification. Perhaps, the three told each other, their release might come soon and even on the same day. Still, prison life was hard and their foremost objective should be to survive. Dongyue told them to guard their health and stay strong. The three made a pact to steer clear of any activity that would give the authorities reason to brand them as common criminals. The regime, they feared, would use any excuse to punish them with the death penalty.

To mark their solidarity, they bought three postcards, with a traditional painting of a chrysanthemum, from the prison co-op. They wrote their names and birth dates on each card. Each man kept one. Prisoners could write to one another only on postcards sold in the co-op, but the trio decided that, once separated, anything they would write to each other could be construed by authorities as incitement. They came up with a plan to exchange seemingly harmless greetings that would pass the censors: every December 25, each would send the other two a postcard on which he would write only "Happy Christmas" and sign his name. The card would communicate a simple message: I am alive. And should authorities keep their families in the dark about their fate, this exchange would be another way to get word out.

Zhijian and Dongyue had parting gifts for Decheng. Zhijian wrote out a recommended reading list of one hundred books. It included Chinese writers like famed Tang dynasty poet Li Bo, but Western titles of philosophy and literature predominated. Zhijian pointed out his favourites among them: philosophers Immanuel Kant and Friedrich Nietzsche, poets Lord Byron and Percy Bysshe Shelley, and novelists Stendhal and Ernest Hemingway. Shakespeare was the only name Decheng recognized. Dongyue composed a poem to encapsulate the three friends' many conversations and the conclusion he took from them, that the greatness of man was his ability to see what was just.

The globe is very small
but mankind is great
the wind of humanity blows across the sweet-scented grasslands
allowing all dreams to thrive.

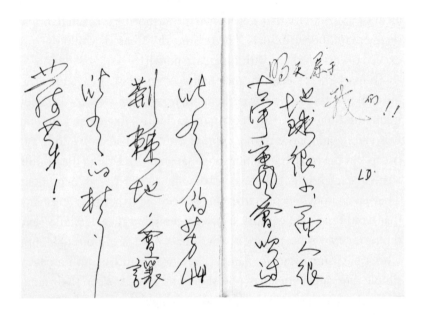

For fifteen *yuan*, a guard took a souvenir photograph of them standing together in the yard, their backs to the high walls. Dongyue, in dark glasses, and Decheng flanked Zhijian. A couple days later, on the last day of March 1990, Yu Zhijian and Yu Dongyue were transferred. Zhijian was sent to Hunan Provincial No. 3 Prison, also known as Lingling Prison and as the Hunan Laodong Auto Parts Works. Dongyue went to Hunan Provincial No. 1 Prison, also known as Chishan Prison, the Yuanjiang Electrical Machinery Factory and the Dongtinghua Farm.

With his friends gone, Decheng kept his distance from others, especially common criminals. Remembering the turncoats who'd denounced Zhijian and Dongyue, he avoided all the 1989 inmates.

He was determined to remain a loner. He saw that as the only way to avoid prison breeding the goodness out of him, turning him to cruelty and violence. He had but one code of conduct in interacting with other prisoners: he would treat the weak, either in mind or body, humanely, regardless of whether they were common criminals or political prisoners.

Qiuping became Decheng's steadying influence. Depending on how she could arrange her shifts, some months she managed two visits. The ache they each felt across the visitation corridor would bring each to tears. But they had already discovered that if they leaned as far as possible across the desktops, they could brush fingertips—something to be attempted only if the guards' backs were turned. Between visits, they wrote to each other. Her letters were fluid and several pages long. In reply, Decheng only ever managed a single sheet.

It would be more than a year before Driver Lu appeared at the prison gates. He would visit every few months, whenever he was able to get a long-distance route out of Liuyang to Hengyang. His letter writing was as sporadic, sometimes two days in a row, then months without a word. His early letters were filled with curses about what a bad son Decheng was, what shame he'd brought on the family. Decheng read them with a mixture of hatred and pity for his father that he should care more about posturing in his letters for the authorities than giving comfort to his son.

Unexpectedly, a crack opened in the prison's cold authority. After one visit, the guard escorting Qiuping out of the visitation corridor slipped her a piece of paper with his telephone number on it. She contacted the guard. He offered to provide a conduit between her and her husband. He wanted no payment for his services; he said he was helping them out of respect and admiration for them as a couple. Kind-Hearted Guard maintained a gruff exterior with the prisoner, but when he had occasion—or excuse, if there was a transaction to be made—to escort Decheng somewhere so that the two were momentarily alone, he shed his mask and spoke to him as a friend. Decheng knew the guard was doing this at great personal risk. To be discovered co-operating would have brought grief to all concerned, including the families of both guard and prisoner.

SOON AFTER THE TRANSFER of Yu Zhijian and Yu Dongyue, all the study groups ended. With orientation over, Decheng would now begin reform through compulsory labour. Like so many dictates of the Party, the philosophy of compulsory and unpaid labour for prisoners was embedded in the belief that faulty thinking and treachery arose from being a class enemy and that a new sense of solidarity with the proletariat could only be cultivated through bitter toil. Every morning, Decheng lined up to wait for roll call, after which guards escorted his work brigade through the double set of iron doors and down a steep ramp leading underground, where most of the workshops were located. Only the vehicle-repair workshop was above ground.

Prison cadres assigned inmates to workshops according to their risk of "resisting reform"—that is, attempting escape. Corrected activists monitored prisoners at their workstations. On his first day, Decheng had already made up his mind: *Prison jobs are meaningless, a waste of my time.* He refused to take his place at his workstation. "Either ask me to work in the vehicle-repair workshop or I won't work at all." He knew that only the most trusted prisoners, corrected activists all, were assigned to that workshop, given the opportunities for escape from there and for contact with the outside. Vehicles were constantly coming and going, and the workshop had a telephone with an outside line.

A cadre threatened Decheng: "Work or we will punish you!"

"I wouldn't work even if you punished me."

They did. The guards handcuffed his wrists to the bars of a window, hanging him just high enough that his feet barely touched the floor. He was left there for several hours, until his feet were badly swollen. Still, he refused to work.

Decheng saw through the guards' action. *They're trying to make an example of me, trying to show me, "We can do this to you any time we want."* He threatened the guards in return: "You can restrain me, but try beating me and I will petition authorities higher up than you. I will fight you!"

The guards neither handcuffed him to the window again nor beat him. The prison's leniency suggested to Decheng that there was another controlling hand—one higher up in Beijing. He spent his days sitting handcuffed in the workshop. Decheng observed the pitiful life of the prison labourer. At whim, guards and trustees refused breaks or extended hours; they singled out prisoners, citing them for being lazy or having a poor work attitude or not following rules. Near day's end, panicked prisoners tried to buy production quota from others who worked faster. Guards held back those who had not fulfilled their quotas, so that they missed what little free time there was in a day, or missed supper. If the prison was facing a delivery deadline, then all prisoners stayed. Or they might be called back to work after supper and forced to work far into, and sometimes through, the night. Sunday, their one day off, was often lost to work.

If the prison authorities responsible for compulsory labour were frustrated by Decheng, his political education officer, Cadre Wu, was especially excited at the prospect of remoulding one of the famous three from Liuyang into a new socialist man. Cadre Wu faced Decheng in his political study class for two hours, four evenings a week. One evening, Warden Liu dropped in. The class was just under way, beginning as always with the singing of "Without the Communist Party, there would be no new China" and "Socialism is good! The Communist Party is good!" The warden spotted Decheng's stony face and his unmoving lips. He leaned over to Cadre Wu and hissed: "Why isn't that person singing?" The rule book was clear. According to Chapter One, "Basic Rules," Article 5, prisoners were to "sing songs loudly and clearly." Cadre Wu's reply silenced the warden: "That's Lu Decheng!" Decheng interpreted what he heard in the cadre's tone: *It's just a song; it's his mind we want.*

After three months, the authorities offered a compromise. They would assign Decheng to the vehicle-repair workshop. He would not be allowed to work as a mechanic nor to enter the workshop itself, but rather would teach a vocational course on auto mechanics six mornings a week. Prison officials told Decheng that it was highly unusual for someone with only a junior middle school education to teach. "However, we respect people's talents and knowledge," they explained. *They're just trying to save face*, Decheng told himself. He knew that teaching positions were preferable to labouring at a work-station, that they were reserved for prisoners with connections or money to pay a bribe to get themselves out of the tedium and harsh environment of the workshops. But he saw how the authorities still managed to punish him by deliberately setting an early hour for his class: five to six-thirty in the morning. The four-thirty wake-up shortened the night for already exhausted prisoners. Some of his students, desperate to catch a few minutes' extra sleep, would roll under their beds to hide from the guards, only to be cruelly jolted by their probing electric prods.

To compensate, Decheng decided to spend the early hour enjoyably. He told his students that when it came to teaching or learning vehicle repair, little could be learned without hands-on experience.

He promised that when it came time for their exam—prepared by him—he would teach them what they needed to know to pass. He was also willing to tutor any individual outside of class. But, in class, he would devote a good part of the time to conversation about whatever they liked. A favourite topic was sports.

Decheng soon realized that his teaching assignment afforded him time to himself, something other prisoners longed for. Their lives were controlled from the moment the rooster crowed until the ghosts whispered at night, but teachers were given the rest of the working day, outside of their classes, to prepare their lessons. Decheng used this time to educate himself, as Zhijian and Dongyue had always encouraged. As a teacher, he had access to the prison library. The guards who escorted Decheng there and back, who were themselves often illiterate or had little education, assumed he was looking at books about auto mechanics. He began with something quite different: a dictionary. Back in the cell, guards and those prisoners considered too great a security risk to labour outside their cells would see him hunched over the metal table he'd been provided for his teaching and assume he was preparing his lessons. Instead, Decheng started working on his Mandarin. He studied pronunciation to correct his heavy Hunanese accent—something Mao himself never achieved. Word by word, Decheng expanded his vocabulary, spoken and written. He turned his slow printing into a more flowing cursive style. Kind-Hearted Guard got him brush and ink, which were better for practising the art of character strokes.

Yu Zhijian and Yu Dongyue were Decheng's inspiration, but Qiuping provided his motivation. *Since she's so determined to stay with me, I'm going to make myself into a better person*, Decheng vowed. The more he studied, the more energized he felt, focused on cultivating himself into a person worthy of her steadfast love.

A SHORT MIDDLE-AGED MAN named Zhao Dehuang worked in administration doing bookkeeping and compiling statistics. His work required him to make the rounds of the cellblocks. One day, when passing Lu Decheng, he slipped him a piece of paper. "We can talk tomorrow, in the yard," he said.

In the note, Zhao introduced himself as an "old revolutionary." His note detailed his charges and sentencing as if presenting his credentials: he'd been arrested twice on charges of sedition, had served eight years the first time, and was now in his third year of a fifteen-year sentence. "We're both here for political reasons," Zhao wrote.

In the yard the next day, Decheng fell into step with Zhao. His new friend congratulated him on what he and his two friends had done in Tiananmen Square. Like Decheng, Old Revolutionary Zhao had also refused to labour in the workshops, and finally the authorities put him to work in administration. As a young man in 1975, when Chairman Mao was still at the helm, Zhao had formed a party that he satirically named the Political Democratization, Economic Privatization Party. He was its only member; he recruited no one to it. For that he served eight years. When he left prison, Deng Xiaoping had taken over and market reforms were forging ahead. In 1987, Zhao was arrested again, at the Beijing railway station. He had been riding the train between the capital and Hunan, selling leaflets denouncing corruption and profiteering among high-placed officials and their sons and daughters. During that time, Decheng himself had bought many such leaflets.

Decheng and Old Revolutionary Zhao began a daily routine of meeting in the yard to talk politics. Early on, in an act that established supreme trust between the two, Zhao lent Decheng a book by General Chiang Kai-shek, *Soviet Russia in China*. Had this been the Cultural Revolution, to be caught with a book by Mao's arch-enemy would have meant certain execution. Even now, it would mean a lengthened sentence at the very least. Decheng read it in two days, during which the book never left his possession, hidden on his person even as he slept.

Perhaps sensing his friend's isolation, Zhao regularly wrote poems for him. They were intended as spiritual sustenance, to encourage him to hold fast to his beliefs, even as he faced his own long sentence. The first was a note of solidarity:

Facing the Same Fate and Difficulties as Lu Decheng

This body has been promised to the country. No fear is in my mind as I am locked up for the second time. This heart is as strong as iron until the day I die: the blood of a good man flows, but his tears do not.

Decheng's morale slid when he heard worrying news about his two friends. An inmate who'd transferred from Zhijian's prison told him, "Your friend is being uncooperative with the guards." Smoking was forbidden and Zhijian, in full view of guards, had been defiantly lighting up. Decheng knew for certain that Zhijian's provocations were serious when Kind-Hearted Guard passed on advice: "Tell your wife to contact Zhijian's family; they should tell him not to challenge the guards so directly. He has to use other tactics to resist."

Dongyue wasn't keeping a low profile either. The newspaper for inmates, *Teaching You a New Life*, published by Hunan reformatory authorities, contained several uncharacteristically sentimental poems by him.

Decheng told Old Revolutionary Zhao that this wasn't like Dongyue. "This is an unhealthy way for him to express his feelings. The poems say nothing; they're bland, like hot water, without any taste."

Zhao was concerned. "Your friend shouldn't write anything more. His poems may not appear to be political, but the slightest idea or word could offend the authorities."

His words were prescient. Another prisoner transferred to Hengyang brought news. "Your friend's gone a bit crazy in the head," he said. "The guards dented his skull in, front and back." Decheng wanted to believe the devastating news was untrue. At Christmas, he had received two postcards.

IN LATE AUGUST 1991, there was more news of upheaval in the Communist world. Hardline Communists in the Soviet Union, upset with Mikhail Gorbachev's policies of *perestroika* and *glasnost,* attempted a coup. It collapsed when tens of thousands of Muscovites heeded the call of Boris Yeltsin, the new Russian president loyal to Gorbachev, and surrounded the Russian Parliament.

Some weeks later, Warden Liu paid Decheng a visit. "What is the state of your thinking about what happened in the Soviet Union?" He would have expected that this was a prisoner who would embrace an opportunity to demonstrate progress in his reform. The prison system had treated Lu Decheng well: he had an easy reform-through-labour assignment. He had suffered no beatings, no solitary confinement. He was permitted regular visits from his wife. Any right-minded prisoner would want this leniency to continue.

Decheng did not hesitate in his reply. "It shows the total bankruptcy of Communism."

The warden was apoplectic, caught between anger and shock.

A prison-wide denunciation meeting was called. Handcuffed, Decheng stood alone on the stage beneath a red banner that read "Defend state power and stop the peaceful evolution." Hardliners in the Party had coined the phrase "peaceful evolution"—*heping yanbian*—for what they believed to be the strategy of enemies of the Party and the Communist system, to inculcate Western-style capitalism and values in China. Decheng endured a frightening barrage. The only other times he'd seen lone prisoners face the entire prison, he'd heard their execution orders read out, usually for fighting or attempting escape. The prisoners would be shot outside, then their bodies left in a classroom until the crematorium truck arrived.

Following the denunciation, Decheng wrote the requisite self-criticism. He repeated the slogan on the banner and correctly interpreted it: Western practices, such as Gorbachev's policies of liberalization, would lead to the erosion of Communist principles and the undermining of the Party. Decheng added a line to his self-criticism: "The breakup of the Soviet Union into democratic states is inevitable." He knew it would provoke the authorities.

He was right. Deputy Secretary Zhu Dongyang from the Hunan government's Political and Judicial Committee showed up at the prison, accompanied by police, an entourage of armed guards, and two provincial cadres with fancy cameras. Warden Liu joined them, along with five section heads from the prison's education, propaganda, and political study sections, including Cadre Wu.

Deputy Secretary Zhu was fierce in his reprimand. "Lu Decheng! You have knowledge and yet you are so stubborn!" He ranted about how the prison system had tried to reform his bad thinking. His voice rose. "You must recant! Don't think the Party won't punish you if you keep resisting reform!" Flashbulbs kept going off.

Decheng kept his eyes locked on the deputy secretary's. *I will oppose him with silence,* he told himself.

"The three of you, what you did in 1989 was an insult! We in Hunan province believe it was a very serious crime. We demanded very strongly that you three be executed!" With that, Zhu stormed off, the others scuttling behind.

Nothing of consequence happened after the visit. Months passed. Warden Liu again came to him. Where he had once been confrontational, now he was conciliatory: "What can we do to help you correct your thinking?"

The prison acceded to Decheng's request for newspapers, but substituted its choices. Decheng wanted subscriptions to the *People's Daily* and the *Reference News.* The latter, a digest of excerpts from Western media and from Hong Kong and Taiwan, had restricted circulation to high-ranking Party cadres. The warden arranged for delivery of the *Hunan Daily* and the *Legal Daily,* a compendium of legal developments put out by the justice ministry in Beijing. Without explanation, at the same time as Decheng's newspaper deliveries began, authorities doubled his space in the communal bed, giving him an extra 18 inches. Since every night was no longer a fight for space, Decheng was getting a better rest. There was more. Now he lined up for a tray of food instead of slopping from the wooden vats. He was eating better and more, and started to put on weight.

That Christmas, Decheng sent out two postcards. He received one from Yu Zhijian. Nothing arrived from Yu Dongyue.

In early May, Warden Liu was again at his cell.

"You had a great love for your grandmother."

Decheng saw no need to reply.

"We are very sympathetic to your feelings for your family. We have been thinking that you have not fulfilled your responsibility to tend to your grandmother's grave. She was the widow of a martyr; she raised you. Your duty is to pay your respects at her grave. Do you want to do that? Do you think you should go?"

These prison cadres are laughable, Decheng thought. His grandmother had died more than two years ago. At the time, they cared nothing for his feelings. "Of course I should go. Why shouldn't I want to?"

"You have been a well-behaved prisoner and have observed prison regulations," said the warden. "We are giving you one week on the outside, to return to your old home for a family visit."

Other prisoners were enormously envious: "The prison is so good to you."

A policeman from the Hengyang Public Security Bureau made Decheng sign a pledge that during his week off he would not attempt to escape. He couldn't wait to go home, though he wondered what would be asked of him in return. Days later, he was given civilian clothes; still, with his shaved head, there was no disguising his status as a prisoner. A van, carrying a policeman from Hengyang, five section heads from the prison, including the keen Cadre Wu, and the prisoner, pulled out of the prison gates and onto Tongxin Road, heading for the train station in Hengyang. It was late May. Rice shoots were reaching for the sun and yellow crystal pears were only a couple weeks from harvest.

EIGHT

UPON HEARING from the hospital staff that Housewife Wang had taken his wife home, Decheng rushed to find Elder Brother, who had always taken his sister's side against their controlling mother. He told Decheng that his mother had locked Qiuping in a small room at the back of the family's flat. The room was windowless, making rescue or escape difficult.

"The situation for you two is dire," said Elder Brother. "My mother has engaged matchmakers—she's not going to let Qiuping out until she's got her married off."

Decheng had one lonely obligation to fulfill before anything else. He buried their infant son in the countryside, near the house on the hill. He said farewell to his little boy and apologized to him that his mother couldn't be there.

With his life unravelling, Decheng took refuge at Grandmother Lu's and considered how he could put it back together. Once Housewife Wang found out—if she hadn't already—that Qiuping was married to him, she would surely force her to divorce him. His only course of action, he decided, was to call on Qiuping's parents. He would ignore his acrimonious history with Housewife Wang, he would be calm and respectful, he would make no accusation of her latest effort to sabotage his relationship with her daughter, and mount no defence of their love for each other. Instead, he would appeal to his in-laws' sense of propriety, if that explained their vigorous objection to the relationship and their cruel refusal to acknowledge the short life of Baby Jinlong. He would offer to marry their daughter in a traditional ceremony.

Decheng told Grandmother Lu his plan. She insisted on helping out, slipping Decheng money she had squirrelled away. Decheng spent more than a hundred *yuan* on simple but expensive gifts. In accord with tradition, spending a lot of money on presents would show that he considered the Wangs to be close family.

When Housewife Wang answered the door at the opera troupe's dormitory, Decheng stepped inside before she could shoo him away. He set down his basket of gifts and told her why he'd come. He was deferential: "I ask you for your consent and for your blessing."

The woman was outraged. She reached for a laundry paddle and struck Decheng. He stood his ground. She took his offerings and heaved them, item by item, outside, while letting loose one profanity after another. Wine bottles broke, yardages of Dacron cloth fell open, and cigarette cartons, biscuits, and candies bounced down the alleyway.

"You ruined my daughter!" Housewife Wang screamed. "You're responsible for everything bad that has ever happened to her. Get out of here. Get out!"

Decheng turned on his heel. As he stepped over his gifts strewn in the alleyway and dodged neighbours scurrying to help themselves, he shot back, "Qiuping is the only girl I will ever marry!"

A day later, using a spare key he'd found, Elder Brother freed Qiuping from her week in captivity. She made for the home of Hongwu, who sent word to Decheng at Grandmother Lu's. The old lady felt as victorious as they did when she welcomed the couple back under her roof.

DECHENG COULD FIND NO PEACE over Baby Jinlong's death. He was haunted by their delay in seeking medical care, their indecision about which hospital to go to, and the precious time lost when they chose the wrong one. "I blame the authorities," he told Qiuping. "They are the ones who forced us into our predicament."

She came to terms with her infant son's death. Poverty had made them stumble. If they'd had more money, they would have been able to afford a better roof over their heads and the best treatment possible for the baby. "You have to get over it," Qiuping said gently, seeing her husband's solitary grief. "We were responsible for our own tragedy."

It did not take long for the women responsible for family planning to show up at Number 35 Clear Water Alley. They were furious that Wang Qiuping had not aborted the pregnancy. "You had an unauthorized child from a non-marriage," they said. "The child is dead, but don't think the matter is over!"

Baby Jinlong's death had already prompted an investigation. The Residents' Committee checked recent births in hospitals and clinics in and around Liuyang and turned up Wang Qiuping's name at the Ji Li Bridge clinic. That led them to Dr. Bei. For delivering a baby with no childbirth permit, he was demoted and fined one year's salary. A further check at the marriage registry turned up the irregularity in the couple's reference letters. For failing to verify their respective ages, which would have revealed that they were underage, Administrator Yu at the bus station was slapped with a steep fine and Qiuping's acquaintance lost her job with the Residents' Committee. For her oversight in issuing the marriage certificate, the clerk at the marriage registry was also fined.

Guilt weighed heavily on the young couple that punishment, even ruin, had come on their account to well-meaning and decent people. Decheng recalled how pleased Administrator Yu had been to help a young couple anxious to marry, and how proud the kindly Dr. Bei had been at the moment of birth.

The family planning women paid another visit to the couple. They asked for their marriage certificate. "It's problematic," they said.

Decheng had no intention of surrendering the document. The only reason to do so was divorce. He made an excuse about not immediately being able to get his hands on it. The women came back. At Decheng's continuing refusal, they threatened him: if he did not give them the certificate they would fine him for having had an unauthorized child in violation of the one-child policy. He would find himself in difficulty, they warned, because they would give him only three days to pay the fine. And if it remained unpaid after that, they would confiscate his possessions.

Decheng was not afraid. "Impose whatever fine you like. What do I have? Nothing." But never did he imagine that they would go as far as they were about to. They didn't fine him; they imposed a "social child-raising fee" by docking his monthly salary by one third. The state regarded the fee, typically not lifted for years, as compensation for the valuable resources that an unauthorized child took up.

Decheng was forced to moonlight to support Qiuping and himself. He contacted a couple of master mechanics, who'd left the bus station to go into business for themselves. He offered to work on cars between shifts at the bus station, if ever they were so busy they needed help. After two months, Decheng was exhausted from running between the station and the other mechanics' garages. But beyond his fatigue, the cruelty of working in order to pay a fee for raising a dead child was just too much to bear.

He went to the family planning women with his own ultimatum. "If you don't lift the penalty, I will simply quit my job."

It was their turn to scoff. How could anyone be so stupid as to give up a secure state job and the benefits of belonging to a work unit?

Decheng kept his word. He quit.

The year of Baby Jinlong's birth and death, the National Population and Planning Commission called on local officials to make an all-out effort to enforce the one-child policy, telling them to conduct "crash drives" against illegal, unauthorized pregnancies. 1983 would turn out to be a banner year for the one-child policy, aided by a near doubling in the number of "remedial measures" over the previous year: primarily abortions, but also vasectomies and tubal ligations. That year, the United Nations would award China, together with India, its inaugural Population Award.

Decheng and Qiuping didn't stay in town to find out how the Residents' Committee would respond to his leaving the bus station.

The couple retreated to the familiar countryside outside Liuyang. They traded work for food or shelter, and did odd jobs. Briefly, they considered moving to one of the four coastal towns in the south that Beijing had designated Special Economic Zones in 1980 to attract foreign investment. Three years on, none of the SEZs had taken off, but people were still applying in great numbers for residence permits there. Then Decheng found out that prospective residents needed letters of reference.

Pursuing another idea, Decheng took a trip to Guiyang City, the capital of neighbouring Guiyou province. He and a son-in-law of Ironworker Li, a butcher who'd been laid off, looked into importing dog meat to sell to butchers and eateries in Liuyang. Dog was a seasonal dish, considered best eaten in midwinter when the *yin* (cold) and *yang* (hot) of one's blood had to be balanced by "hot" foods. Both Decheng and the butcher thought dogs were plentiful, and therefore, cheap, in Guizhou because of a popular curse in Liuyang, "Dog of Guizhou!" But the two found they were the same high price as at home.

The trip opened Decheng's eyes in another way. One of Guiyang's many cinemas advertised an American movie, *Rambo: First Blood*. Decheng and his friend had never heard of it; neither had they ever seen a film from a non-Communist country. Liuyang's only cinema was a year behind getting any current movies. They bought tickets and emerged two hours later bursting with talk about what they had just watched. Decheng was especially taken with the Rambo character, played by Sylvester Stallone. In the film, John Rambo, a disturbed Vietnam war veteran, takes on a sadistic, small-town police force. "He's a great heroic figure," Decheng said, "especially since he was always outnumbered."

With the approach of winter, Decheng and Qiuping decided to end their vagabond life. They both longed to restore some stability to their lives and knew they needed to build some financial security. The couple would return to town, and Decheng would try to set up his own vehicle-repair shop.

He went to Grandmother Lu to discuss moving back in. Nothing pleased the old lady more, even if it meant the Residents' Committee would soon be knocking on her door again. Decheng rented a space in a garage in town. He set his rates low, hoping to attract business from long-distance truck drivers passing through town. The early days of his enterprise were marked by frustrating inconsistency, either long, dead stretches of idleness or so much business at once he had to send his customers to his competitors.

In 1984, happiness bloomed in Decheng and Qiuping's life. She was pregnant.

The family planning women, reinforced by the male head of the Residents' Committee, came marching in rank formation down River Road to rap at the door of Grandmother Lu's. They barged in, sat themselves down, and railed at the couple.

"Here you are, pregnant again! You are going against the one-child policy. You illegally cohabited. You married early. You already had a child, and now you are having another. You did not obtain permission, so you are exceeding your quota. You are not the correct age. All in all, in every way, you have been conducting yourselves illegally!"

The women again demanded the surrender of the couple's marriage certificate and that Qiuping arrange an abortion.

Decheng and Qiuping grew only sadder.

As Qiuping's pregnancy progressed, the women showed up more frequently. Their hectoring was so aggressive that Decheng worried the stress might cause Qiuping to lose the baby. He started watching for the women through a crack in the back door, which gave him a clear view up River Road. If he saw them approaching, he called out to Qiuping to hurry out the front.

Qiuping soon amassed a loyal army of little children in the neighbourhood. When they caught sight of the hated women, they went running back to the house, the patter of their feet and their voices sounding a warning. "They're coming! They're coming! Three of them!" or "Four of them!"

Decheng's childhood friend Zefu came to visit and was distressed to see the toll that the harassment was taking on his friend and his pregnant wife, who was near term. As it happened, he was there when the children alerted them. Normally mild-mannered, an irritated Zefu took off out the back door. He ran up River Road to intercept the old women.

He was as angry as he was pleading. "These two people are really in love with each other. A tragedy has happened once already; the child died because they tried to run away from you people!"

Nothing he said, however, could put the old women off.

The standoff continued. Just when Decheng and Qiuping were feeling defeated, he suddenly saw everything clearly. He'd been repeating a pattern begun with Baby Jinlong. *The softer I've been, the harder they've been hitting back.*

He told Qiuping that, in hindsight, he realized that he himself had helped the authorities to create the circumstances that led to their son's death. "Because I gave in to them. I ran away, I quit my job, I gave them what they wanted." But now he was angry. "I'll show them!" he vowed.

The next time the contingent came to the back door, Decheng grabbed a broom and raised it menacingly. The old women waddled away like scared ducks. While the responsibility of the women was to campaign against feudalistic beliefs like superstition, they didn't want to chance being cursed by years of bad luck if hit by a household broom, lest it was inhabited by spirits (as kitchen objects were often believed to be). Decheng's voice boomed after them: "Do whatever you want, just don't ever talk to me about this again! Don't show yourselves here again!"

They didn't. Decheng realized that the battle was a psychological one: he didn't belong to a work unit, he didn't have a state salary with state benefits, the women had nothing else to take from him. The couple had learned from their experience with Baby Jinlong. They showed up at the People's Hospital when Qiuping was in an advanced state of labour. Admissions asked for the childbirth permit.

Decheng acted flustered. "I'm sorry, we were in a terrible hurry. I brought the marriage certificate by mistake. The childbirth permit is at home."

The clerk glanced at the certificate and registered the expectant mother and father. After an uneventful delivery, the People's Hospital recorded the birth of a baby girl to the couple under false names Decheng had provided at admissions. There would be no paper trail to implicate either them or the medical staff. Decheng had contacted a couple of former classmates who were nurses at the hospital. He had confided in them about their lack of documentation and asked them to put in a good word with their colleagues so that no one would betray them should the Residents' Committee come poking their noses into the matter.

The family planning women braved a reappearance at the house. They were irate. "Where was your baby born? Answer us!"

Decheng refused to tell them, and his friends at the People's Hospital made sure that no one could be connected to the baby's birth.

Qiuping chose the name Xinfeng, "Good Fortune in Abundance." When their little girl reached her Full Month, when it is considered safe to assume a baby will live, the couple hosted a banquet of ten tables that took over both Grandmother Lu's house and Carpenter Yi's next door. Only siblings came from the couple's immediate families. Housewife Wang and Deputy Director Wang stayed away. So too did Renqing. Never was there any question of Stepmother Meilan appearing.

WITH A NEW BABY and a vehicle-repair shop that had become very busy, the couple's life was hectic day and night. Decheng hired two young apprentices. He could manage fixing vehicles and supervising his two recruits, but running the business turned out to be a huge headache. Customers were late paying up or never paid at all, making it difficult to keep enough cash on hand to meet daily expenses. Decheng was run ragged. Rare was it that he didn't either miss dinner or have to return to the garage to work on vehicles promised for the morning. He was getting precious little sleep and, on some days, none.

One morning, however, he awoke feeling unusually refreshed. The night before, Qiuping had invited his two sisters for dinner and she had done all the shopping and the cooking for five, including Grandmother Lu. Most mornings, he had to drag his body out of bed and didn't speak unless he absolutely had to. But this morning, he awoke chatty and ebullient, before hopping onto his bicycle and tearing off down the road. At day's end, he felt none of his usual fatigue. That night when he lay down, he was unable to sleep, but also felt no need to. His vigour and wakefulness spilled into the next day and the next. He was brimming with things he wanted to say, the words lining up to get out of his mouth.

Qiuping was alarmed by her husband's talkativeness. She asked the opinion of Carpenter Yi and his wife and they agreed, Decheng was behaving erratically and out of character. She hurried down to the

garage to question the two apprentices. She wondered if the three of them, facing more work than they could handle, had ingested something to boost their energy. They were as bewildered as she, especially seeing how Decheng was so talkative, even with strangers.

On the third day, neighbours spoke up. "He's young and energetic, but this is out of control. You should take your husband to the hospital."

When his wife suggested it, Decheng didn't protest. He had been thinking that to go so long without sleep was abnormal. At the People's Hospital, doctors admitted him and gave him a dose of sleeping pills. He woke three days later, still in a state of nervous excitement. Doctors had extracted some bone marrow and run some tests, but they revealed nothing of his condition. They had one theory, that he had ingested an overdose of ginseng. Qiuping was guilt-ridden. She'd bought the ginseng on the spur of the moment. Out shopping in the market for the dinner, she'd thought about how tiring and stressful her husband's work had been of late. Though she had no experience with medicinal herbs, she bought a large budding root of ginseng, simmered it, and brewed a tea especially for him. The dinner that followed included a soup made from an old hen, a soup traditionally given to women after childbirth and to those recovering from illness. The rich soup, Grandmother Lu deduced, must have redoubled the ginseng's effects.

The doctors wanted to keep Decheng in hospital. His instinct was that nothing was seriously wrong with him. And he didn't want to run up a hospital bill. He discharged himself to recover at home.

Decheng's two sisters dropped by the house. They'd visited him in the hospital, but he'd been sedated at the time. Concerned about his condition, they'd gone to tell their father that his son was in hospital. But of course, he had waited to see Stepmother Meilan's reaction. She had been dismissive. As long as one had the security of money, she'd told her stepdaughters, one didn't need a son in life or to see one off to the afterlife. She'd invoked a saying: "If you have a large basket of grain under your bed, you need not worry that no one will cry for you." Renqing had taken his cue from his wife. "Your brother's health is not my concern," he'd said.

Hearing of his stepmother's crass remark, Decheng felt a sharp pang. How he missed his mother and her easy, genuine affection for him! And hearing of his father's reaction, Decheng saw how easily the man let himself be manipulated. How repressed he was, nothing more than a servant for Stepmother Meilan! Perhaps no one, not even he, knew his true feelings! Decheng was struck by an idea. He thought back to people's reactions when his state of agitation had come on. Acquaintances that he'd bumped into on the street gave him odd looks or even backed away from him. Some said laughingly, without a shred of sympathy, "Hey, Decheng! What's happened to you?"

Decheng decided to prolong the appearance of his affliction. He would feign an unknown illness, disorder of the mind. For good measure, he'd add a loss of appetite. His ruse would test the affection of those closest to him. Qiuping's and Grandmother Lu's concern he held to be genuine and unwavering, but to keep his cover he could exclude no one. He would drop the masquerade only once he'd unmasked the true feelings of everyone in his family.

In the next days, he kept a mental tally of those whose reactions he deemed "positive and normal." From the start, Qiuping and Grandmother Lu were both very much frightened. Qiuping was desperate that a cure be found. Grandmother Lu, at eighty-one years old, climbed the more than one hundred steps up Green Sun Hill to make an offering at the Taoist temple. Decheng moved down his list. His sisters each made repeated visits to the house. "I can say I'm well satisfied," he said, checking them off. As he expected, Stepmother Meilan did not visit or send word. He was still holding out for his father, who had not shown his face.

Distressed at her husband's worsening condition, Qiuping went to Hongwu. "Decheng needs you to go to him!" He was perplexed. *How can this be? I designed such a good life plan for him. Decheng has settled into a life with some stability, has a wife and child, a roof over his head, a business.*

What could possibly have gone so wrong now that they'd need me? He returned with Qiuping to Grandmother Lu's.

One look at his friend, who was sitting on a low-slung bamboo chair, his head back, eyes staring at the ceiling, told Hongwu all he needed to know.

"Decheng, you're pretending to have a mental disorder. You do not. There is something in your mind that you can't get rid of, that's all."

Decheng said nothing. His chin dropped to his chest and he began to cry.

"You haven't eaten or slept for several days. If this continues, you *will* go crazy. What is it? Have you lost money in your business venture? If so, you have to forget about it, at least for a while."

Hongwu kneeled beside Decheng. He grasped his friend's hands firmly. "Listen to me. I designed a plan for you and now you're undoing it. Even if you are not crazy, keep this up and you'll be seen as psychologically unstable. Do you want a good future? Do you want a good life?" His tone turned stern: "Then you have to eat, tonight!"

Decheng pounded at his chest and began to weep.

Qiuping took her husband a bowl of noodle soup and he received it gratefully. She cared only that the illness that had begun with the ginseng didn't appear to be permanent. And whatever his intentions, he hadn't been healthy and couldn't be entirely faulted.

Hongwu was already formulating a way to make sure this episode didn't ruin Decheng's future. Driver Lu should take his son to Changsha to a hospital of Western medicine with a department of mental health. The doctor there could verify Decheng to be of sound mind. Driver Lu could get something in writing from the doctor, and show it to his superiors at the bus station and, in particular, to the Political Education Committee there. This would ensure that word about Decheng's mental stability would spread through Liuyang from the highest levels of the Party on down.

Immediately, Hongwu went to see Driver Lu. He spoke of Decheng's mysterious illness and impressed upon him that, as a father, his responsibility was to find the treatment for his son that would also confirm that he'd been cured. The best option would be the Western hospital in Changsha.

"He's not a good son, he's done nothing to give our family a good name."

Hongwu had already considered the obstacle to his plan: Stepmother Meilan's ongoing contrivance to come between father and son. "You are a pioneer and a model worker in the bus company," he told Renqing. "He's your only son. If you don't find a cure, you will suffer too. Your reputation will also go downhill."

Where Decheng's sisters could not persuade their father to see his son, Hongwu did. Driver Lu returned with Hongwu to Number 35 Clear Water Alley. His son's fragile state frightened the bus driver. He arranged to take two days off work and drove Decheng into the countryside, seeking herbalists and practitioners of traditional medicine, even a shaman, to determine if an evil spirit possessed him. *My father is behaving admirably*, Decheng told himself. Finally, Renqing followed Hongwu's suggestion to go to Changsha. On the bus there, Decheng enjoyed the sincerity of a father's affection as never before. In Changsha, outside the doors of the hospital, he decided the time had come to confess. He was more than satisfied with his father's reaction. To saddle him with the costs of a hospital stay or to risk taking treatment when he wasn't ill was unwise. After he was told the truth, Renqing cursed Decheng as a bad son who'd cheated his own father. On the bus ride home, he scolded Decheng non-stop. The entire time, Decheng was smiling inside, deeply content.

DECHENG REDEDICATED HIMSELF to winning over his mother-in-law. He invited Housewife Wang to one of Liuyang's new restaurants to celebrate her birthday. She and Deputy Director Wang accepted, and Decheng and Qiuping shared an evening with them. Despite many awkward silences, the occasion marked Housewife Wang's acceptance, not necessarily of Decheng, but of her daughter's affections for him and the young couple's determination to stay together.

Just when Decheng thought that all was calm in their lives, he returned home from the garage one day to find Grandmother Lu angry and upset. She told him his father had shown up, wanting to speak to Qiuping. He'd scolded her, had spoken disparagingly about her living in an illegal marriage and having an illegal child, not just once but twice. He'd demeaned her, blamed her for the shame she had brought on his good name and that of his wife. Qiuping had scooped up Little Xinfeng and run out of the house.

Decheng went to Hongwu's. His wife and daughter were not there. A day later, Elder Brother brought word from his sister that she was hiding out with the baby at a friend's. Decheng rushed over and found his wife deeply hurt and profoundly upset at what his father had said, and refusing to return to Number 35 Clear Water Alley.

Grandmother Lu had it out with Renqing. She had delighted in having her grandson and his family under her roof. "I got Decheng back and you drove him away!" she reproached him. Decheng was more sympathetic to his father once he learned what had prompted his father's outburst. The women from the Residents' Committee, yet again employing the tactic of "attacking from all sides," had shown up at his father's workplace with senior bus executives in tow and threatened him: "Tell your son to give us the marriage certificate or you will suffer serious consequences!"

Decheng decided to find lodgings in the countryside, in hopes this sacrifice would convince the committee to leave his father and the bus station management alone.

Some weeks later, Renqing visited Decheng's garage for the first time. He came with a proposal. He had spoken with the executives of the bus station, had argued for his own value as a long-time employee and for Decheng's talents as a mechanic, and had persuaded them to hire both Decheng and Qiuping. They were prepared to offer Decheng a position as a mechanic and Qiuping a job in the ticket office. Renqing had also explained Decheng's dispute with the Residents' Committee, which would have to be resolved before the couple could join the work unit. "I can't control this son of mine,"

Renqing had told his superiors. The bus station took Decheng's side and convinced the committee to drop the matter of the marriage certificate, and to legally recognize Little Xinfeng's birth.

Decheng was only too glad to leave behind the stress and long hours of running his own business, and the couple welcomed the second income. The only shortcoming in the job offer was that it contained no provision for housing. No flat in the dormitories was available, nor was one likely to come up. In twenty-eight years, Driver Lu himself had not climbed any higher on the priority list for a bigger flat. However, the bus station was willing to let Decheng and his wife unofficially move into one of the tiny single rooms available for travelling bus company staff. His *hukou* would retain his legal residence as Number 35 Clear Water Alley.

The couple juggled their shifts so that one or the other could look after Little Xinfeng. But when both parents were working at the same time, they needed a babysitter. Grandmother Lu babysat once or twice, but she was getting old. And there were times when Qiuping had overnight trips away, when she was assigned to sell tickets on board long distance routes.

A happy solution was found.

The couple's last landlord in the countryside had been Ding Peiling, a martial arts master. He and his wife and his two married brothers lived in a compound. Their respective children were all grown. Aunts and uncles and cousins came and went in a way that recalled for Decheng the household of his mother's birth family. Ding had become a trusted friend and the couple had bestowed on him the honour of being their daughter's godfather. Godfather Ding agreed to take in Little Xinfeng. Qiuping and Decheng would visit her from time to time and pick her up to stay overnight with them at the station.

AT THE WORK UNIT, Decheng settled into a stable life echoing that of his father's generation. He dared to think that he might now reap the happiness that was long overdue.

One pleasure Decheng reclaimed time for was friendship. Among his boyhood friends, Yu Zhijian had gone to college, graduated, and had now returned to Liuyang. Zhijian taught science at the local high school. He wasn't unhappy about the college posting him here, apart from the fact that teaching was the lowest-paid state profession. Few from Liuyang in his graduating class got assignments other than teaching. One of his college mates who did end up with a lucrative post was Tanxu, who went to work at the county propaganda bureau. But he had connections; his father was a Party member. Zhijian was not at all envious. "Teaching allows me to lead a politically unambiguous life," he told Decheng.

After his return to town, Zhijian became the hub of a widening group of friends. His guiding principle when meeting new people was "defence without defence." He assessed a person's character before he became close to them, but he also made it a rule to be as open to people as he was to ideas—he would talk to anybody, to college graduates and workers, intellectuals and Party members alike. Decheng knew several of Zhijian's friends, but only as acquaintances. They were unmarried and had day jobs, whereas he had to balance the demands of family and shift work. More to the point, he felt inferior, being less educated.

Zhijian and Decheng would meet for long chats in a corner of the Big Marching Ground. Mostly, Decheng listened. He admired his friend's ability to comprehend and interpret current events, to form insights and express them with ease. Having decided at college that he could teach himself more by reading books than by following what was taught in class, Zhijian had spent his college years haunting bookstores and searching out people with private libraries, paying them for borrowing privileges. Despite the inferiority that Decheng felt, Zhijian greatly respected his friend. He looked to him as a man who had experienced adulthood as he had not. In these respects, Decheng's intuitive, emotional personality complemented Zhijian's rational, disciplined mind.

NINE

DECHENG KEPT STACKS of ledger books pasted with news-paper clippings inside his metal desk. The books formed his version of the world beyond the prison walls. He'd begun clipping his newspapers when no other prisoners had shown an interest in sharing them, and saved the articles in ledger books supplied by Old Revolutionary Zhao, who had access to office supplies. At first, he collected items in the order that they caught his eye—Bill Clinton's bid to be the Democratic presidential nominee for 1992, the cost for a student in America to attend a year of university, government crackdowns in China against the manufacture of fake cigarettes and fake medicines. Quickly, he became more systematic and organized his legers by topic: daily life, health and medications, corruption, legal news, and foreign news.

On board the train to Changsha, the first leg of his trip home, accompanied by the policeman from Hengyang, Cadre Wu, and the four other section heads from the prison, Decheng contemplated the small corner of the world that he would see in his week out of prison. Of course, on this "family visit," he would fulfill the warden's expectations—visit Grandmother Lu's grave, call on relatives, spend time with his wife and Little Xinfeng, now seven years old. But he also had goals of his own.

Cadre Wu took a seat beside Decheng and spoke to him in a kindly way about the prison's compassion and care for his well-being, and his own commitment to help him become a new person. Decheng wondered what the man was working up to. He soon got his answer. He saw too that he had been fattened and rested for a reason: "When you are home in Liuyang, you can show your gratitude. You can make a statement that you have seen the error of your ways and of your bad habits, that you will no longer commit foolish acts as in the past." Cadre Wu told Decheng that the officials had brought along camera and sound equipment to record his statement. Decheng said nothing.

Into the trip, the five section heads from the prison had a serious falling-out. There was a foul-up—no one had brought along the recording equipment. Cadre Wu was sorely disappointed. "This is very, very regrettable. We've missed the chance to show the international community how nice we are to Lu Decheng." But the finger pointing stopped when they realized none of their sections possessed either such equipment or the authority or budget to purchase it.

DURING DECHENG'S WEEK in Liuyang, two policemen—the one who'd come along from Hengyang and one from Liuyang—would come to the bus station every morning to ask his plans for the day. At day's end they would return to verify that he was back in his room with Qiuping for the night. They said that if his week passed without incident, he wouldn't see Cadre Wu or the other prison officials until they reconvened for the trip back to Hengyang.

In his and Qiuping's room at the station, Decheng was most curious to see what the police had taken in their search of the room three years ago. As he expected, the leaflets were gone. He was surprised to see they'd also removed his entire collection of old *Red Banner* magazines. He'd had two stacks, each a metre high. Some issues he'd paid dearly to acquire. Decheng didn't see how magazines published by the Party could have had any bearing on his case.

He looked in the wardrobe. Qiuping had saved his letters to her. She'd also tucked away newspapers and magazines containing the first reports of what Decheng and his two friends had done. He wasn't surprised at the regime's response. Predictably, the articles expressed the "great shock of everyone," extolled the "great respect that society has as a whole for Chairman Mao," and concluded: "How dare they go against the moral standard and universal will of the whole nation!"

Two articles, however, unsettled Decheng. The bylines on both looked to be obvious pen names. The first criticized the conduct of Yu Zhijian and himself in the interview broadcast on May 23. Yu Zhijian talked about the incident "as if he couldn't care less." And when Lu Decheng explained how egg and paint came to be stuck on his sweater, he comported himself as if he were conducting "a university physics class," when "in fact, he has only a junior middle school education." Decheng was affronted: *The writer is throwing stones at us when we're in the well.*

The second article explained more about who the three agitators were. Dongyue was "a kind and sincere fellow." His accomplishments in calligraphy and painting were lauded, and his career as the arts editor at the *Liuyang Daily* described as "well on its way." But Zhijian was maligned.

> [Yu Zhijian's] favourite foreign writer is the Russian poet Vladimir Vladimirovich Mayakovsky. He would go to class dressed like Mayakovsky. He was asked to tone it down by the school but he was one to carry on as he pleased. He failed two of his core courses and had to return home to Liuyang to teach . . . In his one year of teaching there he was controversial. He would not stick to the given curriculum and at times overwhelmed the students with too much material. At other times he would forget to bring his notes and had to send students to retrieve them from his dorm. Due to his poor teaching he had to change schools several times . . .

What Decheng read about himself made him out to be a hooligan, which was how his first cellmates in Beijing had suggested he portray himself:

> Since [Lu Decheng] was young, he has enjoyed playing
> pranks on people . . . For these pranks he often received
> punishments in class . . . He did mischievous things that
> also disturbed one of his neighbours. In 1980, in order to
> take revenge on this neighbour, he poured pesticide into
> his thermos. Fortunately, this was discovered in time and
> Lu was not charged for murder but was sent to jail for
> two months . . .

The personal details about all three of them left Decheng wondering if the article could have been written by someone who knew them. He had his suspicions about who would finger Zhijian and himself but keep their hands off Dongyue. The source of information, if not the author, might be a college mate of Zhijian's. A bureaucrat named Tanxu, who worked in the county propaganda bureau, had been one of the nine who'd met at Dongyue's flat to discuss going to Beijing. Decheng remembered him as the one who used big words and flowery language about what a meaningful experience it would be to join the student protest in Beijing, only to stay home. Decheng guessed that Bureaucrat Tanxu—if indeed he was the author—might have calculated that it was better to sacrifice friendship with Zhijian than to direct scrutiny on the *Liuyang Daily*, Dongyue's work unit.

IN KEEPING WITH THE OBLIGATIONS of his family visit, Decheng went early on to visit his grandmother's grave at the cemetery on Green Sun Hill. He did the rounds of relatives. What they saw was not what they had expected: he was terribly underweight, but not shockingly so, his senses were intact, and he had no visible scars. "We're so glad to see you are not suffering," they said.

Seeing Qiuping outside the confines of the visitation corridor, where every outsider brightened the dreariness, Decheng realized that his incarceration was taking its toll on her. Qiuping, whose black hair held early hints of grey, lamented that she used to look so much younger than him, but not anymore.

"What will happen if by the end of your sentence, I am not pretty anymore? Will your love for me fade?"

"I will love you as before. Or, if you're not as pretty, then I will love you even more."

Qiuping received Decheng's answer with great amusement.

They and Little Xingfeng went to a studio and sat for two portraits: one of father, mother, and child, and another of the couple alone.

AS THE WEEK WOUND DOWN, Decheng's excursions became sorties. He took a stroll by Number 35 Clear Water Alley, which his father had rented out since Grandmother Lu's death, and "chanced" upon his former neighbours, Carpenter Yi and his wife. She was jittery, not wanting him to linger, but the old man was delighted to see him. "I never knew you could be so gutsy! Well done! Ignorant people called the three of you blockheads, but I'm proud that Liuyang produced three *liaobuqi*." He'd used a word for a "terrific person"—one who'd also passed a moral test through political action. Walking back to the bus station along People's Road, Decheng stopped at the ancestral home of Tan Sitong, now a memorial hall. Decheng saw the shops out front and thought they cheapened the residence. He bought an entry ticket. The rooms upstairs were still residences for local Party cadres. He found the exhibit area desolate and deserted.

In his final task that week, Decheng was aided by Yu Zhijian's widowed mother. She'd heard that Lu Decheng was on leave from prison, and made contact with Qiuping. At the end of Decheng's last day of leave, the two policemen arrived as usual. Decheng told them that since it was his last night, he wished to go out for a walk with his wife. They saw no problem with that and bid him good night. The couple left the house and parted company at the market, Qiuping as if on a shopping errand and Decheng to a restaurant as if to grab a bite. By "coincidence," his friend Li Hongwu was dining there with Yu Hongguang, Zhijian's older sister. To be caught having conspired to meet either of them would bring trouble; authorities probably still had their eyes on Hongwu, even though he was the only one of the five from Liuyang who'd gone to Beijing who escaped punishment—the fifth, Teacher Kong, was demoted. Decheng joined their table. All knew that their time had to be short.

Decheng peppered Hongguang with questions: How was her brother? Was he being tortured? What did she know of Dongyue? Was he still alive? Did he have brain damage? Hongguang said that Zhijian was horribly thin, that he'd lost two front teeth from a beating by the guards. She'd hardly been able to see him because he was so often in solitary confinement. Dongyue, she said, had been driven insane. He'd suffered beatings, torture, and solitary confinement. "He's in a very bad mental state."

Decheng asked Hongguang to deliver a message on his behalf. "Tell your brother that our greatest feat will be to get out of prison alive." He left the restaurant, hurrying to meet up with Qiuping for their walk.

BACK AT THE PRISON in Hengyang, Cadre Wu pointedly coached Decheng on what to write in his report on his week-long family visit. The cadre carefully avoided any suggestion that it was a confession, lest he antagonize his charge. "Remember that we allowed you to go back to your old home to help you overcome your bad habits and solve the problems in your thinking. Write what you thought about your trip in a way that analyzes the state of your thinking."

I intend to do just that, Decheng told himself.

Certain that his two friends were being treated harshly, Decheng had returned to prison resolved to face his sentence with commensurate courage. He'd seen how prisoners fared in solitary confinement. They were emaciated from having to live on "non-labouring" rations, psychologically disturbed from being locked up in a dark, dank "dog cave." Kind-Hearted Guard sometimes had Decheng help him deliver a prisoner's belongings to solitary, so he'd seen the cave for himself. Decheng continued to hear news about how his friends had provoked the authorities: a prisoner newly transferred into Hengyang told him that Zhijian had refused to work at iron smelting, arguing that his eyesight wasn't good enough. A guard said that Dongyue had been identified as the prisoner who'd put up a painting of a blackened sun that blatantly impugned the Party's emblematic use of a red sun. He warned Decheng, "You'd better not make trouble. Yours is the same political case."

In accounting for his week off, Decheng wrote extensively about visiting Grandmother Lu's grave and his devotion to her memory. He used the rest of the report to describe Liuyang in the manner of a tourist brochure. He wrote of its fireworks industry and the decorative chrysanthemum stone found in river bedrock. In the middle of the report, he deliberately buried a reference to Tan Sitong:

> Liuyang is also the home of the great hero of the reform movement in the Qing dynasty, Tan Sitong, who was known for his courage and moral uprightness. Although he only lived thirty-three years, his ideas cross all time.

Decheng was satisfied that he'd made clear that his role model was Tan Sitong. Just as Tan Sitong had stayed to face his punishment, he was joyfully returning to prison. Decheng handed in his report.

Cadre Wu had only one question: "What did you talk about with Yu Zhijian's sister?"

They were watching me closer than I'd thought. The guard was right, ours is the same political case. He recovered quickly: "It was a coincidence that we saw each other. We exchanged small talk." His answer seemed to suffice.

A few days later, at Decheng's political study class, a prison official from the propaganda department showed up with a fancy new still camera. He took a photograph, capturing an image of Decheng in his assigned position, on the first bench, directly in front of Cadre Wu. After class, Decheng's fellow prisoners told him, "That camera was bought because of you!"

Senior cadres came to deliver good news: "Lu Decheng, you have been a good prisoner and have observed prison regulations. We are going to apply to the courts to have your sentence reduced by two years, from sixteen years to fourteen years."

Decheng immediately saw Beijing's plan: take the uneducated and backward one of the three, the lesser threat and the softer target who would be easier to win over, treat him with leniency, soften him up even more by giving him a week on the outside, then offer him a meaningless sentence reduction. All to bring him closer to recanting, then use his contrition to discredit his two friends and their political beliefs.

The cadres were stunned when Decheng told them not to bother.

The prison responded by sending a telegram to Driver Lu and Stepmother Meilan, summoning them to Hengyang. On the evening of their arrival, guards escorted Decheng across Tongxin Road to the prison's administrative offices; Warden Liu was hosting a private dinner for his parents. They were eight around the table: the warden, the deputy warden, two section chiefs, one officer, Driver Lu and his wife, and the prisoner. Course after course came. Dishes appeared that were seen at only the best banquets, including Decheng's favourite, succulent fatty pork. He salivated at the feast before him but restricted himself to nibbling. *I have to keep my dignity,* he resolved. He tried to console himself with the thought that rich food would wreak havoc on his stomach, but soon enough, he felt almost sick with revulsion to think that across the road, starving prisoners were eating rotten vegetables and mildewed rice.

Everyone else ate heartily. "The Party has helped our family so much!" Driver Lu said to his host. He took his chance to rage against his son's ingratitude and the "evil" act he and his two friends had perpetrated.

That evening, Driver Lu and Stepmother Meilan stayed in a guest room normally reserved for visiting officials. The next day, Renqing met with Decheng in a small conference room off the visitation corridor, a privilege certain sympathetic guards accorded Qiuping when she visited. The bus driver lectured his son, telling him to accept the prison's offer to seek a sentence reduction.

When those efforts failed to persuade him, the prison ordered Qiuping to Hengyang to try.

At their meeting, her voice carried a hesitancy that was unfamiliar between them. "Is it true, you don't feel the same about being with your family? That you don't have the same feelings as before?"

Decheng was deeply saddened to see the insecurity in his wife's face. He saw that prison authorities had got to Qiuping. They had toyed with her emotions, had planted a notion in her mind that he was refusing the sentence reduction because he'd grown distant from her, that he didn't need her love.

"The sentence reduction is an attempt to win over my mind. I have to reject it."

Both were crying.

"The more you persist like this, I feel as though you're rejecting my love. Didn't you like being free? Being together at home?"

"I did." He wanted to say that he was only "relatively" free.

Qiuping pleaded, "Just go along with them, you'll get out sooner and everything will be fine again."

"I don't care about their one or two years. What's one or two years in my sixteen-year sentence?"

Decheng tried to restore hope in Qiuping, knowing that prison authorities had violated the bond between them. "I'm sure there will be pressure from inside and outside the country to release all three of us. We could be out soon, who knows, maybe even in a year's time."

"You're just being stubborn." Qiuping sounded resigned.

AT MONTH'S END, the cadres told Decheng that they weren't going to bother applying to the courts for a reduction in his sentence. Immediately, his sleeping space in the communal bed shrank and he was back to slopping his meals from the wooden vats.

Beijing had larger fish to fry.

The bidding process, eight years in advance, had begun for cities vying to host the summer Olympics in 2000. That Beijing was in the running at all was a sign that international revulsion over the massacre in Tiananmen Square was fading. But China still faced Western concerns about its human-rights record and political prisoners.

The regime timed two high-profile acts of leniency to make certain they caught the attention of the powerful International Olympic Committee. In March 1993, a month before the IOC's inspection tour of the city, Beijing "paroled" the student who'd topped the regime's most-wanted list of twenty-one student leaders. Wang Dan was months short of completing his four-year sentence. In September, a week before the IOC's vote to decide the winning city, Beijing released the man considered the father of China's democracy movement, Wei Jingsheng. He had served fourteen-and-a-half years of a fifteen-year sentence. Wei, a magazine editor and electrician at the Beijing Zoo, achieved fame owing to his postings on the short-lived Democracy Wall, on Beijing's Xidan Street in late 1978 and 1979. He had called for a "fifth modernization" of democracy, arguing that Deng Xiaoping's vision of a developed modern economy could not be accomplished without first achieving individual freedom.

Beijing lost to Sydney, Australia, by two votes.

Eight months after the vote, the Chinese government rearrested Wei Jingsheng and sentenced him to a second fifteen-year term. Soon afterwards, Wang Dan was back behind bars, serving an additional eleven-year sentence. Both were cited for subversion. The former angered the regime by raising money for victims of the Tiananmen massacre and meeting with an American politician, the latter by accepting foreign donations and enrolling in a history correspondence course at the University of California, Berkeley.

AWARE THAT ITS PENAL SYSTEM was coming under international scrutiny, Beijing was making efforts to show that there was more to prisoners' lives than compulsory labour. At the Hengyang prison, a prisoners' musical troupe gave a performance in the great hall. They opened with a spirited singing of "Without the Communist Party, there would be no new China." Afterwards, a troupe member sought out Lu Decheng to pass along a book from Yu Zhijian, a Communist perspective on the collapse of the Soviet bloc. Decheng found a cryptic note inside. "As old as I am, I am old."

Decheng found Zhijian's message to be of enormous spiritual support. Old Revolutionary Zhao pronounced it "rich in sentiment and logic." He agreed with Decheng's interpretation: Stay strong, Dongyue has been beaten into a precarious mental state, but "I'm the same old me."

Another distraction from the drudgery of Decheng's life came by way of a book sale. Hunan's Yuelu Publishing House brought in boxes of overstock and out-of-print books. Most prisoners snapped up anything to do with marketing, business, and economics. Decheng found himself perusing books that didn't interest the others. He came across the ancient and sacred texts of the Confucian canon, *The Four Books* and *The Five Classics*. The price was steep, forty *yuan*. Decheng decided to buy the set, because he wanted to understand history from a Confucian perspective.

Decheng browsed further among the dusty books. He was surprised to find a historical work he'd heard of but never before seen. The *Comprehensive Mirror to Aid in Government* was written a millennium ago by Sima Guang, a Confucian scholar and poet who held high office to a Song dynasty emperor. A chronological narrative of fifteen centuries of China's history, from its creation in the fifth century B.C. until the time of the work's publication in the tenth century A.D., it comprised four volumes totalling more than four thousand pages. For almost one thousand years, until the last days of imperial China in 1911, China's governing elite routinely consulted the *Comprehensive Mirror* as a record of events and figures in history, and as a guide to methods and strategies that brought success or failure. In that time, only the Confucian canon would have been more read.

While there were always buyers for books on Confucianism, the clerk from the publishing house was staggered that anyone, much less a starving prisoner who laboured unpaid, would buy the arcane *Mirror*. The price was sixty *yuan*. She felt compelled to warn Decheng, "This contains weak and contemptible knowledge!" Back at his metal desk, Decheng pored over the *Mirror*. Curious guards and prisoners who saw him hunched over the thick books would take one look at the classical Chinese characters and shake their heads. "You're from another planet," said one.

When Decheng got to the end of the four thousand pages, he started over. He took to heart the stated purpose of the work: "to reveal that the good should be the law, and the evil put aside, to make history a mirror for the good of society." He pushed himself to think deeply about what China's rulers did, especially in periods of authoritarianism, treachery, and cruel deaths, and the difference between what was *apparently* right and what was *really* right. He took up his pencil. He underlined passages and in the margins he rewrote names, copied out text, translated phrases of classical Chinese into modern Chinese and dynastic dates into modern ones. He folded corners of pages top and bottom, added exclamations and question marks. His marginal comments spilled over into his notebooks.

The phrases Decheng underlined, rewrote, or added began to look like a moral critique:

Slogans are a deceit, a tool for officials to continue their banditry and cheating.

Those who are burdening the people with taxes are brilliant gentlemen; those who are killing the people are loyal officials.

The more people you hurt, the better an official you become; the more people you kill, the more loyal a member of the government you are.

This is the horror of dictatorship, where the government doesn't care if or how many lives are destroyed or people are killed.

From their mouths come words of virtue, but in their hearts they are like snakes and vipers.

One of the oldest stories in the *Mirror* remained as controversial today as it was twenty-four centuries ago. Known as the *Emperor and the Assassin (Jing Ke Ci Qing Wang)*, the tale takes place during the period of the Warring States, when the state of Qin fought for domination over six other powerful feudal city-states. The crown prince of the neighbouring state hired an assassin, Jing Ke, to kill the hated and brutal king of Qin. Jing Ke laid plans to gain an audience with the king by an offer to cede territory. He convinced a Qin general to kill himself as sacrifice, took the general's severed head and a map in which his dagger was concealed, and came face to face with the king. The assassin failed and the king of Qin went on to complete his bloody conquest.

He proclaimed himself "the first emperor." By unifying the states, the emperor, in effect, created China. But debate raged on to modern day about whether the brutality and empire building of the first emperor was worth it. While he brought in progressive laws to centralize state control and to allow for economic and military expansion, his tyranny and violence did not abate. He ordered book burnings. He buried Confucian scholars alive. And in the end, the Qin dynasty lasted only two decades.

In 1974, the debate over the first emperor's legacy was revived when farmers drilling a well near Xian hit what turned out to be a terracotta soldier, one of an army of thousands buried with the first emperor in his tomb. At that time, the Gang of Four, led by Mao's fourth wife, Jian Qing, who were the main proponents of the Cultural Revolution, vigorously defended the first emperor, arguing that brutality and repression could be justified. The *People's Daily*, for example, likened Jing Ke, the failed assassin, to the "counter-revolutionary buffoons" plotting against Mao's regime.

The edition of the *Mirror* that Decheng purchased had been published in Changsha in 1990. The publisher's postscript to the final volume quoted Mao Zedong's nurse: "Chairman Mao read this work repeatedly and had a copy of it beside his bed. Eventually it was worn out from so much reading." After a year, Decheng's volumes were so thumbed that the titles of each were faint then disappeared, the bindings loose, and the tissue-like paper greasy from handling.

DECHENG DECIDED to put the failures of man to the test in prison. He challenged himself: find a good man and show that goodness could survive even here.

One day, the guards came to ask him to help them convince a new prisoner to vacate their office. A corrected activist had taken him there to be disciplined for so minor a violation that the guards themselves wanted to drop the matter. In protest for having been brought there in the first place, Zhong Guiyou, an illiterate peasant, was refusing to budge. Decheng understood why the guards had enlisted him, thinking he and the new man shared the trait of stubbornness. He was impressed, seeing before him a man of principle. Left alone with the man, Decheng learned why Peasant Zhong was embittered. He was serving thirteen years for a crime he said he did not commit—supplying the knife that someone had been killed with in a fight. Even under torture, he had protested his innocence. After having his say with Decheng, he agreed to leave the office.

This is a good person who could turn into a bad apple in prison, Decheng thought. Like the prisoner whom Zhijian and Dongyue and their followers had rescued from the Rigid Control Team, Peasant Zhong—young and muscle-bound—could be eyed as useful brawn by the cell bosses. Decheng decided to take him under his wing. He extended his friendship, but Peasant Zhong, being from the countryside and never having gone to school, declared himself of too low a class to befriend someone like Decheng. "Never feel that you are inferior!" Decheng said. "We start by being equal and we stay equal."

He set out three principles for their friendship: Peasant Zhong would seek to educate himself; each would point out if he felt wronged by the other; and trickery, guile, or boastfulness had no place between them. The new understanding benefited both men. Decheng arranged for his young friend to be transferred into his mechanics course, and Zhong taught Decheng a regime of daily physical exercise to maintain muscle strength. On Sundays, in the hour for relaxation, the two played cards, inventing a rule that the loser had to crawl on his belly under a table, rationalizing this to be exercise and not gambling. Once, when Decheng had lost several times in a row, his friend offered to crawl under the table for him. "No!" Decheng insisted. "Rules are rules!"

Politics was never a subject of conversation with Peasant Zhong, and it was all that Decheng and Old Revolutionary Zhao ever talked about. But both friendships persuaded Decheng that even in a harsh environment like prison, equality had meaning, and honesty and trust could survive. But by early 1995, Peasant Zhong was transferred to another reform-through-labour camp, a coal mine. Then Old Revolutionary Zhao received notice that he was to be released early, for which the prison gave no reason.

Old Revolutionary Zhao wrote a final poem for Decheng.

Manjianghong [The River Runs Red]

Though I am in pain, I still have the will to live. The East [China] *remains in darkness, the night is long. After living for half a century, I have endured so much hunger and labour. Being locked up for sixteen years, my body and heart can no longer be healed. I shed my blood, but never shed tears. My bones are still warm.*

The hatred between the classes is imprinted on my heart. The revenge between the nations is carved in my bones. I pray to the sky to nourish the flames of the Communist movement.

Corruption needs to be ended, bandits and village chiefs need to be rid of, policies need to be corrected, and people's trust needs to be restored. My heart will only be in peace the day a nation stands tall and strong in the East.

Zhao wrote his poem in the style of an original by the same title that, according to folklore, was written by Yue Fei, a Song dynasty hero. General Yue was someone about whom enemy troops said, "It is easier to move a mountain than to defeat a Yue Fei army." The emperor threw the general into prison, which led to the origins of the term *mo xu you*, a "trumped-up charge." Yue Fei, executed at the age of thirty-nine, remained such an enduring hero for his valour and patriotism that in the 1930s and 1940s, *Manjianghong* became an anthem of the resistance movement against the occupying Japanese.

At forty-two years old, Zhao was going home to his aged mother, whose only wish was that he find a wife. The old revolutionary told Decheng, "If I never marry, the loss to the world is a small family with one child, but if I give up my political life, I lose the hope of a democratic revolution in China." Decheng committed Old Revolutionary Zhao's poem to memory and ripped the paper it was written on into tiny pieces.

NEVER CERTAIN HOW LONG his sentence would last, Decheng drew a bead not on his remaining time but on his purpose— continuing to educate himself. He read, studied, filled his notebooks and clipped his newspapers, expanded his vocabulary, practised his calligraphy. He acquired other historical books, including the dynastic histories, and, to round out his understanding of modern China, the collected works of Mao Zedong. He branched out in his reading. He asked college-educated prisoners if he could borrow their books, which had titles like *Male Psychology* and *Organizational Behaviour*. Decheng grew ever more satisfied with his progress: *I'm on track.*

Qiuping's own life had become busy. Sometimes she'd miss a visit, or even two in a row, because the bus station had called a meeting or their daughter or her parents were making demands on her time. But her letters kept Decheng up to date. Little Xinfeng was doing well in school, Qiuping had bought a colour television and installed a telephone—one with caller identification, no less.

In late July, Qiuping arrived for a visit. Her brusque manner and the red flush in her face tipped off her husband: something was wrong.

"Lu Gao, I'm asking you for a divorce." She removed from her purse a set of documents and set them on the table.

Decheng sat impassively.

The guards were stunned. They never imagined that such a romance could come to an end.

Qiuping said if the two of them agreed, the marriage registry would allow the governor of the prison in two months' time to conduct the divorce proceedings and to issue a divorce certificate. "I've already signed the document," she said.

Decheng felt a sense of calm. He looked at Qiuping. "Okay," he said and affixed his signature.

Abruptly, Qiuping stood up. She reached into her purse again and took out a carton of cigarettes made in Changsha, the kind she always brought for him, left it on the table, and stormed out.

Back in his cell, Decheng sat feeling serene and in a contemplative mood. He had long believed that divorce was the moral thing to do, under their circumstances. He had been the first one to ask for it, right after his sentencing. Now that divorce was Qiuping's choice, he felt that he had done the right thing by agreeing. She had suffered the strain of his incarceration for six long years and untold more could lie ahead. By saying yes he had set free the woman he loved.

In the two-month waiting period, the thought occurred to Decheng that perhaps asking for a divorce was an act of love on Qiuping's part. Perhaps she was trying to push him away, to dull the pain of separation for them both. He wrote her a letter:

August 23, 1995
Wangping,
I love you. I love you. I love you.
Your Lu Gao

As the date of the divorce proceedings drew near, Decheng had panicked second thoughts. He found himself dwelling on why Qiuping had ended their last meeting so abruptly. Was she just being stoic? *I know she's a tough character,* he thought. Or was she angry because she had expected him to protest?

Suddenly, he was convinced that the reason she had asked for a divorce was to test his love for her. He was filled with great regret. They still loved each other, beyond doubt. They should discuss rationally, then, whether or not to divorce, and not make such a decision in anger. Decheng began a letter. He wrote furiously. His letters to her were usually two pages at most. He wrote five pages, ten. Twenty pages. He mopped his brow as his pen flew, piercing the paper unevenly. When finally he was done, he'd written thirty pages. He knew his thoughts were confused, his sentences repetitive and full of contradictions. But all that mattered was she'd see the one line he'd written that showed that he had come to accept her view, that love was uppermost—"Politics and all belief in politics can go to fucking hell!"

He faced an immediate problem. The post would not get his letter to Liuyang before Qiuping left for the prison, where the divorce proceedings would take place. He asked two guards a favour, to travel to Liuyang, to deliver the letter themselves. They had to ask prison authorities for permission. As Decheng expected, it was granted. He knew they weren't acting out of compassion: the prison needed Qiuping in his life as insurance that he would, as he'd written in his letter, forsake his politics.

The guards panicked when they found out that his wife had already left home for Hengyang. They went to the long-distance bus station in town and waited for buses from Liuyang. When Qiuping arrived, they handed her Decheng's letter.

"I don't want to look at it. I don't want to see it!" she said. The two guards insisted she take it. She did, only to throw it on the ground, leaving them to pick it up.

On arriving at the prison, Wang Qiuping was all business. Decheng could see how determined she was that the governor of the prison begin the divorce proceedings immediately. Decheng stared at her until she returned his gaze. "Surely you still love me."

She looked coldly at him.

Decheng could not believe that she could be so unfeeling, so hostile toward him.

When the proceedings turned to dividing matrimonial property, Decheng asked only that upon his release, Qiuping return letters, photographs, notebooks, and books belonging to him. He agreed that custody of their daughter would go to her—after

all, he didn't know how long he would remain in prison. With these issues resolved, he exchanged not another word or glance with her. Deliberately, he behaved as if he weren't affected in the least by what had just transpired. As the paperwork was being completed, he spoke lightheartedly to the guards about meaningless things. And when a prison officer came to take his photograph of record for his prison dossier, he kept up the same pretense—that the divorce meant nothing to him.

THAT EVENING, Decheng fell violently ill. His bowels ran, he had a high fever, and his body broke out in a rash that looked like melon seeds. Three days later, when the fever and rash had abated and he'd otherwise recovered, he felt no rancour toward Qiuping. He had been selfless and he had freed her from an impossible situation. Feeling inspired, he decided to quit smoking. The timing was bleakly perfect; October 1 was National Day and he felt as bitter toward the day that marked Mao's founding of the People's Republic of China as he did about shedding an enjoyable habit.

In the new year, Driver Lu came to the prison, requesting a visit with his son. Renqing's stooped posture suggested bad news. His eyes held tenderness, and his voice expressed a degree of concern that Decheng had not heard from him before.

"Wang Qiuping has remarried."

Decheng was devastated. "This too will pass," said Renqing, his voice cracking. Days later, Decheng's two sisters arrived together for a rare visit, sent by their father to console him.

In short order, Decheng received a letter from Qiuping. He didn't recognize the name of the man she married, Xiaohu, who was younger than them both. But his eyes passed over the news written in Qiuping's own hand and came to rest on how she had addressed him—"My friend, Decheng"—and how she had signed off—"Your friend, Wang Qiuping." How could their love be reduced to this?

When Decheng reread her letter, he found its tone forced. Her thoughts didn't flow. He was sure she was hiding torment behind the words. *Of all people*, he thought, *I know her best.*

He calculated the timing of her remarriage. He was forced to consider another reason why she'd requested a divorce—she was pregnant. Alas, Decheng saw the other man must have been in the picture months ago. But he'd been so secure about the love between himself and Qiuping and so caught up in his studies that her missed visits last spring and summer had aroused no suspicions in him. He thought back to her appearance last July. Now he saw that the flush in her face might have had more to do with her being pregnant than with the oppressive summer heat or the stifling prison air.

Decheng was resolute. If Qiuping were suffering, he would want to comfort her, pregnant or not. He asked prison officials if they could arrange a meeting between them. The prison sent Qiuping a telegram, summoning her to Hengyang.

The meeting went poorly. What little talk there was, he did most of it. Clearly there against her will, Qiuping was cool and unreceptive. With the meeting going nowhere, Decheng couldn't help himself. "Do you really not love me anymore?" he asked.

"I don't love you even a little bit," she snapped.

Decheng felt as though he were falling to the bottom of a well. In the ensuing days, he became obsessed with his suspicion that she had been pregnant when she'd asked him to divorce. That he had agreed to it may well have driven her to marry the baby's father. The thought of his complicity tortured him.

He arranged to bribe a trustee so he could use the telephone in the vehicle-repair workshop. Knowing Qiuping had caller identification, Decheng let her phone ring and ring. Even if she didn't answer, she'd know he had called. He remained in the booth, hanging up and redialing, which at three *yuan* a call was adding up. He was about to dial for the seventh time when the telephone in the workshop rang. He picked up the receiver.

He couldn't get a word in. She ranted, the words barrelling out of her like a car going down a hill without brakes. She scolded him non-stop. She called him cruel and insensitive. She accused him of caring only about himself, of always putting himself first. She became hysterical. "You have no heart, no feelings. I have no more tears to cry!" With that, she slammed down the phone.

It was several minutes before a bewildered Decheng put the receiver back in its cradle. An older prisoner in the car workshop had observed him dialing and redialing, then eagerly picking up when finally she—it was most certainly a woman, to make any man so anxious—rang back. Later, he would tell Decheng that going into the telephone booth, he had the look of a proud rooster in his prime. Coming out, he looked like the loser of a cockfight, drained and exhausted.

ONE WEEK LATER, his heart heavy, Decheng took out a sheet of paper. He wrote with deliberate, neat strokes.

April 13, 1996
Last Will

After I die, please take out my heart and give it to the one
that I have loved most, Wang Qiuping. We arrive and
leave this world naked, without attachments.
Communism is the source of all evil.

Wishing in my next life that I will not be a human being,
Lu Decheng

He bit his finger until he drew blood and pressed it above each
of the three characters of his name, folded the will and hid it among
his belongings.

The days passed. At month's end, still tormented by their last
one-sided exchange on the telephone, Decheng decided to write
Qiuping a last letter. He chose a salutation that was resonant
with meaning: he replaced the proper character of her name, *Ping*,
meaning "lotus leaves on the pond," with one that sounds the same
but means "peace."

At the top of the page, he wrote "The Last Outpouring," a title he
chose as much for himself as for those who would read it—Qiuping
and the prison authorities. Decheng tried to respond to Qiuping's
accusations. "It wounds me deeply that you should doubt my character, that you should think I am a man who acts only for his own
profit. What you see is the result of my internal struggles." He
hoped she'd hear something that the authorities reading his letter
would not. "Who is the real Lu Decheng? If ever I get out of prison,
I will give you the facts and the truth." He wrote and wrote, his
words a muddle on the page. He tried to address her anger and hurt,
only to produce his own. His words turned bitter and reproachful.
"Why did you have to talk about divorce when my confidence was
at its lowest, in China and in life? How naive of me to think that I
could end your sadness and agony with divorce." He rambled on

about the nature of love. "It's the cruelest thing to be misunderstood by the one you love most. When you have loved to the extreme, there is no other place for love to go." Twenty-five pages later, he signed off, replacing the proper character for his name with one that could mean "no love" or "no feeling."

The guards sent the letter. When it was returned, unopened, Decheng slid into despondency. He'd lost his precious love; he'd failed in his marriage. He'd resolved to serve out his sentence, but for what? After seven years what political goal had been achieved? He thought back to the naivety of him and Zhijian and Dongyue, to think that they could motivate the students, maybe even the entire country, to rise up and refuse to accept autocracy. Instead, he—and they—sat in prison, cut off from each other, cut off from the outside world, forgotten, misunderstood.

Decheng stopped sleeping. His eyes swelled up; one had shut entirely. His breathing became shallow. A prisoner had to be on the verge of dying before the clinic would arrange for him to be seen by a doctor or send him to hospital. He consulted a prisoner knowledgeable about traditional medicines, who told Decheng part of his problem was likely his thyroid. He suggested that Decheng get hold of some spirits and drink a little every day. But he also issued a stern warning: "You have to improve your mental health first if your body is to heal itself."

In his notebooks, Decheng found a self-test for depression that he'd copied from a medical text. He had saved several self-tests covering various health problems, thinking they might come in handy if ever he needed an objective opinion on his own well-being. The test on depression asked whether one agreed not at all, somewhat, quite a lot, or very much to several statements:

It's hard to concentrate on reading.
I've lost interest in what was once important to me.
I feel like a failure.
My future seems hopeless.

I feel more dead than alive.

I've spent time thinking about *how* I might kill myself.

Decheng took the test and scored in the range of "moderate to severe depression." His score climbed from one week to the next. Week after week, he took the test again. On the week that he agreed with the test's final statement, his score vaulted into the highest range.

Having identified himself as "severely depressed, with a serious tendency to suicide," Decheng ran through the inventory of ways that he could kill himself: slit his wrists, hang himself with his trousers, fall in the path of a delivery truck, dash toward the front gates so the guards would shoot him. As once before in his youth, Decheng contemplated the aftermath of suicide. He saw people laughing and making a mockery of his life.

He reread Qiuping's letter that reduced them to friends. *After all the reading and studying I've done, what have I actually learned? Why did I not see this great failure of my marriage coming?* Decheng had an epiphany. Instead of hurt at Qiuping's use of *friend*, he now felt gratitude. She had given him renewed purpose: he would seek to understand how the two of them had come to this failure, how they had let love slip from their grasp. Decheng thought about his two friends, one driven insane, one "still the same old me," and the pledge the three of them had made to survive. *I must leave this prison alive and with my sanity.* He formulated a plan to achieve all his purposes.

WHEN DECHENG ASKED Renqing for money to deal with his health problems, the bus driver readily agreed. He'd noticed his son deteriorating rapidly since the divorce. He looked perilously thin and Renqing had become extremely frightened that his son might become seriously ill and die.

Decheng led his father to believe that he was using the several thousand *yuan* he delivered to Kind-Hearted Guard as bribes to get him a doctor's appointment or, if necessary, hospital care. Instead, Decheng bought food. He'd come to the conclusion that prison fare, which had worsened with reforms as the state cut prison budgets, would ruin what remained of his health. He'd seen how well the warden and his officials ate, so he knew that fresh vegetables and meat could find their way into the prison. With the guard acting as his banker, Decheng funnelled money to trustees and prisoners in the vehicle-repair workshop who got him food, for which he paid prices ten times what they were on the outside.

His plan had a second part. To re-evaluate the love he and Qiuping once had, he turned a "comprehensive mirror" on human nature, to examine the mirror-image of goodness in order to take the full measure of man as a moral being. The Song dynasty scholar drew inspiration and example from history. Decheng surveyed the panoply of human weaknesses that surrounded him in prison. He sought out those he once shunned: cell bosses, corrected activists and trustees, drug addicts, thieves, and murderers. He had only one rule: engage only in one-on-one conversations, in order to avoid the influence of a gang mentality on him or on his subject. Decheng warmed to his fellow prisoners, chatted with them, shared their wine, played cards with them. His students declared him a lively instructor. He tried out the tedium of forced labour, making Christmas-tree lights, hand-sewing beads on sweaters and novelty ties, cutting fake diamonds, and mixing counterfeit Western-brand shampoos with other prisoners labouring in his living area. All in all, Decheng observed a range of the worst tendencies and excesses—stubbornness, paranoia, jealousy, vengefulness, hatred, cruelty, and brutality.

In understanding human weakness, Decheng came to better recognize his own. He saw that as a child, though he had possessed some moral intuition, he'd had no sense of how to express it other than opposing his father at every turn. His father had bullied the weak and feared the strong, and consequently rejected the virtue of his mother and remarried to a shrewish woman. In his father, Decheng saw the Chinese people generally: from the dictator at the top down to the man and woman in the street, they had lost their moral compass. He laid the responsibility for this tragic state of affairs at the feet of the Communist Party. Authoritarianism had emptied the Chinese people of their humanity. People like his father were its unwitting victims, any responsibility to think for themselves replaced with a constant fear of pitiless reprimand.

In one of his newspapers, Decheng came across an advertisement for a pharmaceutical company. The ad contained an illustration of a man, wearing the slippers and pyjamas of a hospital patient, squatting before a bird in a cage. The man is valiantly trying to minister to the sick bird, feeding it medicine. But the man and the caged bird are themselves enclosed within a larger bamboo cage. Decheng clipped the illustration and pasted it inside the cover of his ledger book devoted to corruption. He knew he was taking a risk. The authorities could choose to see something subversive in his saving the illustration, whether or not they saw it as he did, as a metaphor for the plight of China and its people. The entire country was infected with a sickness, and as long as its people lived under the Party, they would be no better off than caged patients, ministered to by those who were no more well, or free, than they.

T E N

URING BREAKS OR WHILE WAITING for the foreman to assign jobs, most of Decheng's colleagues in the garage at the bus station watched television and videos or played mah-jong. Besides him, only two other mechanics were interested enough to read the newspapers that the work unit subscribed to— the *Liuyang Daily*, *Hunan Daily*, and *People's Daily*. They sometimes commented on what they read to Decheng, though rarely more than a word here or there.

When the *Hunan Daily* started publishing a four-page weekly economic supplement, the vehicle-repair shop didn't take delivery. Decheng bought it himself. To his dismay, the writers referred to the economic reforms as if everybody was happy with them. That might have been so up to 1985; most people didn't grumble much when price controls were lifted and prices rose because they had money to spend on goods unheard of before the reforms, like electric fans and televisions. But after 1985, people wondered if the reforms were operating for the benefit of officials. Under the new "dual-track" system, state-run enterprises could have a foot in both the planned and the market economies. As before, these enterprises delivered a quota of production to the state, and were protected with low, fixed prices for inputs. But now they could also sell any extra production on the market. The potential for abuse was so obvious that journalists immediately invented a word for such profiteering, *guandao* ("exploiting rents"): an official in state agriculture, say, could obtain fertilizer at the low, fixed price, and then turn around and sell it to a private company for as high a price as he could get, and pocket the difference. The writers at the supplement took a timid approach not only to uncovering *guandao*, but to analyzing any fallout from reforms. They were willing to report inflation, but only according to the official rate announced by the government. The supplement reported that in 1986, inflation was already running at half the 12.5 per cent recorded in 1985. Yet most people faced annual increases of 20 to 30 per cent. When the government removed staples like pork, eggs, and vegetables from rationing, prices shot up 30 to 60 per cent overnight. On a mechanic's salary, Decheng couldn't keep up.

As disappointed as Decheng was with the supplement, he reminded himself that it was still a Party organ, published to instruct the people on the Party line. Still, it at least covered these issues, and Decheng bought it every week—it was cheap enough, one *jiao*, one-tenth of one *yuan*—and read it cover to cover.

MOST PEOPLE GOT THEIR NEWS from television, and were used to the Party deciding what they should care about.

One story on the seven o'clock news got the whole country talking. Someone had broken into a bank vault in Changsha and made off with two hundred and forty thousand *yuan*. Workers at the Liuyang Long-Distance Bus Station could hardly imagine that much money. Even the most senior workers made only about six hundred *yuan* a year. Officials from the national Public Security Bureau appeared on the news to announce a nationwide manhunt for the robbers. They vowed a "swift resolution" to the crime and the "harshest punishment" for its perpetrators.

To the shock of people in Liuyang, the thief turned out to be one of their own. Within a month, police arrested a high school teacher named Zhang Rongwu. News reports said the teacher's bungling had led police right to him; he'd repaid a couple of creditors ten thousand *yuan* each with bills still bundled in the bank's security tape. Within days, the teacher was sentenced to death.

Decheng had just heard about the verdict when Hongwu knocked at his door. He had come directly from seeing the teacher's parents. Certain their son's arrest was a mistake, he'd gone to them intending to help them pursue justice.

Hongwu had last seen the teacher six months earlier. He had dined with his younger brother, who'd been a classmate of his. The teacher, whom Hongwu had never met before, had joined them. He taught at the rural Peaceful Bridge School and on weekends rode his bicycle back to town to see his wife and their two-year-old. They lived there with his parents at the dormitory of the Liuyang Printing Company, where his father worked. At dinner, the teacher hadn't talked much, except to lament that he couldn't support his wife and child on a teacher's pay and that he was thinking of going south to try his hand at private business.

Hongwu told Decheng that he had found the parents of the now-condemned man terrified and confused. They had protested that they hadn't seen their son in weeks and refused to talk to Hongwu. "I told them, 'There's nothing to be afraid of, we have to find the truth.' The family has lost their conscience out of fear. We have to think clearly for them."

On the face of it, Decheng agreed with Hongwu that the police either hadn't got at the truth or they'd arrested the wrong man. A respected teacher seemed an unlikely criminal. And it seemed ludicrous to think that anyone could be so smart as to break into a vault and so foolish as to leave the security tape around the stolen *yuan*. Would a teacher know how to break into a high-security bank vault? Had no one asked if security guards or other insiders were involved? Or maybe the teacher had found the money and thought heaven had delivered a windfall.

Hongwu and Decheng, determined to bring new evidence to the police, went together to Changsha to look up the younger brother. They found him at his work-unit dormitory. He was shaking with fright. His head had been shaved. "Tell us everything you know," urged Hongwu.

"Please go away. Don't get involved, you'll get into trouble. Please don't ask me anything. Don't worry about it."

"If we don't help your brother, nobody will."

"We can appeal to a higher court," Decheng added. "Things ought to be done properly."

They persuaded the brother to take them to the prison where the teacher was being held. But the prison refused their request to visit and refused again a day later, when Hongwu returned with the man's wife and child.

Hongwu would not give up. He and Decheng pressed the parents, who finally confided that their son had taken a leave from his teaching position and gone south to start some unknown business. On a visit home, he made a single extravagant purchase, a motorbike, and gave his mother the bundles of money to pay some debts. When police searched the home, they found additional missing cash, seized the motorbike, and confiscated the father's government bonds (cash-strapped work units used bonds to pay workers' salaries).

On the ninth day after sentencing, the parents revealed to Hongwu that any appeal for clemency was due on the desk of the governor of Hunan province by eight o'clock the next morning. Afraid of reprisal, the family hadn't wanted to appeal. That evening, Hongwu drafted a letter pleading for the teacher's life. The next day, at 7:40 a.m., he and Decheng were talking their way past the guardhouse of the provincial government buildings in Changsha. At 7:55, they were shown into the governor's reception room. At 7:57, they came face to face with the chief secretary, only to learn that the governor was in Beijing and not due back until later that day. The secretary promised them he would show the governor the letter. They left. Hongwu was encouraged. "Let's see if the letter gets the government moving."

The two stopped for a bowl of noodle soup, then called on Rongwu's younger brother. When they learned that he'd left earlier in a rush to Liuyang, they made a dash to catch the nine o'clock bus.

Some two hours later, on the outskirts of Liuyang, the bus came to a halt. Traffic in both directions had pulled off to the sides of the road. Hongwu and Decheng disembarked. A voice crackling over a loudspeaker ordered people to stay back: "A criminal is being transported for execution." Roadside chatter had it that Zhang Rongwu was being taken to the Peaceful Bridge School to be shot—criminals were executed at either the scene of the crime or at their work unit.

Decheng saw the teacher, gagged and handcuffed, standing in the back of a truck as it passed. A wooden placard hanging from his neck had his name with a red X through it, and below that, "Robber, Thief, Criminal."

Once traffic started to move again, the two friends hitched a ride from a car near the front of the line. Just short of the school, traffic stopped. The two jumped out and ran ahead. Hongwu was distraught. "What a shame! We don't have the power to save him!"

They heard the report of gunfire: the bullet to the back of the head.

By the time they reached the school, the convoy was gone. The placard lay on the ground, blood stained the earth. "We need a new sun for China," Hongwu cried out. Decheng could only sigh heavily.

In the days following, government notice boards in town posted details of the crime: the ladder that the teacher used to climb through a window at the bank, the specialized tools he'd used to open the vault. Decheng suppressed a cold laugh.

More chilling was the ridicule that town folk heaped on the dead teacher. "Why wouldn't he have hidden it? Or spent it little by little?" "Secretly invested it in a small business?" "How could anyone be so stupid!" No one questioned how he got the money. Decheng wanted to ask these detractors, so quick to condemn a dead man, who they thought would speak up for them if they found themselves suddenly arrested and facing charges.

When Decheng was a boy and had attended public announcements of execution orders, he'd searched the faces of the condemned, curious about their emotions during their last moments. If they showed anything, it was anger. Mostly, Decheng saw a deadened look in their eyes. What he'd seen, however, on the teacher's face haunted him—a mix of frustration at injustice and determination to put up a show of courage.

ABOUT THAT SAME TIME, Yu Zhijian introduced the name of an astrophysicist, Fang Lizhi, into their conversations. Fang's speeches and writings calling on intellectuals to play a role in the reform process were well known in elite intellectual circles. The purpose of reform, Fang argued, was to achieve a modern, democratic society in all aspects. Zhijian picked up Fang's argument, that economic progress was only one measure of the success of China's reform, and that bad results will always come even of good policies without democracy.

Fang, a pudgy fifty-one-year-old with a mirthful laugh, was vice-president of the acclaimed University of Science and Technology of China in Hefei, the capital of Anhui province. In a rousing speech at Peking University in the fall of 1985, he had called Marxist ideology old thinking and said academics had "bent backs" from their subservience to the Party. He had a message for the intelligentsia: stand up to the Party, think for themselves, and speak their minds. Though the university had a long liberal tradition, professors and students weren't used to someone, who was himself a Party member, so openly challenging the Party—and doing so with wit and flair.

One year later, Fang was on a speaking tour of campuses in major cities. In faraway Liuyang, Zhijian and Decheng couldn't get their hands on the progressive journals from Beijing or Shanghai or major dailies that were giving Fang laudatory coverage, but they were able to follow his tour on shortwave radio. Fang attracted international attention—his ability to speak English making for an even livelier interview. Decheng tuned in both Voice of America and the British Broadcasting Corporation. The latter broadcast twenty-four-and-a-half hours of original programming in Mandarin every week. On shortwave, Decheng and Zhijian listened to news that the Chinese media would be slower to report or wouldn't report at all. They heard Fang urge young intellectuals to clear their minds of Marxist dogma. People couldn't take the "first step toward democracy," he argued, without rights as basic as being able to think and to speak freely.

While Fang was speaking his mind with seemingly no repercussions, Zhijian ran into trouble for doing just what the astrophysicist urged. He dared to criticize his school administration and the curriculum they asked him to teach. The county education bureau responded by transferring him to a high school in a village 30 *li* away. Zhijian, his popularity with his former teacher colleagues un-diminished, still came into town often, staying at home with his parents. Decheng asked a favour of Grandmother Lu, to allow Zhijian and his girlfriend to occasionally spend the night at Number 35 Clear Water Alley—she obliged but criticized Zhijian's loose morals when he showed up one night with a different girlfriend.

For a brief few weeks, Fang's views sparked a series of student demonstrations. They began at his own university. In Hefei, on December 4, Fang told students, "Democracy is not granted from the top down; it is won by individuals." The next morning, they marched in the streets of Hefei. Over the next twenty-two days, tens of thousands of students marched in twenty other large cities. Their demands ranged from better food for students on campus to speedier political reforms. Then, abruptly, on December 26, Beijing banned student demonstrations. On December 31, students at Peking University defied the ban and set out to march the 10 kilometres to Tiananmen Square, only to be thwarted by fire trucks spraying water to turn the streets and the square to ice, forcing them to either turn back or vacate the square.

Decheng read the ensuing two-week barrage of editorials in the *People's Daily*, criticizing Hu Yaobang, the general secretary of the Party—and the man Deng had charged with overseeing the reforms—for his "bourgeois-liberal tendencies" and his "laxness" toward the demonstrations. When Hu resigned in disgrace, Decheng remained indifferent. He saw him as just another casualty of yet another power struggle. But he noticed cynicism of another sort from others in Liuyang. People weren't mad at Deng Xiaoping for ending the career of one of their most famous native sons, they were mad at the general secretary himself. "What a dummy!" people said. They felt let down. Hu had made it to the height of power but failed to deliver largesse to Liuyang, and now it was too late. People contrasted this with what lesser-ranking Communists from the county had delivered. Vice-premier Wang Zhen arranged to have a silk factory built. General Wang, a steel bridge. The woman general, Li Zhen, did even better. She developed several mines in the region.

Zhijian and Decheng remarked on how another casualty of the student demonstrations had gone unnoticed in Liuyang. The Party made sure Fang Lizhi disappeared from public view. Beijing reassigned him from his high-profile position to a research position at the Beijing Astronomical Observatory. The regime forbade him from giving speeches or talking to the media, and it expelled him from the Party. This punishment more than any disappointed the two friends; expulsion from the Party usually marked the ruin of someone's career. Equally discouraging, for them as for any of the students and intellectuals Fang had inspired, the government launched the "Anti-Bourgeois Liberalization Campaign."

ZHIJIAN HAD NO INTENTION of keeping his own silence. He paid yet again for speaking out, this time for criticizing the administration of the village high school. The authorities in the county made their displeasure clear: they not only transferred him even farther out—to Tantou village—but demoted him to teaching primary school. This demotion cost Zhijian more than just obscurity or isolation. Rural primary teachers had a demoralizing job; their schools relied on local funding, and money was as scarce for books and teaching supplies as it was for teachers' salaries.

In the summer of 1987, Bureaucrat Tanxu introduced Zhijian to Yu Dongyue. The two had met through Tanxu's propaganda job, which brought him into contact with staff at the *Liuyang Daily*. Dongyue had recently been transferred to Liuyang to serve as an arts editor, his job to take photographs and draw illustrations to accompany stories in the paper.

Dongyue, Zhijian, and Decheng became fast friends. Nineteen years old, Dongyue was five years younger than them. A child protégé of a nationally renowned painter, Dongyue graduated at age seventeen from the same teacher's college as Zhijian. He got a prestigious first assignment as a fine-arts teacher at a vocational school in Xiangtan City that recruited students nationwide, then was transferred to the propaganda job in Liuyang. Dongyue was cerebral like Zhijian, but he also shared Decheng's physical prowess. He was an excellent basketball player, he swam daily, and in a spirited display of independence he spent his summers hitchhiking and hopping freight trains to the frontiers of Tibet and Xinjiang.

Dongyue's generous living quarters above the offices of the *Liuyang Daily* gave the three a room where they could meet. Its tall windows, glass-panelled doors, and high ceilings made it airy and welcoming. The three friends gathered amongst Dongyue's piles of books, magazines, journals and newspapers, photographs and drawings, canvasses stacked several deep, paintings in progress on easels, and scrolls hung to dry on clotheslines. The chaos suited their wide-ranging discussions. Zhijian recited poems from the six volumes of *Three Hundred Tang Poems* or from the *Dream of the Red Chamber* just as easily as he discussed emerging film directors. He liked to roll new expressions off his tongue, trying out what he'd read in the works of modern Taiwanese novelists and playwrights. Dongyue, who had poems and artwork published in Hong Kong periodicals, was constantly experimenting with stream-of-consciousness poems and painting in styles both realistic and abstract. Decheng didn't even know there *were* styles of painting. Of the foreign novelists the other two mentioned, he recognized only Tolstoy and Dostoevsky, and he didn't know the difference between a political scientist, an economist, and a philosopher. He held his two friends in awe. *Those two are so far ahead of me, I can't even see the back of them.*

WHEN DENG XIAOPING SPOKE, the Party listened. Hardliners and reformers in the Politburo had been waiting to see which direction the regime would take after Hu Yaobang's dismissal. The hardliners wanted to pull back from opening to the West and from reforms; the reformers wanted to speed ahead. In mid-1987, Deng affirmed the open door policy, and the government's plan to press on with market-oriented reforms. The steam went out of the Anti-Bourgeois Liberalization Campaign in its very first year.

Intellectuals didn't have to worry as much about "mistakes" in their thinking, but the regime still didn't want them speaking their minds in public. Ordinary people could also be more relaxed about the opinions they shared in private, as long as they didn't publicly criticize the regime.

However, citizens found a way to anonymously exchange information and views in what was known as "small news"—underground leaflets. In Liuyang, these leaflets were hard to come by. Typically, they were produced in Beijing or Shanghai, and distributed by people travelling on the railway. Whenever Decheng was in Changsha, he'd go to the station, buy a platform ticket, and try to spot someone concealing leaflets under their jacket, or uttering a phrase advertising the contents of one. He'd even travel on the train for a few stops, just to find someone selling them on board. Cheaper leaflets, priced at one *yuan*, reprinted articles from journals and magazines, or contained unsigned opinion pieces criticizing the Party. Decheng paid as much as three *yuan* for leaflets that reprinted information from the restricted Party newsletter, or that leaked secrets about domestic policy debates or factional struggles in the Party leadership.

Decheng began to save leaflets that named high-placed officials and their families who'd become multi-millionaires, many of whom ran successful private trading companies. The leaflets often repeated rumours that these officials engaged in nepotism, made backroom deals, and traded power and Party connections for money, and that the private companies they or their sons and daughters ran were no more than "briefcase companies." As gossip about corruption among officials circulated, the term *guandao* settled in the language of people on the street.

"Everybody knows it's happening," they'd say.

DAYS INTO THE NEW YEAR of 1989, the trio of friends in Liuyang gathered in Dongyue's flat, excited by a name that had reappeared in the international news after almost two years' silence: Fang Lizhi. On January 6, Fang was writing an academic paper on supernovae, and the subject of explosions in the universe gave him an idea to write to Deng Xiaoping, to suggest a way he could mark the new year:

> Dear Chairman Deng:
>
> This year marks the fortieth anniversary of the founding of the People's Republic, and the seventieth anniversary of the May Fourth Movement [a nationalist movement which arose out of students protesting the terms of the newly signed Treaty of Versailles, which ceded German territories inside China to Japan]. There must be many events commemorating these important dates, but the people are perhaps more worried right now about the future than about the past.
>
> In order to better evoke the spirit of these days, I earnestly suggest that on the fortieth anniversary of this nation's founding, you grant a full amnesty, especially for political prisoners such as Wei Jingsheng. Whatever one's assessment of Wei Jingsheng might be, a full pardon for people like him who have already served ten years in prison would certainly be considered consistent with a spirit of humanity [...]
>
> My best regards,
> Fang Lizhi

Fang addressed his letter to Deng at Zhongnanhai, the headquarters for the Party and residential compound of the Politburo, and dropped a copy into a postbox outside the observatory. The next day, a colleague came for tea, as did an American professor, Perry Link, later the same day. Fang shared his letter with them both. The colleague sent copies to dozens of other academics in Beijing. The American shared it with foreign reporters.

At Peking University, beginning that winter, a student named Wang Dan had been holding weekly "lawn salons" to discuss Western democracy and problems in Chinese society. Students met at the school's statue of Cervantes—a gift from Spain in honour of the developing relationship between Spain and China. Wang's own ambitions were to see student-organized associations, including even a student-run newspaper, exist independently of the Party or without having to be sanctioned by the Party. He began to invite speakers to the salons, including old Democracy Wall activists and Li Shuxian, a physics professor, and her husband—Fang Lizhi.

ON APRIL 15, Hu Yaobang died, having suffered a heart attack a week earlier. Decheng read the eulogy in the *People's Daily*. It made no mention of Hu as a reformer, remembering him only as a "loyal Communist fighter" and "great proletarian revolutionary." People in Liuyang raised their eyebrows when they saw on television students in Beijing grieving for their native son. Mourners came from Peking University to Tiananmen Square to lay wreaths at the Monument to the Revolutionary Martyrs. The last such spontaneous outpouring for a member of the Politburo—though ousted as head of the Party, Hu had remained in the ruling group—happened in 1976, and ended in what became known as the Tiananmen Incident. Thousands of ordinary citizens had come to the square to mourn Premier Zhou Enlai. The day had ended with police clubbing mourners who'd protested the removal of their wreaths. Students not only laid wreaths for Hu, but hung banners from the obelisk of the monument and shouted slogans against *guandao* and dictatorship. On the third day after his death, tens of thousands of students in the square turned from commemorating the man who'd taken the fall for their demonstrations two years earlier to staging an overnight sit-in outside

Zhongnanhai. They demanded that Premier Li Peng hold talks with their "organizing group," and that the government recognize it as legal.

In Liuyang, a teacher at the high school, a former classmate of Decheng's, organized a memorial march for Hu Yaobang. Decheng declined to take part but came out to observe. A handful of teachers and students, perhaps twenty-five or thirty, donned black arm bands and marched down People's Road behind a banner that read, "Painfully Remember Comrade Hu Yaobang." Decheng thought they didn't look pained at all.

Decheng had no interest in watching the broadcast of Hu's memorial service, held in Beijing at the Great Hall of the People one week after his death. Later that afternoon, the bus station in Liuyang buzzed with more immediate news: drivers and travellers brought eyewitness accounts of crowds in the streets of Changsha angry about high prices and *guandao*. But it wasn't just in Changsha. Listening on his short-wave radio, Decheng learned that a similar protest had broken out that same day in another provincial capital, Xian, in the north.

For the next two days, the national television news carried extended coverage of the two "commotions"—the government's word for the anger that had spilled into the streets. News reports portrayed the protestors as lawless troublemakers who beat police, looted, and smashed property.

THREE DAYS AFTER HU'S MEMORIAL, April 25, every state radio and television channel broadcast the next morning's editorial in the *People's Daily*. Decheng picked up the paper in the vehicle-repair shop the next day. The editorial ran under a banner headline on the front page:

IT IS NECESSARY TO TAKE A CLEAR-CUT STAND AGAINST DISTURBANCES

... [A]n extremely small number of people with ulterior purposes continued to take advantage of the young students' feelings of grief for Comrade Hu Yaobang to spread all kinds of rumours to poison and confuse people's minds. Using both big- and small-character posters [*dazibao*], they vilified, hurled invectives at, and attacked Party and state leaders. Blatantly violating the Constitution, they called for opposition to the leadership by the Communist Party and the socialist system . . .

. . . Flaunting the banner of democracy, they undermined democracy and the legal system. Their purpose was to sow dissension among the people, plunge the whole country into turmoil [*luan*], and sabotage the political situation of stability and unity. This is a planned conspiracy and a turmoil. Its essence is to, once and for all, negate the leadership of the Communist Party and the socialist system. This is a serious political struggle confronting the whole Party and the people of all nationalities throughout the country.

If we are tolerant of or conniving with this turmoil and let it go unchecked, a seriously chaotic state will appear . . .

A couple days later, the three friends gathered at Dongyue's flat to discuss the editorial and the reaction of students in Beijing. The students had been angered, not cowed as the regime had surely expected. The day after the editorial, 50,000 students had marched on Tiananmen Square, a turnout that astounded even student organizers. The three friends saw in the regime's behaviour a familiar pattern whenever it wanted to suppress dissent, this time by students: evoke a crisis of *luan*—turmoil and instability—which the Party considered to be the greatest threat to the country, label the students' motives unpatriotic and subversive, call their protest a conspiracy, then arrest and imprison a few individuals, and in doing so strike fear into everybody else. Maybe it had even played up the unrest and anger in Changsha and Xian, and distorted the truth of what really happened. In that way, the Party could keep people preoccupied with the economic fallout and deflect calls for democracy before they gained support beyond the student movement.

The same teacher who'd organized the memorial march for Hu Yaobang on People's Road found enthusiastic volunteers to help him organize a second. Decheng again said he wouldn't be joining in. *This is Liuyang, not Beijing.* Even so, he didn't think any number in the streets could make an impression on this regime: public opinion didn't count. Zhijian and Dongyue helped out the teacher, writing out posters calling for democracy. Hongwu put up flyers at bulletin boards where the *China Youth Daily* was posted, and he himself wrote out *dazibao* reading "Anti-*guandao*." A few days later, two hundred people shouted slogans and marched down People's Road.

ON THE LAST WEEKEND OF APRIL, Decheng and Qiuping held a gathering to mark Little Xinfeng's fourth birthday. Decheng and Godfather Ding started talking about the editorial in the *People's Daily.* To Decheng's surprise, his friend was dismissive.

"Whoever is king is none of my business."

Decheng prodded him. "Any system is okay?"

"It doesn't matter to me. Our purpose is to earn money and put a meal on the table."

The next week, if for no reason other than a sudden desire to spend time with his daughter, Decheng arranged to take four days off and picked up Little Xinfeng from Ding's home in the countryside. Father and daughter made the rounds of their relatives, including, of course, Grandmother Lu. She was eighty-five years old and showing some frailty. When Decheng went to leave, he gave his usual, "See you later." She called out to him, "*Yazi.*"

Decheng hadn't heard that endearment since he was a boy. The term, a melding of "duck-egg-son," was used for only the very young.

"Child," Grandmother Lu spoke firmly, "you must be straightforward and honest with yourself." These were the last words the old lady would ever say to him.

On May 4, Decheng began to see the student pro-democracy movement in a different light. He watched a televised address by Zhao Ziyang, the general secretary of the Party, to two thousand delegates at the annual meeting of the Asian Development Bank. Zhao said there was no *luan*. He went further. "There's no big risk in opening up a bit," he said, "and reporting the demonstrations and increasing the openness of the news." Immediately, Decheng wondered if there was a fissure opening in the Party's leadership. He also saw on television a student leader who impressed. A twenty-one-year-old education student at Beijing Normal University, Wuer Kaixi, an ethnic Uighur with a mop of hair and a memorable name, stood in Tiananmen Square and called for a "new May Fourth manifesto based on democracy"—echoing the "science and democracy" slogan of the nationalist movement in 1919. Decheng dared to hope that the students—with leaders like that—could exploit the divisions in the Politburo.

A day later, Hongwu told Decheng that some friends were considering making the journey to Beijing. Decheng perked up. "If people are going, without hesitation, I'm going." However, over the next week, most students in Beijing, their interest in activism petering out, returned to their classes.

The protest looked to have run its course.

Until, that is, two days before Mikhail Gorbachev was due to arrive in Beijing for the first Sino-Soviet summit since 1959. Wuer proposed that the students do something radical, as the government prepared to receive a world leader with its traditional welcome in the square. His idea: stage a hunger strike. On May 13, the students began fasting and the waning student pro-democracy movement reversed course. A student named Chai Ling vowed that students would fast until death, that they were willing to risk their lives for the future of the country. Her impassioned speeches swelled the sign-up list of hunger strikers from forty to three hundred. By day two, the number grew to twelve hundred and, by day three, May 15—the day Gorbachev arrived—three thousand. Beijingers thronged to the square. People across the country gathered at televisions. In Liuyang, along People's Road, eateries angled televisions toward the street as a way to attract customers. Even Qiuping planted herself in front of the television in the workers' club at the bus station. The strike had begun in pleasant weather by day, but night brought plummeting temperatures. By the third day, an early heat wave had driven the daytime high to 31 degrees. Ambulance sirens wailed constantly, as students who had fainted or collapsed were rushed to hospital.

Decheng did not think the hunger strike alone would sway the Party leadership. From what he'd seen on television, the hunger strikers continued to dilute their calls for democracy with expressions of discontent with reforms. They penned posters such as "Corruption is the cause of turmoil" and "The people cannot provide for parasites." However, his hopes rose. Gorbachev's visit and the 1,200 foreign journalists who'd come to cover it had put the Chinese regime under the glare of the international spotlight. But most of all, he was optimistic that, in the presence of a model reformer, the students might be inspired to focus on democracy.

On Tuesday, May 16, Decheng ate supper alone. Qiuping was away on an overnight shift. He headed to the communal bath for a shower. He ran into Yin, a university student and an administrative trainee who was briefly working under him in the vehicle-repair shop. Since the teenager was new to Liuyang, Decheng made an effort to be friendly and they chatted about the hunger strike. Decheng noticed that Yin seemed moved by the students' sacrifice. Decheng ventured to show where he stood: "I'm even thinking of going to Beijing. If you could, would you?" The teenager's ardour suddenly cooled, so Decheng said no more.

Later, Hongwu and Zhijian stopped by the bus station. They were spreading the word to interested friends: a meeting tonight, nine o'clock, at Dongyue's flat, to talk about going to Beijing. Originally, Bureaucrat Tanxu had suggested people meet in his office, then thought better of it, given his position in the propaganda bureau.

The teacher who'd organized the two marches begged off the trip because he was newly married, but he'd sent a colleague, Kong Zhongshen, in his stead.When the meeting began, they were nine, young men all in their early twenties.

Zhijian chaired the meeting. They decided first on a name for their group: the Hunan Student Movement Support Group, Liuyang Branch. In making the case for going to the capital, Zhijian spoke eloquently of the value of seeing for themselves what was happening, and he stressed that the opportunity to advocate so openly for democratic reform might never come around again in their lifetime. Bureaucrat Tanxu spoke about "the glorious struggle of the student movement." Someone worried that the authorities might stop trains travelling to Beijing. Others were undaunted. "We *must* go." "We'll hijack a vehicle if we have to."

Discussion turned to slogans. Zhijian talked about Fang Lizhi, to persuade the group that they should focus on political reform, on democracy rather than *guandao*. He had several suggestions. "The government of old men brings calamity to the country and harms the people." Or, "Until Qing Fu is gone, the crisis in the state of Lu will not be over," a proverb taken to mean that there will always be trouble until the troublemaker is removed. Bureaucrat Tanxu argued that all of Zhijian's proposed slogans were too extreme and would undermine the group's solidarity with the student movement. In the end, everybody agreed on two others:

> *Down with Deng, support Fang*
> *End one-party dictatorship and build up democratic China*

If Decheng had found the confidence to speak up, he would have said that developments appeared to be turning in favour of the students, that there was mounting evidence of a rift in the government leadership. He'd have pointed to an exchange he'd heard on the radio at dinnertime between Zhao Ziyang and Gorbachev, in which Zhao, replying to a question from Gorbachev, said that resolving the matter of the students' occupation of the square was "up to Deng Xiaoping." Decheng said nothing, however, and admonished himself: *I'm the perfect example of the saying, You can put dumplings in a teapot but you won't be able to pour them through the spout.*

Zhijian set a time and place for those going to Beijing to meet—noon the next day, at the Changsha railway station. The Number Two Guangzhou–Beijing train departed Changsha in the evening. Two or three spoke up to say they wouldn't be going, including Bureaucrat Tanxu, who conceded that "all things considered" he probably should stay home. "No one should go out of a sense of obligation," Zhijian assured them. "This is a voluntary democratic decision. We welcome your support, but if you do not wish to come with us, we appreciate your decision. But anyone who does participate is a *liaobuqi* taking a first step toward democracy." Decheng thought that the decision ought to be easy, that anyone with a sense of justice in their heart should go to Beijing.

By two in the morning, everyone had left, except Zhijian, Dongyue, and Decheng. They raised the possibility that none of the others would turn up in Changsha. Not even Hongwu. No one had participated more enthusiastically, but, cautioned Zhijian, "He lacks ideals or principles." The three went out for a walk. The streets were dark, as Liuyang's street lamps were turned off at midnight. For the next three hours, they did the same circuit of the town, along People's Road, up New Culture Road, across Station Road, along the Changnan Road toward the river, and back to People's Road, talking all the while, bursting with hope for China, of a future as never before, for change.

As the hour approached when the first bus of the day would leave for Changsha, Zhijian said that he didn't have to stop at home. He explained that he had nothing to pack, that a pen was all he ever needed. At Dongyue's, the other two waited as he filled his yellow backpack with his notebook, a writing pad and pens, and a camera that belonged to his work unit, then slipped a note under the door of the office on the ground floor to say that he'd borrowed it. At the station, the other two stood outside while Decheng decided what to take with him. Thinking the nights might get cold in the north, he put on half long johns under his trousers and a woolen sweater, and over that, his jacket. He grabbed a toothbrush and a washcloth and changed into his good leather shoes. He searched the pockets of clothes in the wardrobe where Qiuping hid their money and took thirty *yuan* of what he found. Finally, he wrote her a note and left it on the table. He set a cup on it to hold it in place.

THE TRIO FROM LIUYANG disembarked the bus in downtown Changsha and walked to the railway station. Two huge characters— the name of the city written in Mao's familiar swift handwriting— adorned the rooftop of the Soviet-style terminal, located at the end of the Boulevard of May 1st. The station bordered a public square, with a cavernous post office on another side of the square and the railway ticket office opposite. On the hour, the carillon in the station's clock tower played "The East Is Red" in its entirety. Travellers, at eight o'clock already anticipating the day's coming heat, crowded beneath any available overhang. Students stood clustered in groups, distinguished by flags bearing the names of their vocational schools, colleges, or universities. Some groups carried banners, many with the same slogan: "The rise and fall of a country is everyone's responsibility."

Zhijian, Dongyue, and Decheng went first to the ticket office and lined up at one of its more than two dozen wickets. The Number Two to Beijing hadn't even left Guangzhou yet. It departed at noon, putting it into Changsha at eight-thirty. If it stayed on schedule, they would arrive in the capital twenty-three hours later. The train was sold out. The three were not discouraged. They had the rest of the day to figure out how to get themselves on board. After a bowl of noodles, they walked up the boulevard and bought supplies to make their own silk banner and paper posters.

Back at the square, in the post office, Dongyue laid out his materials on a long counter. Using black ink on white poster boards, he wrote

"End one-party dictatorship and build up democratic China." On a 5-metre length of red silk, using yellow paint—paint manufactured for use on metal, to give his calligraphy a sheen—he wrote the four characters that meant "Down with Deng, support Fang," and then the group's name. One clerk looking on commented to Dongyue that his calligraphy was worthy of a master, surprising for someone so young. Others scolded him when yellow paint seeped onto the counter. Later, when Zhijian came back and asked the sympathetic clerk if he could borrow a chair so he could reach to put up posters on a lamppost, she offered him a roll of tape too. She wasn't the only one who'd showed them kindness that morning; a sidewalk vendor selling bamboo poles, which they needed for the ends of the banner, and a seamstress, who sewed pockets in the silk to hold the poles in place, had both refused payment. A worker at a concession stand had found them a suitable cardboard carton that they could use to collect donations.

Around noon, Hongwu arrived. He was given the task of finding a way to get them on the evening train.

A short time later they were joined by Teacher Kong, the quiet colleague of the newly married teacher. The five set up near a lamppost. Decheng took charge of the donation box. He noticed that mostly older people gave, and that they gave the most generously. At Zhijian's signal, either he or Hongwu and Dongyue—Teacher Kong remained a bystander only—hoisted the banner, and Zhijian spoke to their slogan. His speeches drew only a handful of people, all of whom seemed to be spectators, come to look at the student groups and their posters. Decheng saw one or two who, by the way they lingered, could be plainclothes police, though they seemed to listen with genuine interest.

Zhijian's remarks persuaded half a dozen teenagers, all male, to commit to going with them to the capital. Dongyue recorded their names in his notebook, and gave each a slip of paper as if it were a membership card, complete with the group's name and his signature. Many of the teenagers had to go home to pack a bag or tell their parents.

All afternoon, curious passersby stopped to comment or ask questions. Decheng would never have imagined that he'd be speaking openly to strangers. Their reactions, whether encouraging or critical, enlivened him. Everyone knew "Deng" on their banner to be Deng Xiaoping. Some would read only the first half of the slogan "Down with Deng . . ." and scold, "You dare to raise such slogans!" "You are attacking the Party!" "This is anti-socialism!" Decheng would explain: "We don't mean get rid of Deng—it's not that at all—we're saying we don't like living under a dictatorship, we'd rather have liberty and freedom." Others would clap or say "Good!" Some asked who Fang was. The rare time anyone knew his name they called him the bourgeois liberal who wanted all-out Westernization for China. Decheng found he couldn't help straying into hyperbole: "He's an icon of liberalization, he's the hope for the modernization of China."

One teenager took offence to their slogan about building a democracy. "Let us get rich first," he said. Decheng shot back, "You mean the children of the first wife should get rich and never mind the rest of us, born to the concubines?" Immediately, he regretted his sarcasm.

The next time someone approached, he tried a new tack. "I want to ask how you would feel if you came across this situation. Just as a general example—I'm not speaking for myself. What if your wife was pregnant, about to deliver, and the planned childbirth people came and dragged her off to have an abortion?" People murmured in recognition. He had another example. Rarely did he get further than mention of two men from Changsha who were hastily executed for raping a woman before the crowd took over, finishing the story of how the woman, a prostitute, had initially gone to police to get even with two clients she thought had left without paying. Too late to stop their execution, she found the banknotes they'd insisted to police they'd left—"the police obviously didn't bother to search"— wedged between the mattress and the wall. Out of remorse, she kept telling the truth to anyone who would listen.

Late afternoon, the line began forming for the Number Two train to Beijing. The five rolled up their banner, discarded their posters, and emptied the donation box. They were astounded to count ninety *yuan*. The group handed the money over to Dongyue to manage and joined the line. By the time the teenagers coming with them caught up, Hongwu had figured out how they would get on the train. He'd found passengers holding tickets willing to purchase platform tickets on their behalf (rules permitted travelling passengers two platform tickets each for people to see them off). Once on the platform, they'd clamour on board. If a conductor came into their car to check for train tickets, Hongwu reasoned, they could buy their tickets from him.

Hongwu's plan worked. When the train pulled out, every two-person seat held three, every three-person seat, four. People sat in the aisles with their legs under seats. The five from Liuyang crammed into the space at the end of a car, outside the toilet and next to the sink. An attendant, an older man, suggested they pile their bags in the sink, and lent them collapsible canvas stools. At stops beyond Changsha, people had to climb in through the windows. Helping hands reached out to make sure anyone who wanted to go to Beijing was not left behind. Zhijian and Dongyue spent almost the entire trip with their heads together, trying out arguments to advance in Beijing and crafting them into a speech. Between the noise and congestion and having to sit up straight, Decheng found sleep next to impossible. He was entertained whenever some nearby students, Beijingers by their accent, started a conversation. Remarkable, he thought, how casually they made such sarcastic assessments of the Party and the leadership.

THE TRAIN ARRIVED in Beijing late Thursday evening, on May 18. As Decheng and his friends disembarked, they almost immediately lost the teenagers from Changsha. Inside the station, railway workers with megaphones instructed students to exit by one gate and all other passengers by another. The five from Liuyang followed the students. Normally, exiting passengers had to show a valid ticket to an inspector, but on this night station masters hurried the students through and waved them out of the station.

The passengers emerged to a roar of cheering and applause from a vast crowd lining both sides of the street. The five unfurled their banner, adding to a dense jungle of silk. Student delegations around them began chanting their slogans: "Down with corruption, starting with the central government and starting now!" "Down with policies that keep the people ignorant!"

The five shouted their own: "Down with Deng, support Fang!"

"Wow, all the way from Hunan."

Flashbulbs popped continuously.

"Look, the native province of Mao Zedong. That's terrific!"

The column of students moved like a long dragon, exuberant and noisy. Decheng guessed that they had to be nearing Tiananmen Square when the crowds began pressing in. Eventually, the crush of bodies forced them to lower their banner. They went from marching five abreast, down to three, then two. By then, they realized that they had lost Teacher Kong. Eventually, their progress was measured in inches. Only when Decheng caught sight of the huge portrait of Chairman Mao that hung at the gate of Tiananmen did he realize that they had entered the square.

LATER THAT NIGHT, they explored west of Mao's portrait, toward Zhongnanhai. Under a bright street lamp, they saw a large crowd. Someone with a megaphone was addressing them. The four recognized the determined voice of Wuer Kaixi.

Zhijian became agitated, fairly shaking with excitement. Wuer had recited an old slogan, *Chairman Mao is the red sun in our hearts.* "Mao" and "sun" were words in many revolutionary songs that remained part of everyday life, from the cheerful children's melody—*I love Beijing's Tiananmen/ The sun rises there/ The great leader Chairman Mao leads our forward march*—to the ubiquitous "The East Is Red"—*The east is red, the sun has risen/ China has brought forth Mao Zedong.*

"The image of Mao is shining too much, too brightly!" said Wuer.

"Bravo!" shouted out Zhijian.

"People can't even open their eyes!"

"Excellent!"

Wuer paused. He put his hand on his heart. A student took the megaphone to say that Wuer was suffering the effects of fasting and had to leave.

Many hours earlier, Wuer had risen from his hospital bed, where he was being treated for an inflamed heart muscle brought on by fasting. Premier Li Peng had made an unexpected offer to student leaders of a one-hour, nationally televised meeting in the Great Hall of the People. Li Peng apologized for his lateness, owing to the streets being clogged because of the hunger strike, and then announced why he'd called the meeting: to ask all hunger strikers to end their fast and to go to a hospital. Interjecting, Wuer Kaixi rebuked the premier, telling him he was not five minutes late but one month late in replying to the students' appeals to meet with them, and that the students, not him, would decide what would be discussed. Wuer's fellow student Wang Dan bluntly asked that the regime retract the April 26 editorial and recognize the students' actions as patriotic. All that anyone who watched could talk of afterwards was Wuer's cocky and assertive performance, all the more memorable because he appeared in his striped hospital pyjamas and paused repeatedly to take oxygen.

As Decheng watched the student escort Wuer away, he wondered if the young man might be given to affecting drama for the sake of the crowd.

Zhijian was brimming with enthusiasm. "We have to write a new speech." He was impressed with Wuer's ability to connect the historical and the present. The four found a spot to sit down, and Zhijian and Dongyue fell deep into discussion. When dawn broke and there was enough light to write by, they wrote furiously. An hour later, they had a draft. Zhijian asked Decheng and Hongwu to approve it. "That's not necessary for me. I have total confidence in you," said Decheng. Even as Hongwu had his say, Decheng was thinking, *He's making the mistake of going off on a long speech.* However, Hongwu did have one sensible suggestion, that before Zhijian delivered the speech, they ought to determine if there had been any developments in the students' or the government's positions.

IN THE LIGHT OF MORNING, their first full day in the capital, the four got their bearings and took stock of the student occupation of the square. Decheng was curious enough to ask someone about the boxes, draped in black cloth, high up on the lampposts—he was surprised to learn that they were surveillance cameras, which the students had covered up.

To show solidarity with the students, the four tied red cloths around their foreheads. But they quickly discovered that students kept to themselves. Not only did they associate with only other students, they appeared even to stay within their school groups, sometimes even within departments of their schools. Many were themselves new to the capital; since the start of the hunger strike, thousands from the provinces had been pouring into the city every day. Still, mindful that he would be reporting back to the group in Liuyang, Zhijian made every effort to talk to students, even if they mostly ignored him.

On this morning, the four had their first taste of northern fare. Vendors did a brisk business selling *jian bing*, a hotcake. Thinking the red cloths might earn them sympathy, Dongyue tried to bargain. The hawker, detecting their thick accent, said, "Ha! Country folk! If you don't have money, you shouldn't eat!" The four found the hotcakes delicious. Vendors made the snack to order: they swirled a paste of milk and mung bean powder onto a hot griddle, tossed on some scallion and sesame seeds, and, if requested, hot chilies, then rolled or folded it in half around *youtiao*, a fried bread stick. A single *jian bing* cost fifty *fen*. For an extra thirty *fen*, vendors added an egg while the mixture was on the griddle.

To keep pace with developments, the four kept an ear to the students' Voice of the Movement. When not broadcasting statements, petitions, declarations, or notices, or giving instructions to students on the square, the station announced the news, and filled any time between broadcasts with the Communist anthem, "The Internationale." Nearby shops and restaurants played televisions and radios all the time. When the ubiquitous government loudspeakers came on, they drowned out everything else, including conversation.

Dongyue kept the draft of Zhijian's speech tucked in his backpack. The day's biggest development had happened before dawn. In the early hours of this morning, May 19, Zhao Ziyang and Li Peng had paid a visit to the students' hunger strike command, housed in a parked bus near the hunger strike encampment. Chinese Central Television was on hand to capture a grim Li Peng, who stepped out of his black limousine, shook a few hands, urged students to end their fast, and then left. Zhao Ziyang stayed for fifteen minutes, talking to students. When a student handed him a megaphone, he spoke sorrowfully. "We have come too late. We deserve your criticism." Television images showed him close to tears. The hunger strike command followed Zhao's appearance with an announcement asking students not to chant inflammatory slogans attacking government leaders. Throughout the day, talk heated up of a power struggle between the reformer Zhao and the hardliner Li Peng.

AT FIVE O'CLOCK in the afternoon a rumour circulated that the government would declare martial law imminently. The mood in the square turned tense and fearful. At six o'clock, the government loudspeakers burst with static. A state radio broadcast all but confirmed that the capital would be under martial law beginning on May 20—as early as midnight that night.

In the early evening, Beijingers rushed to the square to bring word that troops and army vehicles had been spotted in the southern and western suburbs of the city. Since the hunger strikers, many of whom had fasted for seven days, were too weak to respond, student leaders rallied thousands of others in the square to help citizens barricade routes into the city. Beijingers showed up in cars and trucks to ferry students to city outskirts. At bridges and major arteries across Beijing, people dragged steel garbage cans, sewer pipes, bicycle lane barriers—anything not bolted down—to prevent army trucks from advancing. The four from Liuyang hopped on the back of an aging Liberation-model truck and ended up several kilo-metres away, at Six Mile Bridge.

At midnight, government loudspeakers throughout the city blared a live bulletin. Premier Li Peng and Mayor Chen Xitong gravely intoned that the People's Liberation Army was readying to enter the city.

In the early hours of the morning, the four friends found their way back to the square. They were anxious to see how the student leaders had decided to express their opposition to the regime's pending declaration of martial law. They saw that the students had ended their hunger strike and converted it to a sit-in.

"It's fine and good to have a sit-in, but it's hardly an effective way to argue against the legitimacy of martial law!" declared a bewil-dered Zhijian. They heard the students singing—enthusiastically—"Without the Communist Party there would be no new China" and "Socialism is good! The Communist Party is good!" They could not believe their ears. "This is taking patriotism to ridicu-lous lengths," said Decheng.

Just as perplexing were the new posters that the students had raised: "The People's Army won't attack the people," read one. Others quoted Mao's code of conduct that he devised in 1928 for his nascent Red Army: *Three Rules of Discipline and Eight Points for Attention.* Zhijian and Dongyue explained the historical reference—rules that were intended to ingratiate the army to the peasants (obey orders, do not take a single needle or thread from the masses, turn in everything that is captured, speak politely, do not steal, return what is borrowed, pay for what you damage, do not hit or swear, do not damage crops, do not harass women, do not mistreat captives)—but they found mention of it now downright bizarre in the face of hun-dreds of thousands of soldiers converging on the capital.

The four friends didn't know what to make of the students' strategy. They appeared to have no clear position on the government's imposition of martial law. Or perhaps they had no strategy? Searching for explanation, they blamed Zhao Ziyang's early-morning appearance. His apologetic words had drawn the students' compassion, but in doing so, had also muddled their thinking and undermined their ability to stand on principle, leaving them unable to choose clearly between supporting or opposing the government. Decheng swore angrily: "That visit was bullshit!" He belittled Zhao as a soft Mandarin orange—the peel may appear fine but the inside has turned to mush.

What alarmed them was that even if the students were resigned to the declaration of martial law, they seemed to believe that the regime would not use deadly force. Perhaps the students were too young to understand that history had shown the Communists to know only one way to assert their will—with ruthless brutality. Zhijian searched for a way that they could help the students. Just when they needed to stay strong in the face of pending martial law, they had gone weak. An answer took shape: others needed to step forward, to stand beside the students. Those people were the citizens of Beijing.

Zhijian decided that they should issue a proclamation calling for action. They would ask the students to broadcast it. He put two broad questions to his friends: who should the proclamation be addressed to, and what action should be called for?

For the second morning in a row, by the light of dawn, Zhijian and Dongyue wrote furiously. "To the People of Beijing," they began. Then they added, "and of the entire nation." They grounded the proclamation on two premises: the true nature of the Party and the regime is dictatorial; and the imposition of martial law signals that the regime's intention, its goal even, is bloodshed. The proclamation called for a general strike. "Show your opposition to the illegality of martial law issued by the Communist government. Don't go to the factory, don't go to school, don't open your business, don't go to the market." Finally, Zhijian tried to issue their appeal for citizens to come to the aid of students in words as forceful as he could think of: "Do not wait until the troops arrive, for the bullets to fly from the barrels of guns, or all that will be left is for you to collect the dead bodies afterwards." When Decheng read the proclamation's final line—"This power to impose martial law, this political authority in China, who does it really belong to?"— he felt intensely proud of Zhijian. *This authority comes from us, the people.*

Dongyue wrote a clean copy. All four took turns signing their names. When his turn came, Decheng noticed that Hongwu, instead of signing "Li Hongwu," had written "Li Jing," his milk name, a first nickname used by one's parents.

The three of them watched Dongyue from afar as he carried out their plan to persuade the pickets at the monument to let him personally deliver the proclamation to Wuer Kaixi or Chai Ling. He returned and said that he'd handed the proclamation to the pickets, for delivery to the student command and their broadcast centre.

AT NINE O'CLOCK that morning, with the threat of martial law still hanging in the air, an association of Beijing workers began a public registration drive. This was their second day on the square; the day before they had raised a tent and a banner just to the west of Mao's portrait. The student leaders had relegated the workers to that out-of-the-way corner. Workers manning the tent began giving out flyers defending the pro-democracy movement and reissuing the group's support for staging a general strike.

At twenty minutes to ten, the state loudspeakers on the square came to life. The announcer detailed the prohibitions of martial law in effect as of ten o'clock. On the hour, the sound of helicopters shattered the air. Decheng had never seen nor heard the noisy machines. For ten minutes, four military helicopters swooped low over the square and along Changan Avenue, dropping leaflets declaring all demonstrations illegal and ordering demonstrators to leave. The students stayed put.

By mid-afternoon, the citizens of Beijing, in defiance of the new conditions of martial law, packed the square. Zhijian, frustrated that their proclamation had not been broadcast, proposed that they try to align themselves with the workers' group. "I'm willing to consider any organization."

"Too risky," Hongwu insisted. "We're better off to go our own way. And besides, either we wouldn't qualify or we wouldn't be trusted."

Zhijian wanted to join another group, the Dare-to-Die motorbike squad. Local merchants and the workers' group had formed the team to relay intelligence to the square about troop movements on the city's periphery. Decheng was enthusiastic. "They are the most unambiguous group on the square." The four inquired. Its organizers said anyone wanting to join had to show identification from a Beijing work unit plus a *hukou* proving right of residency in the city. In addition, a squad member had to vouch for them.

Evening came. The city saw another night of feverish activity to block roads and bridges to keep the army on the outskirts.

On day two of martial law, May 21, Decheng and Zhijian shared an unease about the calm, certain that the government was readying for drastic, violent action. Students placed strategic buckets of water and distributed cotton face cloths to those participating in the sit-in, in anticipation of tear gas attacks.

When Zhijian saw that the fledgling workers' group had installed a loudspeaker system, he wanted to ask them to broadcast their proclamation. Dongyue would not have it. "We can't give another copy to another party. That would be disrespectful to the first, and unethical."

"Maybe we're just too nervous," Dongyue said of their own tense demeanour and sense of foreboding. He argued that they ought to trust the students to know what they were doing. With all their contacts and their intelligence, the student leaders had to know more than they were letting on. Or maybe they had other strategies that would be revealed in the hours or even days ahead. The others agreed with Dongyue, that their proclamation was in the right hands. It was where it belonged, with the intellectual leaders of the pro-democracy movement—the students.

Regardless, Zhijian wanted them to continue to monitor the Voice of the Movement. However, he agreed that all four of them didn't need to be on the square to listen for it, that only two at a time need stay.

Decheng paired off with Hongwu for a foray off the square. Decheng wanted to get an understanding of the area encircling Tiananmen Square so that they could plan their escape routes should the troops arrive. As they explored the alleyways behind Zhongnanhai, Hongwu proposed an excursion. "Since we're in Beijing, we should look around, see everything there is to see." He suggested Badaling, a restored section of the Great Wall. Or the Ming Tombs.

Decheng was surprised that his friend should want to play the tourist. "That's not what we're here for. We can do that another time."

"Maybe you should see what opportunities are here for you, since you're a skilled mechanic and this city is the economic centre of the country."

Now Decheng felt annoyed. "I didn't come here to do that."

"Well, I should get in touch with some former classmates here. We should have a contact, a foothold, something more than the square."

Hongwu found a public pay phone. Never having seen one before, Decheng had no idea how it worked. He waited with growing impatience as Hongwu dialed number after number from a little black book. Judging from what little conversation Decheng overheard, no one Hongwu called seemed like more than an acquaintance. Every time he heard Hongwu say "Badaling," he felt his blood pressure rise. He told Hongwu that he was going back to the square, that he'd see him when Hongwu returned.

Dongyue heard Decheng's story and felt strongly that the three ought to break off from Hongwu. "Since we arrived in Beijing, he hasn't appeared either very positive or supportive. He only thinks about himself. I don't think his motives for coming were pure."

Zhijian was loath to exclude Hongwu, to reduce their group still further. Decheng was conflicted, caught between Dongyue's astute perceptions and his own deep loyalty to his friend. That night, Hongwu did not return.

Come nightfall, the students added a new strategy. From now on, as morning approached, they would clear all the barriers they'd put in the streets, so that daytime traffic could flow normally and the regime couldn't claim that their occupation of the square was paralyzing the city.

The next day, May 22, Hongwu reappeared. He pulled Decheng aside.

"What I'm saying to you, I don't want Zhijian and Dongyue to know. I'm thinking that we should find some way to get home."

Decheng was taken aback. "We should go home, give up?" Hongwu said nothing. Decheng appealed to his pride. "How can we give up, go home, without having done anything? Without having achieved anything?"

Hongwu remained silent.

"I don't have the money to get home. You don't either." Decheng thought that would end the conversation.

Hongwu had more on his mind. "Zhijian has money." He told Decheng he'd found out, the day before they left Liuyang, that Zhijian had borrowed several hundred *yuan* from a mutual friend who ran a successful pager business.

Decheng wondered if Dongyue was right about his friend.

NEAR MIDNIGHT, on what was now their fifth night in Beijing, Zhijian, Dongyue, and Decheng hoisted themselves up onto a padlocked wooden kiosk near the Great Hall of the People.

They sat shoulder to shoulder.

They lit up one cigarette after another. Dongyue was not a smoker, but on this night he chain-smoked as his friends did.

A week ago, they had gathered in high spirits in Dongyue's flat, filled with hope and optimism. Now they cursed.

They cursed themselves. They had done nothing except worry since the first threat of martial law. They cursed Zhao Ziyang. He had dragged the student movement into whatever power struggle he was caught in. They cursed the students. They cursed the Communists. They cursed the students *and* the Communists: one for thinking the other would listen to reason or react with compassion, for thinking that there could ever be any such thing as an enlightened dictatorship; the other for imposing martial law, for knowing only the language of brutality.

They still believed in the student pro-democracy movement. Barely born, it faced a crucial moment, as did all of China. If the people accepted this abuse of power and cowered under martial law, then they would throw away any chance of democratic reform for perhaps a generation.

But what else could they, three ordinary people, do? They could not have written their proclamation in plainer language.

The three considered returning home to Liuyang. They spoke as much to their consciences as to each other.

"To leave now, we retreat out of fear."

"I feel that if we went home now, it would be an act of cowardice."

But what kind of choice was it to stay and sit defenseless in the square?

"We cannot simply let our boat drift according to the current of the river."

The stress became unbearable.

"Maybe it is better to be dead than alive in such a society."

Zhijian had a way out. "We could burn ourselves alive as a protest. We could do it the square. That would wake people up."

"It would be a liberation from this life."

They discarded the idea. The Communists would just say that they were three insane men who'd burned themselves to death.

They had travelled here from Hunan, home to famous patriots through the centuries, and a proud and long tradition of feistiness and combativeness. But the Party, in the short years since Liberation, had crushed the Hunanese spirit. Ordinary folk like the ones at the Changsha railway station could get angry about narrow injustices, but they couldn't connect that with the absence of human rights. Decheng thought of how even a good and decent man like Godfather Ding was indifferent to politics, unable to appreciate that the students were fighting on his behalf.

The moon was waning, a day or so past full.

They sat, smoking, staring into the distance.

Zhijian settled his eyes on the portrait of Chairman Mao. The Chairman, lighted at night, peered back at him, though he sat in darkness. "It's as if the spirit of the devil is still here," Zhijian said. "It hasn't been vanquished. It's the old Mao who's the cause of all this. That portrait should be removed."

The idea revived them. All along, they had directed their anger at the Party, they had chosen a faceless target.

Zhijian recalled a line from Wuer Kaixi's speech: "The image of Mao is shining too much, too brightly. People can't even open their eyes!"

The emperor was Mao.

The portrait had to go.

This could be their contribution. They would be the ones to remove it. They felt confident that many would support them. Ordinary people, students. Even those caught in the power struggle going on now in the leadership.

But how to remove it? No doubt it was securely anchored to the wall.

Dongyue persisted: they could make the authorities take it down. They could cover up Mao's face, smear it with black paint. They'd need a ladder, rags. But where would they get a ladder? One long enough? It had to be 5 or 6 metres to the top of the arch, that much again to the top of the portrait. Maybe they could get students to help form a human ladder—students hung their banners from the obelisk that way. No, that wouldn't work. All that activity would attract police.

Decheng searched his mind, wandered through his past, trying to think of anything he could offer to help make their plan work. He could swim through a current, hold his breath, dive deep. He could play to his heart's content.

He had an idea.

"Why don't we throw the paint on the portrait? We could put it inside plastic bags, and throw the bags at it." The more the three thought about it, the more feasible it seemed. Someone saw a hitch: the plastic bags might not break. Use eggs, someone else said, the emptied shells would be good vessels for paint.

The three were euphoric. Had the eggs been at hand, they'd have done the deed then and there. However, they quickly settled down. They knew they needed to discuss rationally and soberly what they hoped to achieve, who their gesture would be aimed at, and whether the students would understand its meaning. In the end, they agreed the students' reaction was the only one that mattered. The average person might not comprehend the meaning of what they'd done, but the students at the forefront of the movement would.

Zhijian turned their minds to consequences. Should they fall into the hands of the regime, their punishment could well be death. Plainclothes police—they had to assume they were everywhere in the square—could shoot them on the spot. Or government agents could capture them. If they were arrested, the hardliners would be angry. They'd say what they had done was anti-Mao, anti-proletarian, anti-Party, and anti-socialism. If they went to prison, torture was a real possibility. Zhijian asked both his friends to consider this in making their decision.

Dongyue's resolve was firm. "People have lost their voices because of the fear of reprisal."

So too was Decheng's. "The numbers of courageous people willing to speak up, to step forward, are becoming fewer and fewer. I'm willing to be one of those few people to take the first step."

And if death was the price? They were of one mind, their sacrifice would be a worthy one if, by this gesture, the students in the square were roused from their false sense of security and misplaced faith.

They had talked away the night. The lamplight had gone from illuminating the square to providing a fading glow against the coming dawn.

They were decided. Zhijian would be in charge of the logistics and compose the slogans. Dongyue would determine what supplies were needed. They set the time for their action: two o'clock.

ELEVEN

LATE ONE AFTERNOON, Decheng was waiting in the exercise yard for the order to report for dinner. When the guards called his cellblock, he fell into line. As he reached the doorway to the canteen, a trustee from the Rigid Control Team singled him out: "Lu Decheng!"

"You are not allowed to go in yet. It's not time!"

The trustee, and a corrected activist standing beside him, were two who Decheng knew nursed a hatred for him. Obviously, thought Decheng, the trustee intended to hold him back from the canteen until only the dregs were left, or to deny him a meal altogether. He kept walking.

A brick came down viciously, glancing across his left eyebrow. He pitched forward. The trustee had delivered the first blow; the corrected activist struck next, catching him behind his right ear, opening up a 4-inch gash.

When he was well enough, Decheng, determined to lodge a complaint, wrote to the head of Hunan prisons and copied the letter to the governor of Hunan province. He gave a detailed account of the attack and added that at the prison clinic he'd received fewer stitches than required to properly close his wounds—commonly done to downplay the seriousness of an injury. He cited the legal text "Detailed Rules of Crimes and Punishments for Offenders of the Law," which dictated a punishment of three years in prison. He concluded by stating his intention to sue the prison for thirty thousand *yuan*. Decheng received no reply. He hadn't expected one, but he felt certain that he'd get the attention of Beijing.

THIS INCIDENT ASIDE, the cadres in charge of Lu Decheng's political education commended themselves on the prisoner's enthusiastic participation in his reform. Where he'd once kept to himself,
immersing himself in his labours as a teacher, he now mingled with
the general inmate population. What they did not know was that
Decheng's changed demeanour had nothing to do with their efforts
to remake him into a new socialist man. Nor did they know his
purpose, to hold up a mirror to the contemptible side of man—born
out of the sadness of losing the love of his life.

Qiuping continued to write to Decheng, at least once a year. She
and her husband, Xiaohu, had moved into a flat in the dormitories at
the bus station. They were among a handful of bus company employees who ran a new subsidiary charter business. He was one of the
drivers and she managed the business end.

Although Qiuping's letters never said as much, Decheng detected
an air of disappointment, even misery, in her new marriage.
Decheng himself was at peace. He had peered into the darkness of
man's nature and seen the inhumanity of the Community Party. All
along, Decheng had told himself that authorities had used the love
between him and Qiuping to attack and manipulate him. Now he
saw that the failure of their love was no fault of their own, but rather
a consequence of this cold-hearted tactic; it had left both him and
Qiuping vulnerable, confused about their feelings toward each
other, and embittered.

He did not reply to her letters. Instead, he wrote occasionally
to their daughter. Knowing that Qiuping would read his letters to
Xinfeng, he wrote of his concern for both her and her mother, and
of his lack of bitterness about the divorce. Decheng was certain that
Qiuping would understand his meaning, that when he was finally
released from prison, he hoped to remarry her.

IN EARLY 1997, Decheng had a sense that his freedom might come
soon. Deng Xiaoping's passing, at age ninety-two, cleared the way
for a change of heart in the regime toward political prisoners. While

Deng lived, his name and that of Wei Jingsheng had been inextricably linked. Observers opined that as long as Deng was alive, Wei would never be freed. Even from prison, Deng's enemy had confounded him, penning him open letters calling him a tyrant, and, after the Tiananmen Square massacre, an idiot. If Wei were to be released, then the door would open for other political prisoners to be set free.

Now, every time his father visited, Decheng sent a few ledgers and books home with him just in case his release came suddenly. If it did, guards might either hold back his belongings for close inspection or allow him to take only a portion. Renqing grumbled when he saw the titles: "You're reading all these pointless things. They're not going to get you anywhere when you get out." Besides the obscurity of the subjects, he couldn't understand why his son would want to hang on to such worn and tattered volumes. "They look like they're a hundred years old!"

Decheng defended his pastime. "Reading is what keeps me sane in prison."

In November, Decheng heard that Wei Jingsheng was free, whisked from his Beijing prison and put on a plane to the United States. The news was almost predictable, coming on the heels of a state visit by China's president, Jiang Zemin, at the invitation of President Clinton. Two months after Wei Jingsheng was sent into exile, Cadre Wu, now the warden of the Hengyang prison, came to tell Decheng the good news: he would be released the next day, on January 24, 1998.

Driver Lu received two days' notice to come and take his son home. He arrived with a change of clothes and two zippered plastic bags, one to hold his quilt and the other his clothes, utensils, and toiletries. In sorting through his nearly nine years' worth of life in prison, Decheng gave away his quilt and clothes, including the leather coat Qiuping had given him. In this, the coldest month of winter, the coat could save another prisoner's life. He filled the two plastic bags with his books and notebooks. Cadre Wu took Decheng aside for a heartfelt two-hour parting lecture, reiterating his hope that he would not "do bad things against society again," but offering no explanation for his early release.

Decheng greeted Renqing as a free man. He savoured the genuine happiness in his father's face. *At last,* he thought, *we have achieved a breakthrough in our relationship.* He paid no mind that his father was furious when he saw what he'd packed into the two bags. "I can't believe it," Renqing said. "You had things that could still be put to good use and you bring out completely useless stuff." During the bus trip home, Renqing made a single comment to Decheng on his political action and the price he'd paid. "The shoulder is not as strong as the thigh," he said, an expression that had been popularized by the martial arts. Almost a decade after the government's suppression of the student pro-democracy movement in Tiananmen Square, people like his father still thought of the Party as invincible, which no opponent, try as they might, could topple.

ON HIS FIRST NIGHT in his father and stepmother's flat at the bus station dormitories, Decheng slept contentedly, knowing that Qiuping and their daughter were in a dormitory close by. The next morning, he sent a friend to the office for the bus charters, to let Qiuping know that he had been released and wished to talk with her, that he would meet her there tomorrow at the end of the workday. Decheng reasoned that giving her notice and choosing so public a meeting place would pre-empt any malicious gossip. As well, Qiuping and her husband would have some time to come to their own understanding about her ex-husband's reappearance.

On Decheng's first day as a free man, a policeman came calling. Under the gaze of Chairman Mao, his poster still hanging on Renqing's wall, he had a stern chat with Decheng about conducting himself within the law. The policeman instructed Decheng that he was to meet him at the police station once a week, and that he was to present himself once a month to the local office of the Ministry of National Security.

The next afternoon, Decheng went to the bus charters' office as he'd let Qiuping know he would. About a hundred people, many of them his former neighbours and colleagues, were milling about. Several hailed him, unrestrained in their greeting and welcome. Decheng was surprised to see people behaving this way in public, so spontaneous, talking openly to each other, and to him.

Decheng and Qiuping left together for a quiet restaurant and talked over dinner and a bottle of wine. Their conversation was easygoing, as if the years of separation had fallen away. As the evening progressed, Qiuping unburdened herself, telling Decheng that her husband was not the man he'd led her to believe before they'd married. "All kinds of bad habits come out after marriage," she lamented. At one in the morning, they left the restaurant and bid each other good night. Though Qiuping had seemed deeply unhappy, Decheng told himself that he had to verify for himself that her unhappiness was with her marriage; she may be unhappy through no fault of her husband's.

THE FIFTEEN-DAY CELEBRATION of the new year began the next day. Driver Lu paraded Decheng from house to house. Decheng saw that the years had been fat and plentiful for everyone. They visited relatives, colleagues, and even former neighbours. "This is Lu Decheng! My son!" the bus driver said, beaming and happier than anyone could remember seeing him. Not only had Driver Lu's son survived prison, but he still cut a youthful and handsome figure. Anybody who had avoided the bus driver before, thinking bad luck might rub off on them, had nothing to worry about now.

Under cover of the holiday season, when people travelled to be with family and made pilgrimages to their ancestral villages, Decheng decided to risk a visit to Old Revolutionary Zhao. He told his father not to ask him where he was going. Decheng headed for the Green Mountains, 150 kilometres and an overnight trip away. Following instructions Zhao had given him in prison, he got to a designated village and relayed a coded message, which brought his friend's brother to him on a motorbike. He climbed on the back and Zhao's brother took him the rest of the way. The two former prisonmates talked, delighting in each other's company. Old Revolutionary Zhao was still unmarried. He took Decheng to see the grave he'd dug and the poem he'd carved on a tombstone, so his death would trouble no one in the event he lived out his life alone. Decheng stayed only two hours then left, not wanting to hazard being noticed by police.

After the festive season, Decheng approached the management of the Long-Distance Bus Station. According to Beijing's policy on criminal reform, a prisoner's former work unit should consider him for "rehiring and resettlement" if he'd done well in his reform-through-labour. Decheng had neither a job nor a place to live. Number 35 Clear Water Alley, the address on his release certificate from prison, no longer existed—the entire alleyway, most of the row houses, and part of the steep hill had been levelled to make way for a boulevard alongside the river. Those running the station made it clear to Decheng: they did not want him back.

Decheng and Renqing discussed his dim job prospects. No one in town would hire him. Renqing wanted to buy him a new car to drive as a private taxi, but Stepmother Meilan refused. They settled on a loan to help Decheng buy an old car that he could fix up. The old couple also offered him temporary lodgings until he could afford a place of his own. Decheng accepted, but planned to clear out as soon as he resolved whether he and Qiuping had any future together.

To this end, Decheng sought out Xiaohu's ex-wife and former colleagues. While his inquiries were discreet, their replies were gossipy and disparaging. And so it seemed that Qiuping had, as she'd attested, got herself into an unhappy situation. Feeling full of confidence, and as a matter of courtesy, he went to pay his respects to Deputy Director Wang and Housewife Wang. He expressed his desire to marry their daughter again. They reeled in disbelief: "Wow, you really *are* crazy."

He was undeterred.

DECHENG INVITED QIUPING out to dinner again and proposed remarriage to her.

She was willing to admit that she still had strong feelings for him, and that she had regrets about having married Xiaohu. "But I can't go back," she said. "Too much has happened."

"It doesn't matter that you married again, that you have a young child. You can divorce your husband. I still feel that there is love between us."

"People can be mean. Your father said such unkind things to me."

Renqing had taken the divorce badly. He was unable to forgive Qiuping for abandoning his son when he was unable to defend himself and his home.

"Don't be concerned about what people will say. The only solution is for you to divorce Xiaohu. We will remarry and I will raise your son."

Neither doubted the sincerity or depth of the other's feelings, but where Decheng was optimistic and hopeful, Qiuping could only imagine pain and struggle ahead. "The situation is too complicated, it takes so much effort to be divorced, to be remarried again."

He too was crying. "Wangping, be brave."

"Lu Gao, I'm not strong enough to do all this."

"You and I have been like two foot soldiers. We'll face our struggles together. I have always seen you as strong, I have always respected you as someone who can stand up to any and all hardship."

Qiuping likened herself to a glass bottle: "hard to the touch, but also quite fragile."

STEPMOTHER MEILAN enthusiastically played matchmaker, coming up with names of girls she wanted Decheng to meet. Former colleagues at the bus station told him about female admirers. One worker at the station was particularly persistent. She'd been on a public bus and had seen Decheng board. The driver, recognizing him, refused payment, saying that he'd let Decheng ride for free because he'd once belonged to the work unit. The woman was impressed when Decheng had insisted on paying the fare. She approached Driver Lu, wanting his son to meet her younger sister. She also thought Decheng would get along with their father. "He's always been anti-Mao," she said.

Decheng resisted any and all introductions. He was determined to sway Qiuping's mind. He implored her friends to help. In his regular visits with Xinfeng, he told her that he wished to marry her mother and that he would welcome her little brother.

IN PRISON, whenever Decheng had contemplated the years he'd lost, he'd taken comfort in thinking that Hongwu, his closest friend, would have achieved something great with his talents. Decheng found him living in a tiny flat on People's Road. He was sorely disappointed to find out that Hongwu was earning his living by playing poker and dabbling in fortune-telling. He cringed to hear Hongwu blame his troubles on everyone else, complain that he'd married the wrong wife, and declare that the only satisfaction to be had out of life was in cutting corners, and in ways he knew better than anyone. Decheng spoke frankly: "You have made yourself into a victim of this society without even knowing it." He grieved that his friend had no inkling of how far apart they had grown. Hongwu, he decided, had become, or perhaps had always been, like the man in the illustration still pasted in his ledger. The one person Decheng used to think could be counted on to find a winning way for others could not escape the cage that bound him.

Decheng worked on making the used car he'd bought roadworthy. Driving about town, he saw Zefu, one of his oldest friends from childhood, with his son cradled in his arms, and stopped to offer them a lift. Decheng had heard people in town say that Zefu's child was a "monster" and that he treated it like it was "his sweetheart." The child, now four, had been born with severe handicaps, had stopped growing at age two, and already had the wrinkled skin and bald head of an old man. Zefu confided in Decheng that his wife wanted a second child and the family planning people were willing to allow it, but he'd told her that their son needed all their love and attention. Decheng felt cheered to know that there were people like Zefu, with a great capacity for love.

One of Decheng's first fares got in his cab at the county government offices. After a moment, he recognized the man: Bureaucrat Tanxu. Decheng had heard that his career had advanced very respectably, that he had risen to become the head of the culture bureau.

A question had been bothering Decheng for years. He decided to ask it outright: "Did you write any articles, using a pen name, about the three of us right after our act in Tiananmen Square?"

"A few," Tanxu admitted.

Decheng delivered him to an eastern suburb of town, on Fish Scale Hill, where many senior cadres lived. Tanxu left money for the fare on the seat. When Decheng saw the ten-*yuan* note left for a ride that cost only two *yuan*, he was enraged. He chased after his passenger, right to the door of his unit. Waving the note at him, he demanded to know: "What is the meaning of this?" When Tanxu didn't reply, Decheng threw it at him.

DECHENG BEGAN TO WONDER if there was any point in letting his appeal to Qiuping drag on or whether he was just prolonging the agony for them both.

He went back to her. Sadly, he found her thinking had not changed. He was resigned: "I tried my best. I proclaimed my love for you."

As much out of sentimentality as from a sincere wish that he stay out of trouble, Qiuping said to Decheng, "You should not care so much about politics, because you can never win." Then she admonished him with a variation on the expression his father had used. "The elbow is not as strong as the knee."

Believing that this was the only obstacle—a lingering feeling on Qiuping's part that he had unnecessarily turned the misfortunes of their family into matters of politics—Decheng made a last, valiant effort to convince her. "The predicament we are in—you ending up in an unhappy marriage, my regret about our divorce—is not of our making." He wanted Qiuping to see that, with his proposal to marry, he was offering her the chance to restore the love and happiness that had been taken from them by the Communists.

His large eyes searched hers for an answer.

Qiuping said gaily, "Now, if we had a hundred thousand *yuan*, then we could remarry!"

Decheng's pride was profoundly hurt. She had put a price on their love and he had fallen short. *So there is no hope for us,* he thought. *I'm just out of prison, I don't have a roof over my head. I don't have a secure job. To hell with it then!*

And so, the gulf between them opened impassably wide.

Decheng struggled to accept what had happened to the person he had admired for so long. Qiuping had suffered a loss of spirit, she had lost the will to fight. She had turned into a person like his father. Though even he had found courage, if late in his life.

In keeping with the terms of the divorce agreement, Qiuping returned to Decheng the correspondence that the two of them had exchanged while he was in prison. The nine years of letters filled two large bags. Decheng sorted through it, rereading the letters that had sustained him through his darkest moments. He burned most of them. What he could not bear to part with he put in a small cardboard box, including the photograph she had taken of herself on her birthday, October 2, 1989. He turned it over, read the words he knew by heart, "We will never accept a divorce, neither in life nor in death." He bound the box securely with twine and labelled it, "A dead rose."

TWELVE

ONGWU FOUND HIS THREE FRIENDS easily. They were still sleeping atop a kiosk in front of the Great Hall of the People. He woke them up, anxious to see if, after their fifth night in Beijing, like him, they might be thinking of returning to Liuyang. Zhijian, Dongyue, and Decheng climbed down and shared their plan for that afternoon. "You can join in or not," Zhijian told him, "and you can agree or not, but your views won't change our position." Hongwu listened, made some excuse about personal business, and quickly disappeared.

On that morning, the trio did not tie their red cloths around their foreheads. Inconspicuously, they scouted the area around and below the portrait on the gate at Tiananmen. Steps away, at Zhongshan Park, just west of the portrait, they found the quiet spot where they would ready for their task when the time came.

THE SHOPPING DISTRICT in central Beijing was on Wangfujing Road, a few minutes' walk east along Changan Avenue. Dongyue had prepared a shopping list that suggested a professional artist's supplies: acrylic paints, turpentine, a calligraphy brush, an ink stone, rice paste, and four sheets of sandalwood-bark paper. At the Beijing Number One Department Store, the three friends had little luck. Farther along Wangfujing, at a multi-floored shopping gallery called Dongan Market, they fared better. Dongyue found everything but acrylic paints, so he settled for oils. Before they left the market, Decheng insisted on one more purchase. He splurged on a bottle of the famous Western Phoenix Liquor from Shaanxi province—he'd always wanted to try it—to share in celebration once their deed was done. At twenty-two *yuan*, it cost almost ten times the price of the best liquor made in Liuyang.

Walking back along Wangfujing, the three friends ran into Hongwu. He'd been looking for them. He saw they were in no mood to talk to him and would need some persuading. "You haven't eaten," he said. "I'll take you to eat. I'll pay." They stopped at a snack bar. Hongwu did his best to introduce his argument from the high ground of politics: "The protest you want to do is right and respectful of Confucius. Corruption comes from the centre. But *who* should do it? Who is the proper person to do it? That needs consideration. Let the student leaders of universities in Beijing do it. We shouldn't use coloured paints. We should use drums and banners to spread the word—that's not against the basic laws and policies of the nation. If we throw paint, all the right words on posters won't get the message out. We'll look like crazy people. That will be the worst result and consequence. We have to use the right strategy. We *must* succeed, we *cannot* lose."

The three pushed the table away and left. Hongwu ran after them. "If you use banners to spread the word and use drums and march and take the portrait down and transport it to a museum, then it's like a celebration. If there are no students willing to do that, *then* I might choose to throw the paint with you."

The trio left him standing alone on the sidewalk.

ZHIJIAN GAVE THEM twenty minutes at the post office.

To conserve his supply of writing paper, Dongyue bought envelopes, and told his friends to open them up, write on the inside, and fold them closed to be mailed. Letters sent from Beijing took about a week to arrive in Hunan, and they could well be home before then. But in the event the worst happened, this was their chance to provide a last communication for family or friends, words left behind in their own hand. It didn't need to be said that by later this afternoon the authorities would most certainly be looking or evidence of their intentions, so it would be dangerous to let their ink flow freely.

Dongyue's pen raced. He wrote nine letters. To his employer, the *Liuyang Daily*, he wrote: "I cannot avoid predicting my future yet it is an unpredictable future." The remaining eight were to family and former classmates. He ended every letter with the same line of weighty portent: "I want to learn from *Jing Ke Ci Qin Wang (The Emperor and the Assassin)*." In some tellings of this famous tale, the assassin decides not to kill the king. But the result is the same—a most brutal man lives to create China. Dongyue's pledge: to succeed where the assassin had failed, to act before it was too late, to save China from itself.

With his slow, deliberate hand, Zhijian wrote a single letter. In it, he asked his sisters to read it to their mother, whose eye problems had left her in hospital. "Take care, Mama," he wrote, "and no matter what happens to me, please don't be too worried, don't let your heart hurt too much."

Since Decheng had left Liuyang for Beijing, he'd thought about telephoning the bus station and asking to speak to Qiuping. But he'd pushed the thought away. In Changsha, he hadn't called because he feared his resolve to go to Beijing would weaken. Now that he was here, he feared she'd only beg him to come home. His letter to Qiuping was brief: "We are going to do something big, something that might turn into a big event." Dutifully, he directed her attention to his roles as a son-in-law, a son, and a father: "Please take care of your parents, my parents, and our daughter." He considered how to end his letter. They had always been in love, always would be, but never had they spoken the three words that bound one to the other. Never before had there been the need to. He decided to surrender them to paper: "Wangping, I love you, Your Lu Gao."

THE THREE FRIENDS returned to the gate at Tiananmen to take note of the lunchtime crowds. Now, all that they needed were the eggs.

Dongyue tried to bargain with an older woman selling *jian bing*. He wanted four portions, each with five eggs added. One egg cost thirty *fen*, how much for twenty eggs?

She was adamant, the price per egg would not change.

Then would she crack the eggs in the way he asked? Separate them and reserve the egg white, and save the shells?

She was happy to oblige. With each of the four portions, five times over, she cracked an egg as close as possible to the pointed end, separated it, reserved the egg white in a plastic bag, added only the yolk to the sizzling hotcake mixture, then put the two halves of the shell into another plastic bag.

Dongyue asked if they could sort through her discarded eggshells. They filled another two plastic bags with the most intact ones they could find.

SINCE THE REGIME had declared martial law, student leaders were divided about whether to maintain the protest in the square or to withdraw. At all hours, day and night, arguments raged. No one, not even the students, knew who was in charge, or even how decisions were arrived at. There was the original organizing group of Beijing students, the dialogue delegation, and the federation of students from schools inside Beijing. The hunger strike command had not dissolved, though the strike was over. Arrivals from the provinces now outnumbered students from Beijing. Some student leaders had the idea of a shared command, a "council" with nine seats.

That day, on May 23, a meeting at the Marxist–Leninism–Mao Zedong Thought Institute achieved a breakthrough. For several days a couple of social scientists had been holding secret talks—each day in a different location—between student leaders and intellectuals who wanted to broaden the pro-democracy movement beyond the students. That afternoon, they'd reached a consensus: the Capital Patriotic All Social Sectors Liaison Group for Defense of the Constitution. The group's first decision was to establish a single headquarters: the Tiananmen Command Centre, effective the next day, May 24. Wang Dan would head the group, Chai Ling would serve as commander-in-chief on the square. Students in charge of propaganda were dispatched to get this news out in an interview scheduled later that afternoon with the host of the seven o'clock news.

AT ZHONGSHAN PARK, none of the few passersby who saw the three young men at work seemed at all curious about what they were doing. And even if they had tried to listen to their conversation, they'd have needed to be conversant with the Liuyang dialect to understand anything the three men said.

Dongyue prepared two 1.5-metre-long scrolls, which he made by gluing together sheets of the fine paper he'd bought, end to end. As he was readying his ink and brush, Zhijian revealed the two slogans he'd settled on that summed up their political thinking and captured the meaning of their act. The slogans had come to him fully formed and at the same time:

> *Five thousand years of dictatorship will cease at this point!*
> *The cult of personality worship will vanish from this day onward!*

As Dongyue meticulously wrote the characters, Zhijian took care to point out to Decheng that the two slogans were not a couplet: they did not obey the strict rule of an equal character count.

The three friends sorted through the eggshells. They stood more than thirty in a cardboard tray, fat end down, leaning them against one another. In another tray, they squeezed out the tubes of paint— red, green, yellow, blue, brown. Dongyue added turpentine and the reserved egg whites and stirred the mixture. He explained why he added the egg white: to hasten the drying, to help the mixture adhere to the surface of the portrait, and to create a permanent stain.

Decheng was amused. "Our act is symbolic; we don't need to worry about what happens after!"

Using folded cardboard, the three carefully scooped the mixture into the eggshells, then capped each filled egg with another half shell. When they were done, Dongyue placed another cardboard tray over the top.

Zhijian looked at his watch. Ten minutes past two. The scrolls, stretched out to dry on the sun-baked concrete step, had only to be rolled up. The three decided they ought to mark the occasion with a photograph. "A family portrait," one of them said. Dongyue set the self-timer on the camera. Such was the fine and thin quality of the paper that the scrolls looked like gentle undulating waves. The shutter clicked, capturing an image of three young men and their words set sail on a sea of hope.

THEY PUT ON THEIR JACKETS, gathered their belongings— Dongyue's backpack, the celebratory bottle of liquor, the scrolls, and the cardboard tray of eggs—and began the short walk from Zhongshan Park. They crossed over the central marble bridge, approaching the portrait dead centre.

At the end of the bridge, Zhijian placed their shopping bags and his jacket strategically, in order to help him direct the flow of pedestrians off to each side. He stood with his back to the portrait. "Keep to the sides. Please co-operate," he said, politely directing pedestrians. "We need space, we are going to do something."

At the archway, Decheng and Dongyue's actions were identical. Working on opposite sides of the arch, they applied the rice paste to the wall, then glued the scrolls. When the calligraphy was revealed, crowds began to gather.

The two friends moved back to the spot they had chosen in front of the portrait. The tray of eggs between them, they removed the lid.

Decheng focused on the shape of the egg in his hand and his target. His eyes travelled steeply upwards, climbing from the giant grey lapels to the square chin, to the signature mole on the left side below faintly smiling lips, up over the smooth cheeks, to eyes that seemed to find him, even down here, far beneath the old Mao's towering visage. He leaned back, back, preparing to throw, his neck, shoulder, and back aligned in one taut arc.

The egg broke in his hand; his grip had been too tight. He picked up another, measuring his grip against both the shape and weight.

He took aim and unleashed it. The egg traced its high arc, egg white and a spray of paint trailing like a jet's exhaust on a cloudless sky. The egg broke open against the enormous canvas above, splattering its contents. Another egg took to the heavens. Another and another. With each throw, Decheng learned the power of his arm, better to judge height and distance, so that he could use the remaining eggs to mar the entire image.

Which were his and which were Dongyue's, he didn't know.

An egg skidded across Mao's left eyebrow. A large glob of black paint teetered there.

A man in his thirties grabbed Decheng's arm, momentarily breaking his concentration.

Gravity prevailed. The black glob began to spill, running down from Mao's eyebrow.

"You dirtied my white shirt!" the man said angrily.

Inky rivulets coursed down the side of Mao's nose, past his lips.

"I demand you give me compensation!"

Past his chin, finally disappearing where a peek of white shirt met the collar of Mao's jacket.

EPILOGUE

A T THE TRIAL OF THE THREE MEN from Liuyang, as evidence of the destruction of state property, the prosecution showed photographs, all taken by the management office of Tiananmen Square. Most detailed, stain by stain, the damage done to Chairman Mao's portrait. Among the photographs, however, was one of the red carpet that lined the balcony atop the Tiananmen Rostrum. Prosecutors pointed out broken eggshells and paint and egg stains on it. Some eggs thrown from below had flown clear over Mao's portrait.

AUTHOR'S NOTE

ONE OF THE ILLUSTRATIONS that I include in this book is of a man in a bamboo enclosure, rendered by the artist without a door, not even the hope of a lock. Dressed in the garb of a hospital patient, the man squats and tenderly feeds medicine to his sick bird, itself caged within a cage. Years after Lu Decheng, then a prisoner in a Chinese jail, clipped this drawing from the *Hunan Daily*, a woman, having removed it from one of his scrapbooks, hid it under the clothes she was wearing. Then, she and her eight-year-old son, taking with them a small overnight bag to add to the appearance of their going as tourists on a week-long trip from the mainland to Hong Kong, locked the door of their flat in Liuyang behind them. They did not look back, making for the long-distance bus and eventually, the train south. A few days later, a plane bound for Canada took off from Hong Kong with the two on board. That woman was Lu Decheng's wife, the boy, his son.

Decheng himself had fled China and arrived in Canada a year earlier, in 2006.

Upon his release from prison in 1998, Decheng had no thought of leaving China; he married and started a new family. But after the release of Yu Zhijian in 2000, who had served eleven years, a network in support of dissidents repeatedly made contact with the two, proposing to "rescue" them and help them escape from China. Wary of these individuals, Decheng and Zhijian felt they belonged in China and could not leave as long as Yu Dongyue languished in jail. The support network did not give up. In 2004, a rescue group made mention of a democracy activist associated with them living in the United States, Zhou Yongjun. The two friends knew the name—workers' pickets had held Zhijian in his tent on Tiananmen Square after the three had defaced Mao's portrait. When a picket asked what ought to be done with their captive, Zhou had said, "Let him go." (At the time of this writing, Zhou is in a Chinese jail for the third time, first arrested after Tiananmen Square, twice again after he'd fled China but sought to re-enter, including this last attempt, when he had tried to visit his elderly, ailing parents. In May 2009, after six months without knowledge of his whereabouts, his family received notification from the Chinese regime that he'd been detained on charges of fraud, which the family contends are unfounded.) Bolstered by mention of Zhou, Decheng and Zhijian fled Liuyang that spring. When they reached Yunnan, a province bordering Burma, the two had difficult conversations, divided on whether the fight for democracy and seeking help for Dongyue was best waged from within China or from outside, and on whether one of them ought to stay behind. Decheng urged Zhijian to go onward; he was unmarried, while Decheng had a wife and a young son. Finally, they both turned back. Through the summer, both had second thoughts. When the network approached them again a few months later, they were decided: Zhijian would remain and Decheng, at the urgings also of his wife, would go.

In August of 2004, Decheng left Liuyang. From Yunnan, he made an arduous solo trek over mountains and through jungle into Burma. Bandits traded him from one gang to another, until finally, two and a half months after leaving Liuyang, he reached Bangkok. Immediately, Decheng issued a statement calling for democracy in China and drawing attention to Yu Dongyue's plight. The next month, in December 2004, the Thai government arrested and jailed Decheng, with China pressing for his return. By February 2006, of the three friends, only he remained imprisoned when the Chinese regime finally released Yu Dongyue, after he'd served seventeen years. That spring, under a resettlement program of the United Nations High Commissioner for Refugees, a group of private citizens in Calgary, Alberta, working with the Canadian government, sponsored Lu Decheng as a refugee. He entered Canada on April 11, 2006.

Upon that news, Craig Pyette, an editor at Random House Canada, contacted me. He had wanted to commission a book on human rights in China, and ever more urgently in the face of the unseemly rush in the West to do business there. Of a generation who remembers Tiananmen Square, 1989, I considered how some, in the West and in China, rationalize—or, let it be said, justify or excuse—the lack of, or slow progress on, human rights in China because "times have changed," or because other concerns, including making money, come first, or because rights, freedom, and democracy are somehow different issues there than in the West. With the privilege of being a writer, I saw a personal story about human rights, set in a state that bans dissent and protest, as a chance to understand the morality that is at the core of being human.

In Canada, Lu Decheng took on the life of a democracy activist in exile. He proved to be enthused about and open to my purpose. To gather his story, I interviewed him for days at a stretch over a year and a half.

In late April and May of 2007, I travelled to China. Because of the subject of my book, I quietly and guardedly conducted interviews. The reason for such reticence is to ensure, hopefully, the safety of those in China connected to Decheng's story. Twenty years on from Tiananmen Square, a complete ban remains in place against discussion of the protest and events in the square and the subsequent brutal crackdown and repression—even an accounting of the imprisoned or of the dead is a "state secret." Adding to the difficulty of my doing research, at the time of my trip the Olympic Games in Beijing were one year away; the regime had stepped up its monitoring and surveillance, including of dissidents. Consequently, I took care even in observing and inquiring about life in Lu Decheng's home town. Because of these necessary limitations, to help round out my characterizations of people and portrayal of events, I drew as well upon my own experience from the two years that I lived in China in the mid-1980s, and from my previous travels there. In addition, I followed in some of Decheng's footsteps. Almost eighteen years to the day after the three friends left for Beijing, I boarded a bus from Liuyang to Changsha, then took the overnight train to Beijing. While I was there, on May 23, the anniversary of their act of protest, police apprehended a man who threw a burning rag at Mao's portrait at Tiananmen. The state news agency reported that the man was "insane."

In the interests of protecting Chinese sources, of the meetings and interviews I had in China I can make mention of only one—with Yu Zhijian. I do so only because he and Yu Dongyue are now in the West. With the help of Decheng, the two, together with Zhijian's wife and Dongyue's sister, fled China in the spring of 2008, eventually reaching Thailand. They remained in hiding there until late May 2009, when the United States granted them asylum. Harry Wu, the dissident who founded the Laogai Research Foundation, dedicated to advancing human rights in China and focusing on the oppression of the reform-through-labour (*laogai*) prison system, led efforts to bring them to the United States. On June 4, 2009, in Washington, D.C., Zhijian, Dongyue, and Decheng were reunited at a commemoration of the twentieth anniversary of the Tiananmen Square massacre.

Because I needed an interpreter for interviews, my research was subject to the imprecision and omissions of interpretation and translation. In addition, the Hunanese dialect can be confusing for the Mandarin speaker. Responsibility for any and all shortcomings is mine. Some translations from Chinese are at the writer's choice. For example, I refer to the monument and obelisk in Tiananmen Square as the Monument to the Revolutionary Martyrs; another common translation is the Monument to the People's Heroes.

I benefited from a handful of letters and photographs that Decheng's relatives were able to send to him in the West. Others leaving China carried out limited material. I retrieved for him some books that had kept him company in prison. In *Egg on Mao*, the photographs, illustration, and calligraphy are not captioned but are referenced in the text. Lu Decheng holds all rights to the photographs. The two slogans in Chinese on the cover were conceived by Yu Zhijian. The scrolls with these slogans, which the three friends had put up on either side of the archway at Tiananmen before they threw the paint-filled eggs, have never resurfaced.

I made use of interviews recorded in the film *Tiananmen Survivors Recall Massacre*, produced in 2007 under the "Zooming In" series of Tang Dynasty Television (New York), regarding the controversy over the students' having apprehended the three friends, and the subsequent debate and vote to hand them over to the police. Among the invaluable resources that I relied upon were the works of scholars, writers, journalists, filmmakers, photographers, and artists—among them memoirs by dissidents who fled abroad—recounting and interpreting the events that led to the protests in Tiananmen Square and the aftermath. *Remaking Beijing: Tiananmen Square and the Creation of a Political Space* (2005) by Wu Hung is a fascinating exploration of the many dimensions of the square. That book led me to the art of the Gao Brothers (Gao Zhen and Gao Qiang)—who had an exhibition on in Beijing when I was there in 2007—which also made me see the image of Chairman Mao in new ways. More recently, powerful works of fiction such as *Beijing Coma* (2008) by Ma Jian, which includes an account of the students' detainment of the three friends after they threw paint at Mao's portrait, give the events of Tiananmen Square fresh immediacy.

Regarding the spelling of Chinese words and names in this book, I used *pinyin* and, less frequently, Wade-Giles if a term is more popularly known by that spelling. All persons in this book are real, as are names. Chinese practice is to place the family name first, followed by the given name. Those who appear briefly and those in the Chinese leadership, I referred to by surname after first mention. Others who figure more prominently in Decheng's personal life, I referred to often by given name. Or, to aid the reader, I assigned nicknames, typically referencing the person's profession or trade. I withheld the name of the guard who secretly helped Decheng during his time in prison. In this author's note, to respect their privacy, I do not name his wife and son who joined him in Canada.

Finally, I wish to pay tribute to voices advocating for human rights everywhere. I am honoured to be able to include in this book the poem written by Yu Dongyue in 1990, whose subsequent beatings and torture in prison silenced the artist within him. He wrote that poem with prison authorities looking on, without, therefore, the limitless freedom that the written word ought to make possible.

Decheng once feared that Chinese prison authorities would discover that he'd saved the illustration of the man ministering to his sick bird and deem it subversive. I think of the image that his wife smuggled out of China as binding Decheng to his past, evoking what ails society under a totalitarian regime, and to his future, helping him hold fast to a belief that nothing can imprison man's humanity, that our insistence on human rights can transcend all boundaries.

ACKNOWLEDGEMENTS

IN RESEARCHING and writing this book, I have been humbled by many, by their dedication, knowledge, and professionalism, and their caring and generosity of spirit. At Random House Canada, my editor, Craig Pyette, ever calm and thoughtful, brought clarity to my thinking and writing. He was equally committed to the power of the ordinary and of storytelling to convey ideas. I owe much to Anne Collins from when we first met years ago; her every word contains a joyful wisdom and her every encouragement is an expression of confidence. Ron Eckel believes in being helpful, and I appreciated his enthusiasm. I also extend thanks to Liba Berry and Nick Garrison. I am grateful to my agent, Jackie Kaiser, for bringing me into the embrace of this publishing house. I wish to thank in the United States my publisher, Charlie Winton at Counterpoint. And, as well, Amber Quereshi, who was moved by Lu Decheng's story.

I first met Lu Decheng at Cheuk Kwan's home in Toronto in June 2006. Dedicated to the cause of human rights in China, Cheuk introduced me as a writer to Decheng. I appreciate the faith the two of them placed in me from the start and as well, the welcome from Decheng's private sponsors in Calgary: Paul Cheng, Lap Lam, Allan Cheung, Sam Hui, and William Pang. Together with Jason Kenny, a Member of Parliament for Calgary, they worked to free Decheng from a Thai jail and to bring him to Canada. Another friend of Decheng's in Calgary, Conita Chan, gave me every consideration.

I am privileged to have Diana Lary as a mentor and a friend. She is like family to me. She shared her knowledge of China, helped as an interpreter and translator, and read the manuscript. Her scholarship and insights on China, the breadth of her own experiences living and working there, and, as well, her empathy endeared her to Decheng. A second interpreter who also worked devotedly with me asked not to be identified for fear of jeopardizing his relationships in China; I shall remember how engaged he was by the writer's task. A third interpreter, always obliging, was Lap Lam. So too was Conita Chan. In Ottawa, others kindly helped: foremost among them was Michael To, who did interpretation and translation. Others stepped in to assist, including Pun York Tong and Sam Tang in Calgary, and Frank Zhao in Toronto. A very special thank you to Tony.

I am no less indebted to those, though they must remain unnamed for their own protection, who interpreted for me in China and helped with arrangements there. I include among them contacts made when I lived and travelled in China from 1985–87, when my husband, Roger Smith, was posted to Beijing as the correspondent for CTV, a Canadian television company. He also returned to cover Tiananmen Square in 1989.

Many opened their homes to me on my research trips. I thank especially my sister, Louise Chong, whose artistry inspires me, and Norrie Meth in Calgary. I took over their dining room table, emptied their fridge, and logged miles on their car. My treasured friends, Elizabeth Barr and Stephen Perry in Toronto, indulged both the solitude and company a writer needs. My heartfelt thank you to Lisa Robins and Hervé Pauze in Hong Kong, to Janet Lai, and to Phil Calvert and Chantal Meagher in Beijing. Chantal shared insights on human rights in China, and introduced me to Sabine Nolke in Ottawa, who along with several Canadians in Hong Kong, including Susan Burrows and Gerry Campbell, helped Lu Decheng and friends to unite the Lu family in Canada.

To take on a book is rather like inviting someone to move in with the family, and someone who immediately makes themselves at home and doesn't know day from night. My mother, Wae Hing Chan, knows this from my telephone calls asking for her insights on Chinese traditions. To Roger, Jade, and Kai, thank you with all my heart for living with the making of another book. Roger also read the manuscript and made helpful comments. Jade and Kai often offered encouraging words; I took quiet pleasure in the times the three of us were buried in books, notes, and papers, me at work on my book and you at your homework, too soon over. Finally, thank you to Lu Decheng, Yu Zhijian, and Yu Dongyue for all that your stories have taught me.

DENISE CHONG is the author of the family memoir *The Concubine's Children* and *The Girl in the Picture*, a story of the napalm girl from the Vietnam War. Chong lives with her family in Ottawa.